What kinds of childrearing practice  ing, sharing, and other prosocial beh   and culture play in the development (ok, Nancy Eisenberg and Paul Muss   arly research that has been devoted   cial behavior in children, and exam.   that contribute to children's prosocial development, including the media, parents, peers, biology, culture, personal characteristics, as well as situational determinants. The authors argue that prosocial behavior can be learned and is modifiable, and they suggest ways that parents, teachers, and others can enhance prosocial development.

In addition, the authors attempt to communicate the advances in the study of prosocial development that have taken place over the last decade. The book highlights questions that have not yet been addressed adequately by researchers, and suggests areas for future work.

Cambridge Studies in Social and Emotional Development

General Editor: Martin L. Hoffman
Advisory Board: Nicholas Blurton Jones, Robert N. Emde,
Willard W. Hartup, Robert A. Hinde, Lois W. Hoffman,
Carroll E. Izard, Jerome Kagan, Franz J. Mönks,
Paul H. Mussen, Ross D. Parke, and Michael Rutter

The roots of prosocial behavior in children

The roots of prosocial behavior in children

NANCY EISENBERG *and* PAUL H. MUSSEN
Arizona State University   *University of California, Berkeley*

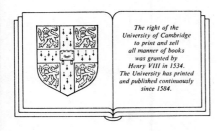

The right of the
University of Cambridge
to print and sell
all manner of books
was granted by
Henry VIII in 1534.
The University has printed
and published continuously
since 1584.

CAMBRIDGE UNIVERSITY PRESS

Cambridge
New York   *Port Chester*   *Melbourne*   *Sydney*

Published by the Press Syndicate of the University of Cambridge
The Pitt Building, Trumpington Street, Cambridge CB2 1RP
40 West 20th Street, New York, NY 10011, USA
10 Stanford Road, Oakleigh, Melbourne 3166, Australia

First published 1989
Reprinted 1990

Printed in Canada

Library of Congress Cataloging-in-Publication Data

Eisenberg, Nancy.
The roots of prosocial behavior in children/Nancy Eisenberg and
Paul H. Mussen.
p.   cm. – (Cambridge studies in social and emotional
development)
Includes index.
ISBN 0-521-33190-0. – ISBN 0-521-33771-2 (pbk.)
1. Helping behavior in children.   2. Socialization.   I. Mussen.
Paul Henry.   II. Title.   III. Series.
BF723.H45E57   1989
155.4′18–dc19   88–37010

British Library Cataloguing in Publication Data

Eisenberg, Nancy
The roots of prosocial behavior in children. –
(Cambridge studies in social and emotional
development)
1. Man. Prosocial behaviour
I. Title   II. Mussen, Paul Henry
302

ISBN 0-521-33190-0 hardback
ISBN 0-521-33771-2 paperback

Contents

Preface

In 1976 we wrote the book *Caring, Sharing, and Helping: The Roots of Prosocial Behavior in Children*, which was published in 1977. The purpose of that book was to organize the limited work concerning the development of prosocial behavior, with the hope of stimulating further research in this nascent field. Now 12 years later, we have reviewed and organized this body of work again. In doing so, it has become strikingly clear how much the field has progressed in little more than a decade. Many issues about which there were few data in 1977 have become foci of interest for researchers; in addition, thinking about the development of prosocial behavior has become more complex and better differentiated in recent years. Thus, it has been exciting and rewarding to see how far the field has come in a relatively short period of time.

Our goals in writing this book are to communicate the advances in the study of prosocial development over the last decade, as well as to pinpoint areas in which more thinking and research are needed. As in 1977, it is our hope that this book will serve to attract attention to the study of prosocial development and will serve as a catalyst for further work. In addition, given the importance of prosocial behavior for interpersonal and intergroup harmony, we hope that this book will provide useful information regarding the enhancement of prosocial proclivities for students studying social development and for parents, teachers, and other potential socializers of children.

Numerous institutions and people contributed to the completion of this book. Support for the first author's efforts was provided by grants from the National Science Foundation (BNS-8509223) and the National Institute for Child Health and Development (KO4 HD000717), as well as by the Max Planck Institute in Berlin (Paul Baltes, director). We are grateful for the assistance from these institutions. In addition, invaluable secretarial services were provided by Lenore Ross, Sally Carney, and Helen Cline. Finally, the authors thank their spouses for support during completion of this project.

1   Introduction

When we open a newspaper or turn on the television or radio, we are bombarded with news about human violence, cruelty, and injustice: Racial conflict in South Africa, wars in Central America and the Middle East, terrorist attacks, hijackings, savage crimes – such are the recurring themes that dominate the news. History seems to be repeating itself endlessly; human history is replete with instances of inhumanity: war, torture, genocide, racial brutality, and crime.

Also in the news, although perhaps less prominent, are stories of large and small acts of helping, sharing, and kindness. During World War II, many people in France, Poland, and other countries risked their lives by welcoming and rescuing Jews and other victims of the Holocaust (Hallie, 1979; Oliner & Oliner, 1988). Less dramatic, but more common, are news stories about needy families or abandoned children who are generously helped by people who hear about their plight. The story of people who worked feverishly to save a young child trapped in an underground pipe in Texas recently was reported nationwide, and stories of heroes who save others during fires or other mishaps are not uncommon.

Given the prevalence of both violent and altruistic acts throughout history, questions arise about what is fundamental in human nature. What traits and behaviors are inherent in humanity? Are humans basically aggressive and violent, or are they basically kind and decent?

In complex societies such as our own, it is evident that there is a wide spectrum of individual differences in nearly all personality traits and patterns of social behavior. Some people seem to be consistently self-seeking – placing their own interests above those of others, and pursuing their own needs, desires, and wants relentlessly. In contrast, other people seem to be concerned principally with the welfare of others and

1

with the good of the larger group. Of course, most individuals lie some-
where between these two extremes on a continuum from unmitigated
selfishness to selfless altruism.

The norms or standards related to selfish, violent, sympathetic, and
kind behaviors and values vary from culture to culture and society to
society. These norms or standards are generally reflected in the behavior
of members of a given culture. Consider, for example, the Ik, the
mountain people of Uganda, described by the anthropologist Colin
Turnbull (1972). This small tribe of hunters had an established social
structure and culture, with laws, rules, and customs, until because of
political and technological changes, they were deprived of their hunting
grounds. Then their social organization disintegrated, and they broke
into small ruthless bands concerned only with personal survival. They
became dehumanized and savage; lying, stealing, plotting, scheming,
deceit, treachery – even killing – became aspects of their "normal" way
of life. No one seemed to have any compassion for anyone else, not
even for mates, parents, or children. Caring for others, generosity, and
kindness (the kinds of behavior we label prosocial) simply no longer
seemed to exist in this group.

In sharp contrast with the Ik disintegration is the traditional Hopi way
of life. In the view of this Arizona Indian tribe, all aspects of the
universe, human and natural, are interrelated and interdependent. Consequently, community cooperation is regarded as essential for survival,
and most, if not all, of what an individual thinks and does has reference
to the group. From earliest childhood onward, nothing is more important to the Hopi than having a "Hopi good heart," defined as having
trust and respect for others, having concern for everyone's rights, welfare, and feelings, seeking inner peacefulness, and practicing avoidance
of conflict. In the Hopi family, the needs of the individual and those of
the household are both served through helpfulness and cooperation;
family interactions are not controlled by rules and regulations. The
ideals of personal characters and the compelling motives of the Hopi
include cooperativeness, industriousness, compliance, and an unaggressive approach to people and to situations. Not surprisingly, competition,
dissension, and self-assertion are strikingly absent from the traditional
Hopi community (Dennis, 1965).

The striking contrast between the Ik and the Hopi regarding values
and behaviors illustrates the variability encountered in human social

interactions and beliefs. People are not fundamentally and irrevocably good or bad. Thus, the age-old question – "What is human nature?" – has not been, and may never be, resolved. An individual's behavior, selfish or altruistic, admirable or deplorable, is the product of a complex interaction among biological, social, psychological, economic, and historical events – the result of both biological (i.e., genetic) potentialities and environmental (learning) experiences.

Definition of prosocial behavior

As mentioned earlier, the traditional Hopi engage in much altruistic and prosocial behavior, whereas the Ik came to display very little. Now that we have given some examples of prosocial behavior (and the lack thereof), we must define our terms explicitly. Although we have used the two terms *prosocial behavior* and *altruism* to refer to positive behaviors, we define these two terms somewhat differently. "Prosocial behavior" refers to voluntary actions that are intended to help or benefit another individual or group of individuals. Prosocial behaviors are defined in terms of their intended consequences for others; they are performed voluntarily rather than under duress. Although prosocial actions are intended to have positive consequences for others, they may be performed for a variety of reasons. For example, an individual may be motivated to assist someone for selfish reasons (to get a reward), to gain the approval of others, or because she is really sympathetic or caring about others. We all know of instances of helping, sharing, or comforting in which the people who assisted seemed to have had ulterior motives; similarly, we can think of instances in which a helper or benefactor seemed to be genuinely concerned about the well-being of another (other-oriented).

"Altruism" refers to one specific type of prosocial behavior – voluntary actions intended to benefit another that are intrinsically motivated – that is, acts motivated by internal motives such as concern and sympathy for others, or by values and self-rewards rather than personal gain. Internalized values that instigate altruism include a belief in the importance of others' welfare or justice. Individuals may reinforce or reward themselves with feelings of self-esteem, pride, or self-satisfaction when they behave in ways consistent with those internalized values, and they may punish themselves (with guilt or feelings of worthlessness) when they do not (Bandura, 1977, 1986). For this reason, some have argued that prosocial acts motivated by values are actually selfishly rather than altruistically motivated (Batson, Bolen, Cross, & Neuringer-Benefiel, 1986). However, we believe that people may act in ways consistent with their internalized values for reasons other than, or in addition to, self-reinforcement or self-punishment.

Altruistic acts may take a variety of forms – generosity, expression of sympathy, sharing of possessions, donating to charity, and activities designed to better the welfare of the community by reducing social inequalities and injustices. What determines whether or not these and other prosocial actions are considered altruistic is the motive underlying the behavior. However, it is usually difficult (if not impossible) to assess the motives underlying prosocial actions.

For this reason, we use the term "prosocial behavior" when discussing voluntary actions intended to benefit another. Only when egoistic motives are not involved can we assume that prosocial behaviors are altruistic. Unfortunately, such situations have been studied relatively infrequently.

Norms and behavior

The principal focus of this book is on prosocial *acts*, that is, on overt responses and manifest prosocial *behavior*. For this reason, from the outset we must draw attention to several important distinctions.

First, the *acquisition* (learning) of prosocial behavior must be clearly differentiated from its *performance*. An individual may have learned a particular prosocial response, but may actually manifest it only on certain occasions or under certain circumstances. Consider this simple instance: A youngster has learned that he or she should come to the aid of another youngster who is being "picked on" unfairly. The first youngster often acts according to that principle. But under circumstances in which this prosocial response is potentially dangerous (e.g., if the aggressors are big and tough and the would-be altruist risks becoming another victim), he or she may leave the scene rather than try to aid the victim.

Knowledge of societal norms may be quite separate from conduct that conforms to these norms. Some prevalent norms (cultural expectations or prescriptions of how one *ought* to behave) are acquired early in life through learning, identification, or imitation of the behavior of others.

For example, according to the *norm of reciprocity*, people should help those who have helped them; that is, a recipient of assistance should repay the benefactor. In contrast, the *norm of social responsibility* prescribes that we should assist others who depend on us and need help. When this norm is internalized, giving becomes an end in itself, and we "act on behalf of others, not for material gain or social approval but for [our] own self-approval, for the self-administered rewards arising from doing what is 'right'" (Goranson & Berkowitz, 1966, p. 228). By the age of 8 or 9 years, children have learned the norm of responsibility, can explain the norm to other children, and judge others' behavior on the basis of its conformity to this norm. Yet this knowledge of the norms per se does not ordinarily instigate prosocial actions; elementary-school children's endorsement of the norm is not significantly related to generosity in donating to the needy (Bryan & Walbek, 1970; Eisenberg-Berg & Geisheker, 1979).

To act in accordance with learned or internalized norms, the child must first perceive the other person's needs, interpret them accurately, and recognize that the other person can be helped. In addition, the child must feel competent in this situation, that is, capable of providing what is needed, and the cost or risk entailed in helping must not be prohibitive (Eisenberg, 1986; Schwartz & Howard, 1984). Unless these preconditions are met, even the child who knows the norm of social responsibility is not likely to render aid. A self-concerned or egocentric youngster, or a child who has not yet developed the requisite cognitive capabilities, may not be aware of the needs of others or may be unable to interpret those needs accurately. In addition, failure to conform with the norm of social responsibility may be the result of ignorance of how to help in certain situations (Midlarsky, 1984; Peterson, 1983a,b). In short, although societal norms bearing on prosocial behavior are widely accepted, even among children, they guide behavior only some of the time and under particular circumstances. Internalization of norms is not sufficient to explain or predict prosocial behavior; in fact, there is very little evidence that knowledge of norms exerts control over children's actions.

Prosocial *behavior* must also be distinguished from moral *judgment*, a term that refers to the *cognitive* aspects of morality – conceptualizations and reasoning about moral issues. In recent years, much of the research on moral development, stimulated largely by the creative theories and investigations of Jean Piaget and of Lawrence Kohlberg, has been centered on moral judgment. As we shall see in Chapter 8, moral judgment and moral conduct are associated, but there is not a one-to-one correspondence between them. An individual with mature, sophisticated concepts and judgments about moral issues may or may not ordinarily *behave* in prosocial ways.

It is important to make these distinctions at this point because all the key variables on which we shall concentrate pertain to prosocial *actions*. Variables such as knowledge of societal norms, motives, moral conceptualizations, and moral judgments are extremely important topics, the subjects of a great deal of important research and theory (e.g., Colby & Kohlberg, 1987; Kohlberg, 1984; Rest, 1979), but in this book we are concerned with them primarily as they relate to prosocial *conduct*.

Purpose of this book

Although it may be assumed that all human beings have the *potential* for acquiring prosocial behavior, the behavior itself – the forms and frequency of prosocial actions – must be *learned*. For example, if a young Ik infant were adopted by the Hopi and reared in the foster parents' culture, he or she probably would act as a Hopi, not as an Ik. And a Hopi raised from early childhood among the Ik would show Ik characteristics rather than Hopi characteristics.

This book is designed to provide an analytical examination of what is known about how prosocial behavior develops and the processes or mechanisms underlying that development. How are children socialized to behave in prosocial ways? What personal attributes or capabilities, and what environmental conditions, facilitate or inhibit expressions of generosity, helping, and comforting behavior? These are some of the primary issues explored in this volume.

Intimately related to these questions are questions pertaining to *variability* in prosocial behavior. Two kinds of variability are of concern: differences among people and variations in an individual's behavior from time to time. Why do some people have a strong predisposition toward prosocial conduct, whereas others show very little concern about others and display little prosocial behavior?

In attempting to understand the first kind of variability (variation among people or individual differences), we must examine biological factors as well as the process of socialization – specifically, children's interactions with, and reactions to, the major agents of socialization: parents, teachers, siblings, peers, cultural and religious institutions, and the mass media. What role do genetic factors play in the predisposition to respond to others' distress? How do the values of culture affect the child's tendencies to help others? What kinds of child-rearing practices or parental attitudes foster or inhibit the development of prosocial behavior? What role do siblings and peers play in shaping the degree and intensity of the child's predisposition to altruism? Do school and the mass media have significant impacts? The key to understanding individual differences in prosocial behavior lies in the answers to these questions.

The second type of variability, variability *within* an individual, is concerned with the fact that everyone's behavior varies from time to time. Most of us have acquired many prosocial responses; under some conditions we *perform* them, but at other times we do not. We shall survey what is known about situational factors – circumstances or events that increase or decrease the likelihood that prosocial responses will be performed.

Because prosocial behavior is acquired, it can be modified. Theoretically, at least, it is possible to find ways that parents, educators, and the media can enhance children's prosocial behavior, thus contributing to improvement of the human condition, society, and the general welfare. Such practical measures will prove to be effective, however, only if they are based on scientific knowledge of how prosocial behavior is acquired and augmented. Such knowledge is derived from systematic research.

A brief historical note and a word of warning

Trends in the behavioral sciences – the issues and questions investigated or theorized about – are linked with social and historical events, as well as with the general tenor of the times *(zeitgeist)*. As the concerns of a society change, so do the research foci of behavioral scientists.

For many years, behavioral scientists have been committed to the betterment of human welfare and the reduction of societal ills, such as aggression, conflict delinquency, and prejudice. When these concerns have been translated into empirical research, the emphasis usually has been on understanding actions that are clearly inimical and directly threatening to society and on providing information that can be used to reduce antisocial behaviors. For example, it is well known that delinquency and violence often have their roots in parental rejection and in an aggressive family milieu (Parke & Slaby, 1983; Patterson, 1982). This information can be used in the treatment and alleviation of these social problems. Similarly, there is a substantial body of information about how tensions between groups develop and how they may be counteracted. This information can also be applied in real-life social actions.

By contrast, the history of psychological research in prosocial behavior is relatively short. Most of the studies reviewed in this book were conducted during the last 20 years. We do not understand all the reasons for the neglect of this area of research until around 1970, but we can suggest some possibilities.

First, problems that threaten to undermine the structure and functioning of the society have a quality of urgency; they demand immediate attention. Scientists are likely to be concerned first with conditions that urgently demand alleviation before they turn their attention to the promotion of positive social behavior. The history of medicine provides an analogy. Until the last few decades, virtually all medical research and practice were focused on the cure or control of illness, disease, and disorder. The field of preventive medicine, emphasizing health education, the promotion of good health, and community psychiatry, and oriented toward better psychological adjustment of whole populations, developed relatively recently.

Another reason for the lag in research on prosocial behavior is inherent in the field itself: The phenomena of interest are enormously complex and difficult to study. There are few standard methods for assessing prosocial dispositions in the sense that there are standard tests for measuring intelligence, language, aptitude, learning, or problem-solving ability. To evaluate children's generosity, different investigators have used different techniques – for example, teachers' or parents' ratings, experimental or situational tests, paper-and-pencil tests, and direct observations of naturally occurring responses (see chapter 2). Because these different measures often are found to be relatively independent of each other, it is difficult to identify the best or most representative criterion of prosocial behavior.

Methodological problems such as these accounted in large part for the apparent failure of early studies of prosocial behavior. For example, in the 1920s, after an extensive study of moral development (Hartshorne & May, 1928; Hartshorne, May, & Shuttleworth, 1930), a group of researchers concluded (incorrectly) (see chapter 2) that school-age children's prosocial behaviors were specific to the situation. That is, they concluded that there was no consistency in children's moral behaviors, such as generosity; rather, children varied their behaviors as situations changed. That study, which was extensive, costly, and widely publicized, highlighted the difficulties of studying prosocial conduct (as well as other morally relevant behaviors) and thus had the effect of discouraging, rather than stimulating, further research on this critical social issue.

In the last 20 years, we have seen increased interest in research on prosocial conduct, undoubtedly related to a change in the spirit of the times. Somehow the general public became more aware of the long-standing injustices suffered by women, ethnic minorities, and the disabled, and this awareness helped to motivate affirmative action programs. Also, American participation in the Vietnam War led to a diversity of activist protest movements, liberalization of laws, and wider acceptance of humane values. Particularly in the 1960s, people (especially the student counterculture) seemed to be searching for a way to improve the quality of human life for all, and humanistic concern for others was seen as one way to alleviate some of the salient social problems. In this atmosphere, behavioral scientists concentrated more of their efforts on trying to understand the growth and enhancement of humane attitudes and behavior (Bar-Tal, 1984).

An unusual dramatic event also served to trigger a considerable number of relevent investigations of helping behavior. One night in March 1964, a young woman named Kitty Genovese was fatally stabbed in the parking lot near her apartment in Queens, New York. There were 38 witnesses who heard her screams and saw her murdered, but none of them did anything to help; no one even called the police until the woman was dead. Extensive press coverage of this episode shocked many people into a realization of how apathetic or unconcerned with each other people can be. That, in turn, spurred some prominent social psychologists to initiate research and to formulate theories about why people help, or refrain from helping, others in distress (Latané & Darley, 1970; see Bar-Tal, 1984).

Much of the initial research that came in the wake of the Kitty Genovese murder was conducted by social psychologists who were interested in the situational factors that affect whether or not people assist others. This work usually was experimental in nature; investigators would set up a situation in which individuals could help and would manipulate various situational factors (e.g., the number of other people available who could help a person in need, the cost of helping for a potential benefactor, or the degree to which the needy other's distress was obvious to an observer). Even today, the bulk of the social psychological work concerning helping is focused on situational determinants of prosocial behavior.

In contrast, in the 1970s, developmental psychologists studying children's prosocial behaviors frequently examined social learning conditions and cognitive processes related to the development of prosocial behavior, as well as the situational determinants of such behavior (Bar-Tal, 1984). In fact, social learning conditions were the most popular focus in that research. That trend seems to have continued into the 1980s; developmentalists examine socialization and cognitive antecedents of prosocial action somewhat more frequently than situational determinants. Thus, developmental and social psychologists complement one another in their attempts to understand prosocial behavior.

In 1976, we wrote a book entitled *Caring, Sharing, and Helping: The Roots of Prosocial Behavior in Children*, in which we attempted to summarize the current state of knowledge about prosocial behavior:

Although interest in prosocial research has expanded substantially in recent years, there are still very complex and troublesome problems regarding methods of investigation. Furthermore, the findings of some studies are contrary to the findings of others. All these things make it very difficult to synthesize research findings and to arrive at general conclusions. [1977, p. 11]

That summary statement is still true today. We know considerably more than a decade ago; indeed, research on prosocial behavior has become quite prominent in the last few years. Nonetheless, as was true then, we must warn the reader that there are numerous questions for which we do not have definite answers. Therefore, as in 1977, our goals are modest: to survey the best research on prosocial development that has been completed, to show how this research has been conducted (examining both the advantages and limitations of various approaches), and to draw reasonable conclusions, with the explicit acknowledgment that in many cases these are tentative. Because we are concerned primarily with *development*, we concentrate on studies of children, citing some studies of adults that have clear developmental implications. We have tried to present the "state of the art" of research on the development of pro-social behavior; in addition, we highlight the areas in which substantial data are lacking and are urgently needed. By doing this, we hope to stimulate further interest in the research on altruism and prosocial development that has blossomed in the last decade.

2 Methodological and theoretical considerations in the study of prosocial behavior

The form and content of acts such as caring, sharing, and helping are shaped by a host of factors – age, personality characteristics, motivations, capabilities, judgments, and the immediate situation – and intricate interactions among them. In recent years, investigators have tried to develop models for prosocial responding that capture some of this complexity and provide guidelines for the study of prosocial behavior (Eisenberg, 1986; Piliavin, Dovidio, Gaertner, & Clark, 1981; Schwartz & Howard, 1984; Staub, 1978, 1979) (see chapter 11). However, no single investigation, no matter how extensive and well designed, could possibly explore all, or even a substantial proportion, of the determinants of prosocial behavior.

Researchers therefore approach the study of prosocial development problems in the only way possible: by selecting one (or at most a few) of the potentially significant antecedents and investigating its (their) contributions to particular forms of prosocial behavior (e.g., sharing or donating to charity). The categories of antecedents that appear to be powerful influences on the acquisition and development of prosocial behavior (e.g., biological, cognitive, and cultural factors) are discussed later in this chapter. In chapter 3–11 we survey what is known about the variables subsumed by each of these categories.

Before proceeding, we must examine how research on prosocial behavior is conducted. The first issue to consider is that of *operational definitions*, the actual behavior the investigator observes or measures when assessing prosocial actions or predispositions. Because various operational definitions and, consequently, diverse criteria of prosocial behavior are used, questions about the stability, consistency, and generality of the measures inevitably arise. Investigators interested in the

12

processes underlying the development of prosocial responses such as donating or helping are seldom interested only in limited set of observations or in transient, highly specific reactions. Rather, they are concerned with more general and enduring personal attributes or social orientations, that is, with traits or recurring states. For the investigator interested in traits, measures are meaningful if they are *representatives* of *classes* or *categories* of behaviors, signs or indices of stable and enduring predispositions (such as the tendency to donate or help in many different situations). We shall discuss this issue of representativeness, consistency, and generality of measures in the next section of this chapter.

In another section of this chapter, theoretical issues are reviewed. In the ideal paradigm of scientific discovery, theory and hypotheses serve as guidelines for empirical investigation. But, as might be anticipated, there is no theory that can adequately account for all facets of prosocial behavior and determinants of this kind of behavior; nor is it likely that such a theory will be formulated soon. We shall discuss the significant contributions of three major (or "grand") psychological theories – psychoanalysis, social learning, and Piagetian theory – to the study of this topic. Each offers insights into different aspects of prosocial development, focusing on specific critical dimensions. Circumscribed theoretical accounts of prosocial responding, such as sociobiological theory (Wilson, 1975b, 1978), Hoffman's empathy-based theory (1984), and Weiner's attribution theory (1986), are discussed in later chapters.

In the final section of this chapter we delineate a framework for classifying the vast number of potentially significant determinants or antecedents of prosocial behavior. Categories are defined, and in subsequent chapters of the book they are used to organize surveys of the empirical literature.

Methods of assessing prosocial behavior

Although standard tests are available for measuring many psychological functions – such as special capabilities (mechanical, mathematical) and personality characteristics (self-confidence and the need for achievement) – there are no generally accepted methods for assessing traits such as generosity or concern for others. Investigators therefore usually devise their own criterion measures or adopt them from others' research.

Most of the relevant assessment techniques fall into one of the five categories described in the following paragraphs.

Naturalistic observations, focused on children's behavior in their "natural" environments, may be made in playgrounds, homes, classrooms, or other settings while children go about their usual activities. The investigator determines the classes of behavior to be observed and defines them precisely (helping others in distress, sharing toys, comforting children who have hurt themselves). An observer systematically records all manifestations of these responses during specified observation periods (e.g., 5 min) on a number of occasions. The frequency of occurrence of a response in a given time period is the individual's score for a given category of prosocial behavior.

Naturalistic observation takes a great deal of time and effort, but, in our opinion, it is likely to provide a highly dependable and accurate estimate of a child's propensities to behave prosocially in the specific settings studied. As we shall see later, measures of prosocial behavior based on naturalistic observations tend to be consistent and stable over time.

Situational tests involve controlled settings designed to elicit a range of prosocial (or selfish) responses. In one typical situational test, children first play a game or perform a task and win some prizes, such as pennies, or coupons that can be redeemed for toys. Later, each has an opportunity to donate some of these earnings to another child or to a charity fund for needy children. Does the child refuse to donate, give only a meager amount, or share generously? The predisposition to help someone in distress can also be tapped by means of situational tests. For example, while playing a game, a child may hear a cry of distress coming from next door (Staub, 1970a,b), or another child or an adult (a confederate of the experimenter) may come into the room where the child is playing whereupon the confederate may appear to sustain an injury, or drop some papers, or express a need for help. How does the child in the study react – with an attempt to give assistance of sympathy, or by ignoring the other's plight?

It is possible, with some ingenuity, to devise situational tests to evaluate many forms of prosocial behavior. A child's responses in this situation will provide only a small sample of the child's total behavior, but investigators generally assume that it is *representative*, an indication of the child's customary or usual way of responding. This assumption can be checked by examining the correlations between performance of prosocial acts, such as helping or sharing in the situational test, and behavior in other settings, such as on the playground.

Ratings are used to assess a child's standing (on a continuum from high to low) regarding an attribute such as generosity or helpfulness. Ratings usually are given by teachers or others who know the children well and have observed their behavior frequently and in a variety of settings. In our opinion, such ratings are most meaningful in research with young children. Nursery-school teachers observe their pupils closely and repeatedly under many different conditions and in spontaneous, free-play situations. However, teachers in higher grades ordinarily observe their students in relatively structured, formal classroom settings, rather than in spontaneous social interactions; consequently, they probably are less well situated than nursery-school teachers to give meaningful ratings of prosocial characteristics.

Sociometric questionnaires are used to obtain information about children's reputations with their peers for kindness, consideration, and other forms of prosocial conduct. The questionnaires, which typically are administered to all or most of the students in a class, may ask the children to name their classmates who best fit certain descriptions, for example, the names of three classmates who are most likely to "consider other kids' feelings" and "to help another kid who is being picked on." (Hoffman, 1963; Hoffman & Saltzstein, 1967). The number of nominations received is a score or index of the child's standing in these characteristics. These sociometric assessments or peer nominations seem particularly appropriate for assessing the prosocial dispositions of children in elementary school. Children of this age know most of their classmates – especially those of their own sex – reasonably well and probably can evaluate their typical social reactions better than can their teachers. There is, however, some danger of prejudice or a "halo effect" in children's responses to questionnaires; in some situations, same-sex peers, or perhaps popular or intelligent classmates, are more likely to be named in the favorable (prosocial) descriptions, even through such nominations do not constitute accurate appraisals. Careful instructions may help to minimize this possibility (Singleton & Asher, 1977).

Questionnaire measures of prosocial responding consist of a series of questions regarding the individual's own performance of prosocial acts, or the frequency of enacting a variety of prosocial behaviors. For example, a child may be asked, "How often have you helped someone to carry packages?" Thus far, questionnaires of this sort have been used primarily with adults (Rushton, Chrishohn, & Fekken, 1981); however, recently they have been adapted for use with older children (Eisenberg, Miller, & Shell, 1988).

Questionnaire measures of prosocial behavior are imperfect indices of prosocial responding because people may try to appear more altruistic than they really are. For example, because helpfulness and consideration are highly valued in our culture, people may want other people to regard them as being strong in these characteristics. Questionnaire indices may be most useful when they are used together with other measures of prosocial behavior.

Whatever method or combination of methods is used, an investigator can assess only a small *sample* of behavior. Is this an accurate index of stable and enduring predispositions toward prosocial conduct? This brings us to the critical issue of the relation between the behaviors sampled and other manifestations of prosocial orientations – the demonstration of cross-situational consistencies in behavior. In our opinion, the accumulated evidence lends substantial support to the so-called consistency (trait or state) hypothesis with respect to prosocial characteristics.

Consistency and generality of prosocial behavior

According to the conclusions of Hartshorne and associates in the late 1920s, moral behavior shifted from situation to situation (Hartshorne & May, 1928; Hartshorne et al., 1929; Hartshorne, May, & Shuttleworth, 1930). For example, cheating in a test did not predict dishonesty in another situation (e.g., when a storekeeper gave too much change after a purchase). Similarly, helpfulness and consideration were not consistent across situations. The view that moral responses, including prosocial actions, were specific habits rather than generalized predispositions was widely accepted after the publication of their work. But reanalyses of the original data of Hartshorne and associates seem to lead to a different conclusion. Specifically, factor analysis showed that there was indeed a general underlying trait of honesty, although not a very strong one, as well as specific components in the honesty tests (Burton, 1963). Teachers who participated in the study agreed on which children were most prosocial, and their ratings of children were highly correlated with a global index of prosocial behavior based on their combined scores on all the situational tests (Rushton, 1980).

Subsequently, a number of other investigators further demonstrated that there is generality in prosocial behavior; they discovered predominantly positive and significant, although not always high, correlations among prosocial measures such as helping and sharing in various situations. This was especially true when these measures were based on naturalistic observations or situations. Assessments derived from contrived, artificial situations, such as highly limited situational tests (e.g., donating to a particular charity on one occasion), were less frequently found to correlate highly with other indices.

In one relevant study, the generosity of 4-year-old boys was measured by the number of candies each shared with a friend, and they were independently rated by their nursery-school teachers. Those who were generous in the situational test were rated high in generosity and kindness and low in competitiveness, as compared with nongenerous boys (Rutherford & Mussen, 1968). Analysis of the data from naturalistic observations in a nursery school showed that nurturance and cooperative behaviors were highly correlated among boys and moderately correlated among girls (Friedrich & Stein, 1973). Similar findings were obtained in another study in which children were observed during free play for 30 hours (Strayer, Wareing, & Rushton, 1979). However, some other studies of children have yielded more equivocal results (e.g., Eisenberg, Pasternack, Cameron, & Tryon, 1984; Yarrow & Waxler, 1976). For example, in one study, the scores on experimental measures of sharing were found to be significantly correlated with the scores on measures of comforting others, although neither of these two scores was significantly related to helping behavior (Yarrow & Waxler, 1976). In another study, there were few significant relations among laboratory or naturalistic indices of preschoolers' helping, sharing, and cooperating (Iannotti, 1985). It is unknown why these differences in results occurred; perhaps they are attributable to differences in the scoring of the various types of prosocial behaviors.

The degree to which children are consistent in their prosocial actions may increase during the early years. In a study of siblings in their homes, older siblings (ages approximately 3 to 6 years) were more consistent over a 6-month period of time in their helping, sharing, and comforting behavior than were their 1-to-2-year-old siblings. However, for both groups of children, some types of prosocial behaviors (e.g., giving, cooperating, and sharing/helping/comforting) were significantly intercorrelated, whereas others were not (Dunn & Munn, 1986).

Consistency across measures of prosocial behavior has also been noted in studies of school-age children (Elliott & Vasta, 1970; Rubin & Schneider, 1973; Rushton & Wheelwright, 1980; Rushton & Wiener, 1975). For example, a composite score based on 6- and 7-year-olds' naturally occurring altruism – incidents of offering help, offering support, and making responsible suggestions to others – was highly correlated with teacher ratings of overall altruism, whereas measures of egoistic behavior, such as dominance seeking, were negatively correlated with this measure (Krebs & Sturrup, 1982). In addition, the frequencies of acts of "offering help," "offering support," and "suggesting responsibly" were significantly intercorrelated in the data from a cross-cultural study that made use of naturalistic observations. These characteristics were found to be negatively related to egoistic behaviors (Whiting & Whiting, 1975).

In a study involving fifth- and eighth-grade pupils, three measures of prosocial behavior were collected: a score on "other-centeredness" (assigning greater importance to values such as "having a world of equal opportunity for all people, races, and religions" than to values such as "living a life of pleasure and comfort"), sociometric measures (peer nominations for kindness and considerateness), and actual donations to charitable organizations. The three measures were significantly intercorrelated in both age groups, and some of the correlations were high (Dlugokinski & Firestone, 1974). In another study of adolescents' naturally occurring interactions on a bicycling or canoeing trip, various measures of prosocial behavior (such as helping a peer to put up a tent, sharing food and possessions, and comforting a distressed peer) were intercorrelated. In addition, individual differences in these actions tended to be stable over several weeks' time (Small, Zeldin, & Savin-Williams, 1983).

Impressive evidence of cross-situation consistency (generality) and the stability of prosocial behavior comes from several longitudinal studies. In one such study, extensive and intensive observations of nursery-school boys and girls were collected (Baumrind, 1971). During the first observational period, nurturance and sympathy to other children, thoughtfulness, and understanding the viewpoints of peers were all intercorrelated in ways that suggested an underlying predisposition to social responsibility and altruism. The same boys and girls were systematically observed again in elementary school 5 to 6 years later. Again, at that time, socially responsible and altruistic behaviors were associated with each other. Most striking from the point of view of across-time consistency or stability were the correlations between behavior indicative of social responsibility and altruism during the nursery-school period and comparable behavior (independently observed) 5 or 6 years later ($r = .60$ for boys and $r = .36$ for girls) (D. Baumrind, personal communication, 1976).

As part of another extensive longitudinal study, 5-year-olds were given an opportunity to share prizes they had earned (prizes earned by performing a task with another child who did not have time to finish the task and therefore did not earn prizes). Those who responded generously had been described by their nursery-school teachers the year before as generous, helpful and cooperative, empathic, considerate, dependable, and responsible. Those who were stingy in sharing had previously been described as aggressive and unable to delay gratification. The patterns of associations among these independently derived measures, taken at different times, are clearly congruent with the hypothesis that tendencies to engage in prosocial actions are consistent, general, and enduring (Block & Block, 1973).

In another longitudinal study, 1-to-2-year-olds were studied in the home, primarily by means of mothers' detailed reports of children's behavior in naturally occurring situations (e.g., when the mother hurt herself). The children also were studied 5 years later. For the majority of children (two-thirds), the ways in which they reacted to the distress of others were stable over the 5-year period. Thus, if children responded emotionally, with avoidance, or with a cognitive, nonemotional response at age 2, they were likely to do so at age 7 (Radke-Yarrow & Zahn-Waxler, 1984).

In a fourth longitudinal study, children's tendencies to donate to needy children and to assist an adult (e.g., by helping pick up paper clips) were assessed over a period of several years. Children who donated a lot at age 7 to 8 years also donated more than other children at age 9 to 10. Similar consistency in donating was found between the ages of 9 to 10 and 11 to 12. In addition, helping behavior, which was assessed at ages 9 to 10 and 11 to 12, was relatively stable over this

2-year time span (Eisenberg, Shell, Pasternack, Lennon, Beller, & Mathy, 1987).

Investigators have not always found correlations among indices a children's prosocial behavior. For example, in one study of fourth- and fifth-grade girls and their younger sisters (who were approximately 7 to 8 years old), the children were observed playing competitive games at home and in the laboratory. Antisocial behaviors such as refusing to help and disparaging one's sister (e.g., by calling her names) tended to be intercorrelated for both older and younger sisters. However, prosocial behaviors such as helping, comforting, and sharing were not associated with each other; for example, children who helped a lot were not especially likely to share or comfort their siblings (Bryant & Crockenberg, 1980). It is not clear why prosocial behaviors have not been found to be intercorrelated in studies such as this one.

It should be noted that the correlations reported in the studies of cross-situational consistency are *minimal* estimates – probably actually *underestimates* – of the "true" or "real" correlations among the various criteria for particular forms of prosocial behavior. This is true for several reasons. First, each criterion measure has some inherent unreliability (error) that tends to attenuate the intercorrelations. When several indices of prosocial behavior (such as generosity in different situations, or collecting jokes and pictures for hospitalized children) are combined (which researchers seldom do), the aggregate generally is more highly related to other prosocial actions (Rushton, 1980). Second, when children's reactions to situational tests are used as indices of such traits as generosity or altruism, it is assumed that they interpret the situation as the investigators do. This may be an unwarranted assumption, because children may perceive the situation as demanding conformity to the experimenter's expectation. A child's reactions may reflect the strength of her tendencies to conform rather than her predispositions to generosity or altruism. If this is so, responses in the contrived situation may have no connection with generosity in natural settings. We can expect to find "evidence of cross-situational consistency only if the individuals in the research sample agree with the investigator's a priori claim that the sample behaviors and situations belonged in a common equivalent class" (Bem & Allen, 1974, p. 510).

The degree of generality or consistency of prosocial responses also

depends to a considerable extent on the *salience* of a prosocial orientation to an individual. Bem and Allen showed that individuals who
regard a trait as highly salient for them are likely to behave more
consistently with respect to this trait in diverse situations, whereas
others are more likely to vary their behavior as external circumstances
change (Bem & Allen, 1974). It may therefore be inferred that children
who regard altruism as a very important personal characteristic will act
relatively consistently across situations in which altruism is elicited;
those for whom altruism is less salient will vary their reactions from
situation to situation, acting altruistically in some situations but not in
others.

Another possible reason for the fact that prosocial behaviors are not
always related is that not all prosocial acts have the same psychological
significance or meaning. Some behaviors may reflect altruistic motivations (e.g., the desire to make another feel better), whereas other
behaviors may be performed for reasons such as obtaining rewards or
social approval (Bar-Tal, 1982; Eisenberg, 1986). Behaviors that reflect
very different motives or predispositions would not be expected to be
intercorrelated.

Two types of prosocial behaviors that appear to reflect different
motives are preschoolers' spontaneous acts of helping or sharing in
the preschool class (i.e., prosocial acts that are not requested by peers
or adults) and their prosocial acts performed in response to a request
from a peer. Spontaneous prosocial actions are related to young children's other-oriented, empathic explanations for their moral decisions
(Eisenberg-Berg & Hand, 1979; Eisenberg, Pasternack, Cameron, &
Tryon, 1984) and to relatively high levels of sociability with peers
(Eisenberg, Cameron, Tryon, & Dodez, 1981) (see also chapters 5 and
8). In contrast, children who perform many prosocial behaviors at the
request of peers tend to be nonassertive and to be the targets of frequent
requests from peers (Eisenberg et al., 1981; Larrieu, 1984b). Apparently,
spontaneous and requested prosocial actions are different types of behaviors. Consequently, it is not surprising that they are not generally
intercorrelated. In contrast, spontaneous sharing and helping are positively correlated, as are the two types of requested behaviors (Eisenberg,
Cameron, & Tryon, 1984; Eisenberg-Berg & Lennon, 1980).

Unfortunately, very little is known about children's ordering or classification of prosocial situations, the meanings they attach to their moral responses, or the personal salience of prosocial attributes. It seems predictable, however, that if data on these factors were available and were taken into account, investigators would discover higher correlations among criteria or measures of generosity or altruism.

In conclusion, the bulk of the evidence indicates that children's prosocial dispositions show appreciable degrees of consistency across situations and stability over time. Although not all studies have yielded significant cross-situational consistencies (e.g., Bryant & Crockenberg, 1980; Eisenberg & Shell, 1986; Iannotti, 1985; Mussen, Rutherford, Harris, & Keasey, 1970; Staub, 1971c), the *pattern* of findings indicating consistency has been replicated often, and the reported correlations probably underestimate the "true" relations between measures. The closest associations between criteria are discerned in studies using measures of the most relevant kind, that is, naturalistic observations or composite scores based on a battery of tasks (e.g., Friedrich & Stein, 1973: Radke-Yarrow & Zahn-Waxler, 1984; Whiting & Whiting, 1975; see Rushton, 1980). Overall, then, the findings are congruent with the theoretical position that there are fundamental and lasting prosocial dispositions residing in individuals as general traits or states. This position is strengthened by the fact that diverse forms of prosocial responses (sharing and helping) are associated with similar learning or socialization experiences (parental modeling, identification, or the use of reasoning in child rearing). We shall elaborate on this in chapter 6.

Some theoretical explanations for the development of prosocial dispositions

Given these consistencies in prosocial behavior, investigators are certain to inquire about the processes underlying the acquisition and development of prosocial predispositions. Each of the three predominant or "grand" theories or approaches to human development – "grand" in the sense that they embrace diverse phenomena and incorporate many interrelated hypotheses – is characterized by distinctive explanatory concepts of moral development, including prosocial conduct. We shall summarize those aspects of each theory that are most pertinent to the investigation and understanding of children's prosocial behavior.

Psychoanalytic theory

According to psychoanalytic theory, there are three major "structures" or systems of personality. The *id*, the oldest and most primitive of the system, is composed of innate, instinctual, irrational impulses, particularly aggression and sexual desires. The primary function of the id is to gratify these impulses and to maintain a tension-free state in the organism. The *ego*, the organized, rational part of personality, develops early and acts as an intermediary between the id and the external world. It copes with reality, protects the individual against dangers, and provides a rational, socially acceptable means of dealing with the tensions produced by the needs of the id. The ego governs the individual's relationship to society, and its functions include thinking, perceiving, learning, remembering, and reasoning.

The third structure, the one most relevant for understanding prosocial behavior, is the *superego*, the internalized representative of morality and the arbiter of moral conduct. This structure, which reflects the standards of society and strives for perfection, develops out of the ego, at about 5 or 6 years of age when the child resolves the Oedipus complex (the boy's sexual desire for his mother, and the girl's sexual desire for her father). Then, identification with the parents replaces the child's mixed feelings of love, jealousy, hostility, and rivalry toward them. Through identification, the child incorporates and internalizes some of the parent's (or other model's) complex patterns of behavior, personal traits and characteristics, motives, moral standards, values, and prohibitions (see chapter 6).

The superego, a major product of identification, is believed to contain two subsystems, the *conscience* and the *ego ideal*. The latter sets the moral standards or ideals, the goals aspired to, whereas the conscience judges and regulates the individual's behavior, punishes transgressions through guilt, and suppresses or redirects instinctual drives that, if acted upon, would violate the moral codes the child has internalized.

In the view of Freudian or classical psychoanalytic theory, human behavior is instigated largely by self-gratifying motives. Instinctual drives and guilt are major determinants of thought and behavior, including social conscience, justice, and moral actions. Freud asserted that "social justice means that we deny ourselves many things so that others may have to do without them as well, or what is the same, they may not be able to ask for them. This demand for equality is the root of social conscience and the sense of duty" (Freud, 1921/1960, p. 67). Guilt, self-destruction, sexual strivings, and conflicts about homosexuality are fundamental forces underlying generosity and altruism (Fenichel, 1945; Glover, 1968).

However, Freud also acknowledged the role of other, more positive impulses in the development of altruism:

Individual development seems to us a product of the interplay of two trends, the striving for happiness, generally called "egoistic," and the impulse towards merging with others in the community, which we call "altruistic." [Freud, 1930/1953, p. 98]

Some more recent psychoanalytic theorists, called ego psychologists (e.g., Breger, 1973; Flugel, 1945), have stressed the dominant role of ego processes, rather than instincts, in the development of personality and morality. They reject the notion that moral behavior and values simply represent the internalization of parental and societal values at the ages of 5 and 6, and they regard identification and moral development as ongoing, creative processes that extend into adolescence and adulthood:

From what he is – more or less angry, demanding, aspiring, loving, anxious; from what the parents do – display certain principles in their own actions (or not), punish, espouse, love or reject; as seen through the framework of a given structure of self and a given intellectual stage; from all of these, the child, over periods of years, transforms himself in new directions....The acquisition of conscience and moral standards is, thus, a part of the more general process of self or ego development; a process characterized by the creative; stage-wise, transformation of self through the internalization of new roles. [Breger, 1973, pp. 256–257]

Furthermore, although parents may contribute the primary content of the child's ego ideal, subsequent identifications with "significant others" (teacher, ministers, peers) also are seen as influential (Settlage, 1972). Many changes in moral orientations, values, and attitudes accompany the maturation of ego structure – changes from fear to security, from aggression to tolerance and love, from moral inhibition to spontaneous kindness and consideration, and from heteronomy (use of external standards and authorities in making moral decisions) to autonomy (Flugel, 1945).

Psychoanalytic theory has proved to be a rich source of hypotheses about the development of shame and guilt, as well as the internalization of prohibitions. However, because of its emphasis on the self-seeking motives, psychoanalysis cannot readily account for the development of altruistic predispositions or humanistic values, which are explained in terms of defense mechanisms and reaction formations (see A. Freud 1937 and Kaplan 1984). Nevertheless, the theory has served to sensitize behavioral scientists to many factors that are critical in understanding the origins, development, and modification of prosocial orientations. One factor involves the potentially enduring effects of early training and experiences in shaping later behavior. Another is the role of identification, a concept formulated and introduced by Freud (1924/1959), but adopted (often with some changes) into practically all personality theories. In our view, identification is of considerable importance in the internalization of humanistic values and patterns of prosocial behavior, as well as in the incorporation of parental and societal prohibitions (processes stressed by classical psychoanalytic theorists). If parents are nurturant, generous, and altruistic, their children may adopt these characteristics through identification. Research on identification (and its experimental analog, modeling) and prosocial behavior will be reviewed in chapters 6 and 7.

Social learning theory and social cognitive learning theory

In contrast to psychoanalytic theory, in which internal (and often unconscious) motives, emotions, instincts, and identifications predominate, traditional social learning theorists generally have emphasized the acquisition and development of overt responses. They maintain that most human behavior is learned, molded, and shaped by environmental events, especially rewards, punishments, and modeling. Essentially, the processes and mechanisms underlying animals' and humans' acquisition of a wide variety of responses, including fears, social skills, aggression, and conformity, are also invoked to explain the development of moral standards and behavior. Conscience, for example, has been defined in learning theory terms as a "conditioned anxiety response to certain types of situations and actions" established through the pairing of punishment or other aversive stimulation with disapproved responses such as hitting another child (Eysenck, 1960). As a result, the pain and anxiety associated with punishment are associated with the forbidden act and

anxiety (conditioned fear)...gradually become[s] the conditioned response to carrying out or even contemplating the naughty action, and...this immediate negatively reinforcing consequence would discourage both contemplation and execution of the action in question. This conditioned anxiety is experienced by the child as "conscience." The acquisition of this "conscience" is, of course, facilitated by labeling, as is its generalization over different types of actions. By calling a variety of actions bad, evil, or naughty, we encourage the child to identify them all in one category, and to react in the future with anxiety to everything thus labeled. This, very briefly and not altogether adequately, is my account of the growth of "conscience." [Eysenck, 1976, p. 109]

From a traditional social learning perspective, prosocial responses are interpreted as the consequents of direct reinforcements (rewards), whereas "moral character" is defined as learning habits and virtues that are inculcated by parents and teachers (Hartshorne & May, 1928). It is easy to demonstrate that if a child is rewarded by praise or attention for sharing possessions or for helping someone in distress, these responses will be strengthened (Gelfand, Hartmann, Cromer, Smith, & Page, 1975; Grusec & Redler, 1980). But how can learning that is due to rewards account for self-sacrifice, helping, and generosity when these are not followed by any apparent reinforcements? Indeed, most prosocial actions appear to be controlled by the individual rather than by extrinsic rewards: "The assumption is that controls were originally external (through the administration of rewards and punishments by an external agent), but that behavior becomes independent of these external sanctions, and the individual comes to administer his own rewards and punishments" (Maccoby, 1968, p. 258). As a consequence of repeated experiences, children learn which responses bring parental praise, and they begin to praise themselves for these reinforced actions.

Principles of conditioning and learning have been used to explain the development of empathy (matching one's own feelings and emotions with someone else's) and tendencies toward altruism. In one study (Aronfreed, 1968, 1970), children in an experimental group formed a conditioned association between feelings of pleasure and the experimenter's expressions of delight. This was accomplished in the following way: The child sat close to the experimenter, who demonstrated the operation of a choice box with two levers. If she pressed one lever, candy was dispensed; if she pressed the other, a red light flashed. The experimenter displayed no emotion when she received candy from the box, but each time the red light flashed, she exclaimed loudly, smiled at the child, and then hugged her. With repeated experiences, the child's feelings of pleasure (evoked by the experimenter's smiles, hugs, and affection) became associated with the experimenter's rejoicing in reaction to the flash of red light. Children in control groups were exposed either to the experimenter's expressions of delight when the red light flashed or to her affectionate responses (smiling and hugging), but not both. Hence, for the controls, feelings of pleasure were not linked with the experimenter's expression of emotion.

Later, each child had an opportunity to operate the choice box while the experimenter sat on the other side of the table. Each participant had to choose between pressing the lever that produced the red light that pleased the experimenter so much or pressing the lever that brought candy. In essence, the child could obtain a material reward for herself or make the experimenter happy. The majority of the children in the experimental group pressed the lever that activated the light more frequently than they pressed the other one, thus sacrificing the candy reward. In contrast, the control subjects typically pressed the candy-producing lever. As a result of temporal contiguity and conditioning, the cues that communicated the experimenter's feelings of happiness had become capable of arousing corresponding emotions in the children. Consequently, the investigator asserted, they were motivated to produce signs of pleasure in the experimenter. The cues originally associated with direct, external rewards (smiling, hugging) gradually acquired a cognitive, internal representation and thus were able to exercise control over behavior.

Over the last 25 years, social learning theory has gradually been changing. Concepts involving cognitive processes have been introduced into the theory, but not without much debate and disagreement. Two important concepts that have been introduced are observational learning and cognitive regulators.

Observational learning. No developmental psychologist would argue against the assertion that direct rewards facilitate the learning of specific forms of prosocial behavior that are exhibited in settings in which reinforcement may be forthcoming. But it is also clear that substantial proportions of the individual's helping and sharing responses are acquired through observation and imitation of a model's behavior, without direct reinforcements. The pioneering work of Bandura and Walters (1963) on observational learning and imitation stimulated a great deal of theorizing and research that has proved highly salient in the investigation of prosocial behavior. In Bandura's view, observational learning involves four types of processes: attention, retention, motor production, and motivation. Thus, individuals imitate only if they attend to a model, store in their minds what they have observed, are able to physically enact the observed behavior, and are motivated to do so. In chapters 6 and 7 we shall examine modeling and identification as critical antecedents of prosocial predispositions.

Cognitive regulators. In recent years, Bandura (1977, 1986) has been revising social learning theory in dramatic ways. Internal cognitive factors are now emphasized more strongly than they were in earlier versions of social learning theory. External influences are believed to affect behavior through mediating cognitive processes. People symbolically manipulate information gained from experience, and thereby they are capable of comprehending events and generating new knowledge about them. Moreover, cognitive activities guide and regulate the individual's behavior.

In Bandura's most recent social cognitive theory, intentions and self-evaluative processes play important roles in the self-regulation of behavior. Through the use of cognitive representations, individuals can anticipate the outcomes of behavior and act in ways that are intended to bring about a desired state of affairs. They also set goals for themselves and evaluate themselves negatively if they do not behave in ways consistent with their cognitive representations of appropriate behavior. Because self-satisfaction is contingent on living up to internal cognitive standards, individuals create their own incentives to persist in their efforts to live up to internal standards.

According to social cognitive theory, children acquire internal standards and rules by imitating models and by understanding socializers' explanations of moral behavior. Others' reactions to a child's behavior help the child to understand its social significance.

In summary, reinforcement, punishment, observational learning, cognitive representations, and self-regulation are all important concepts in current social cognitive theory. Socializers play a major role in the learning of moral values and behavior; however, individuals' self-regulation of their behavior in accordance with internalized rules and standards is also a major influence on moral action. Moral development, including prosocial behavior, therefore is viewed as a product of the interaction between social forces and the individual's changing cognitive capacities.

Cognitive developmental theory

The cognitive developmental theorist's conceptualization of the nature of development contrasts sharply with those of the psychoanalytic and traditional social learning theorists, but is similar in some respects to that of present-day social cognitive theorists like Bandura. Children are not seen as passive, driven by instinctive impulses, or shaped by environmental forces. Rather, they *act on* the environment, often in creative ways, just as the environment acts on them. Each perceives the environment in his or her own way, interprets and organizes stimuli, and behaves as an intelligent being. According to Piaget, intelligence, which includes all cognitive functions, serves the purpose of adaptation. Cognitive development, the result of the interaction between changing (maturing) mental structures and environmental events, proceeds through a universal, invariant sequence of stages. Each stage is an integrated whole that is qualitatively different from the others, and earlier stages are replaced and integrated into later stages. Moral reasoning and judgment, which are manifestations of intelligence, grow and change as other cognitive functions do. The stages of children's cognitive development thus provide a framework for, and impose a limit on, the level of their moral judgments. Social influences are recognized by cognitive developmental theorists, but are assigned a much smaller role in moral development than they are in social learning or social cognitive theory (Kohlberg, 1969).

Proponents of cognitive developmental theory are not primarily concerned with moral *behavior*, or with affects that regulate prosocial actions. Two famous cognitive developmentalists, Piaget and Kohlberg, have described stages in the development of moral reasoning and judgment, and these will be discussed in chapter 8. They explicitly recognized that moral thought, as they defined and measured it, may not always correspond to actions. But Kohlberg asserted that "the fact that children do not always do what they say when the chips are down does not mean that development of judgment and development of conduct go along two different tracks. Verbal judgments may not be 'trustworthy' reports of conducts, but they may still reflect the same basic developmental process" (Kohlberg, cited by Maccoby, 1968, p. 240). Recently, he has tried to demonstrate this relation between moral reasoning and prosocial behavior (Kohlberg & Candee, 1984) (see chapter 8).

In our view, the cognitive developmental theorists have contributed immensely to an understanding of morality and of the development of prosocial behavior by illuminating the nature of age changes in moral judgments and role-taking ability (see chapter 8) and by highlighting the importance of reasoning and other cognitive processes in influencing prosocial behavior (e.g., Bar-Tal, 1982; Eisenberg, 1986).

Determinants of prosocial behavior

None of these major theories can adequately explain all facets of prosocial development. Different aspects of morality are emphasized in the three approaches; each also has its own conceptualization of the basic mechanisms underlying moral and prosocial development. Yet there are some points of agreement among the three approaches. According to all three groups of theorists, children are initially self-centered (egocentric, in the cognitive developmental theorists' terms) and become more oriented toward others as they achieve greater cognitive maturity and gain more experience. Concomitantly, the control of moral behavior shifts from external rewards and punishments (by parents or other authorities) to internalized motives or indivdual principles.

Each theory complements the others by centering attention on aspects of prosocial behavior that the other theories underplay or neglect. Cognitive development theorists underscore the significance of thinking, reasoning, judging, and role taking – functions that are underplayed in psychoanalytic theory and traditional social learning theory. Psychoanalytic theory, on the other hand, stresses the critical roles of emotions and motives, early parent–child relationships, and identification, and all of these are fundamental in the development of prosocial behavior (see chapters 6 and 7). Although there are many similarities between cognitive developmental theory and social cognitive theory, the latter assigns greater importance to socialization agents, whereas the former emphasizes development through a sequence of cognitive stages.

Each of the three theories has generated a great deal of relevant research, but social learning theory, with its focus on overt behavior, has probably been the most fruitful source of hypotheses about the development of prosocial behavior. The impact of social learning theory (and recent social cognitive theory) on empirical research will be apparent throughout this book.

Because no existing theory deals with all the central issues of the formation and development of prosocial characteristics, our approach is pluralistic, reflecting the enormous complexity of this domain of behavior. We are fully aware that we must deal with many subtle, interacting antecedents. We do not propose a new theory, but we shall proceed with orderly and systematic analyses of the major classes of determinants of prosocial behavior, and we shall review relevant studies of the impacts of various determinants. Many of those investigations were guided by theory or were specifically designed to test theoretical hypotheses dealing, for example, with identification, originally a psychoanalytic concept, or role taking, a concept that is of central importance in cognitive developmental theory.

Many empirical questions about prosocial development are derived from sources other than theories: a priori, rational analyses of the components and antecedents of prosocial actions, "minitheories" that deal with restricted issues such as empathy (see chapter 9), observations of children's spontaneous interactions with parents and peers, common sense, folk wisdom. To illustrate, "folk wisdom" says that child-rearing practices have strong impacts on the child's behavior and attitudes. Different ways of handling discipline (harsh punishment, exhortation or preaching, reasoning and explanation) may be expected to have different effects on children's predispositions to prosocial behavior. These issues are obviously important, certainly worthy of investigation; yet none of the three major theories deals extensively with these variables. (The principles of social learning theory and social cognitive theory, however, may be applied in formulating hypotheses about these differential effects).

In brief, to achieve a deeper understanding of the acquisition and development of prosocial behavior, we can be guided by psychoanalytic, social learning/social cognitive, and cognitive developmental theories. But our thinking and research should not be restricted by these. We must also examine other kinds of theories (e.g., attribution theory and sociobiology, to be discussed later), speculations, and empirical studies concerned with critical issues and variables not included in these major developmental theories.

Categories of determinants

It is obvious that many factors are determinants or antecedents of pro-social behavior. These fall into seven major categories: biological; group membership or culture; socialization experiences; cognitive processes; emotional responsiveness; personality and personal variables such as sociability and gender; and situational conditions and circumstances.

Biological factors no doubt play a role in the capacity for prosocial behavior, and some have speculated that there are genetic bases for individual differences in the predisposition to act altruistically. It is well established that genetic factors control the prosocial responses of certain subhuman species (see chapter 3), and it is tempting to generalize from the findings in animal studies to the biological bases of human prosocial behavior. Such generalizations must be made very cautiously.

It is generally accepted that an individual's actions, motives, orientations, and values are, to an appreciable degree, governed by the culture in which the individual is reared (*group membership*). All aspects of behavior and psychological functioning that are acquired rather than inherited "have – at least in their more superficial and peripheral aspects – a cultural tinge" (Kluckhohn & Murray, 1948, p. 59).

But membership in a cultural group can account only for general tendencies; it cannot be used to explain individual variations within a culture in the propensity to act prosocially. In discussing the cultural determinants of personality, Kluckhohn and Murray made observations that apply equally well to the determination of individual differences in prosocial behavior:

If there were no variations in the conceptions and applications of cultural standards, personalities [or predispositions to act prosocially] formed in a given society would be more nearly alike than they actually are. Culture determines only what an individual learns as a member of a group – not so much what he learns as a private individual and as a member of a particular family. Because of these special experiences and particular constitutional endowments, each person's selection from and reaction to cultural teachings have an individual quality.... Deviation from cultural norms is inevitable and endless...[Kluckhohn & Murray, 1948, p. 59]

The category of determinants labeled *socialization experiences*, the "special experiences" referred to in the preceding quotation, encompasses all the child's interactions with the major agents of socialization, such as parents (perhaps the most significant agents), peers, teachers, and the mass media. These socialization experiences are critical in molding the child's prosocial predispositions.

Included in the category of *cognitive processes* are the child's perceptions, interpretations, and evaluations of situations (e.g., attributional processes), the level of cognitive development or maturity and intelligence, the ability to see and evaluate the situation from the perspective of others (role taking), and the child's decision making and moral reasoning.

The variables in the category of *emotional responsiveness* are guilt, sympathetic concern for others, and empathy (an emotional state that stems from the apprehension of another's state or condition). Each of these reactions appears to affect whether or not and when people assist others.

Among the individual characteristics that are associated with prosocial tendencies are gender, developmental level (reflected in age), and personality traits such as assertiveness and sociability. These variables, in turn, reflect the influences of factors we have discussed; for example, age differences in prosocial responses are due in part to age changes in cognitive capabilities and socialization experiences.

External pressures, social events, and social contexts also may be powerful regulators of prosocial reactions. The category of *situational determinants* embraces two different kinds of events. One subcategory comprises events that "just happen" to the individual – for instance, chance or casual encounters that have enduring effects, influencing an entire life course, impelling the individual to become altruistic or selfish. The other subcategory of situational determinants has to do with the immediate social context, the situation or circumstance confronting the individual – for instance, one's mood at the time, or the personal characteristics (such as attractiveness) of others involved in the particular interaction.

The rest of this book is devoted to surveys, syntheses, and evaluations of the empirical evidence concerning each of these categories of determinants of prosocial behavior. It must be recognized that these determinants are not independent; they are, in fact, interdependent, interacting, and they are linked in intricate and complex ways. This is very easily demonstrated. Constraints are set on children's socialization experiences by the cultural milieu in which they are reared; for example, children in some cultures are never spanked, and children in other cultures are almost never reasoned with. In most cases, the child's learning at home (socialization experiences) is congruent with, and reinforces, the norms and standards of the culture in which the child is growing up (group membership or culture). But conflict is generated if the behavior, attitudes, and values stressed by the culture differ from those taught at home, and this conflict is likely to affect the development of prosocial behavior.

Socialization experiences undoubtedly affect cognitive functions and abilities (another category), and the latter, in turn, undoubtedly influence the child's reactions to socialization experiences. In addition, a child's affective reactions and interpretation of the immediate social context are to some extent dependent on the child's cognitive maturity and personality structure, both of which are affected by socialization experiences. Finally, biological factors probably determine, in part, the individual's affective responsiveness and other aspects of personality that regulate prosocial behavior. The complex interrelations among the various classes of determinants will become clearer as we proceed.

3 Biology and prosocial behavior

Sharing, helping, and self-sacrifice – behaviors that benefit another – are not exclusively human. Many animals below humans on the phylogenetic scale, ranging from social insects (ants, termites, bees, and wasps) through such mammals as hunting dogs and dolphins and up to the higher primates, act in ways that at least superficially resemble human prosocial behavior. In 1975, Edward O. Wilson, a prominent biologist at Harvard University, published the stimulating and controversial book *Sociobiology* (1975b). It was essentially the founding work in a new scientific field dedicated to the systematic study of the biological basis of social behavior, and it was rich in examples of actions by animals that appear to be prosocial. We shall sample a few of these.

Some social insects are suicidally self-sacrificing. Honeybee workers attack other insects attempting to intrude into their hive, embedding their barbed stingers in their victims. When this occurs, the bee's venom gland is pulled out, along with much of its viscera, so that it soon dies. Its attack is successful, however, because the venom gland continues to secrete poison into the intruder's wounds, and the odor coming from the sting excites other members of the hive to make further attacks on the intruders. Certain ants and wasps perform similar self-sacrificing defensive acts: "The fearsome reputation of social bees and wasps is due to their general readiness to throw away their lives upon slight provocation" in defense of their colonies (Wilson, 1975b, p. 121).

Members of many other species also will readily risk their lives to defend others, particularly their own young or their relatives. For example, the females of some bird species, such as ducks and partridges, protect their young from predators by feigning injury and acting as though they could be captured easily. When a mother bird spots a predator nearby, she acts as though her wing is broken, stumbling and fluttering at some distance (usually a safe distance) from her nest to draw the predator's attention away from her young. She moves farther from the nest, stumbling repeatedly, leading the predator away from her young. Finally, when the predator is a safe distance from the nest, the female tries to fly away. In many cases she escapes, and so do her young. However, in some cases the predator may capture her, but because of her actions, the young survive.

Various species of animals manifest altruism by sharing food. During one season of the year, for example, packs of African wild dogs live in dens, and some adults must stay at home to guard the pups while others go out to hunt for food. When the hunters return, they give fresh meat to those who stayed at home, or they regurgitate pieces for them. These actions benefit those who stayed at home with the pups, usually including the mother, as well as sick and crippled adults who are unable to hunt. Also, in this species, mother dogs sometimes allow hungry adults to suckle their milk.

According to Wilson, chimpanzees are the most altruistic of all animals. These animals are ordinarily vegetarians, but occasionally they capture rodents, monkeys, or baboons for food. Although the successful hunters dismember the prey and feast on it, other chimps may approach to beg for morsels. The hunters often respond to the beggars' appeal, permitting them to feed directly on the meat or pulling off pieces and donating these; sometimes they even share without being asked. Chimpanzees also help one another by communicating the location of food or by leading others to it.

How can animal altruism, especially of the self-sacrificing sort, be explained? Wilson (1975b, 1978) and some other biologists invoke the concept of *kin selection*, a broadened view of natural selection. Through self-sacrificing actions, it is argued, the animal increases the probability that its close relatives, who share its genes, will survive. Shared genes are preserved by the altruist's sacrifice, and these can then be transmitted:

In the process of natural selection...any device that can insert a higher proportion of certain genes into subsequent generations will come to characterize the species. One class of such devices promotes prolonged individual survival. And others promote superior mating performance and care of the resulting offspring. As more complex social behavior by the organism is added to the genes' techniques for replicating themselves, altruism becomes increasingly prevalent and eventually appears in exaggerated forms. This brings us to the central theoretical problem of sociobiology: how can altruism, which by definition reduces personal fitness, possibly evolve by natural selection? The answer is kinship: if the genes causing the altruism are shared by two organisms because of common descent, and if the altruistic act by one organism increases the joint contribution of these genes to the next generation, the propensity to altruism will spread through the gene pool. This occurs even though the altruist makes less of a solitary contributon to the gene pool as the price of its altruistic act. [Wilson, 1975b, pp. 3–4]

The mechanism can be shown most clearly in termite soldiers, who are genetically programmed to sacrifice themselves when they are attacked by ants or other enemies. To fight them off, the termite soldiers spray a glandular secretion that fatally entagles both themselves and their victims. By sacrificing itself, the termite soldier "protects the rest of the colony, including the queen and king which are the soldier's parents. As a result, the soldier's more fertile brothers and sisters flourish, and it is *they* which multiply the altruistic genes that are shared with the soldier by close kinship. One's own genes are multiplied by the greater production of nephews and nieces" (Wilson, 1975a, p. 42). Similar levels of self-sacrificial behavior have been observed among female worker ants, who share three-fourths of their genes with their sisters (Rushton, 1980). Moreover, among human twins aged 5 to 13 years, identical twins (who share all genes) have been observed to cooperate and help one another more than have fraternal twins (who share half their genes) (Segal, 1984).

The beneficiaries of altruism are in many cases the altruist's relatives, but many animals and people behave altruistically toward nonrelatives as well. For example, female bluebirds occasionally provide foster parenting to nestlings deserted by their mothers (Hayes, Felton, & Cohen 1985). Sociobiologists use the concept of *reciprocal altruism* to explain this behavior (Trivers, 1971, 1983). The fundamental idea is that the altruistic act entails danger (and no immediate benefit) to the altruist, but also may serve to evoke a reciprocal altruistic act by the beneficiary at some future time; that is, the altruist may at some time in the future be the target of the beneficiary's altruistic acts. For example, a female bluebird who helps a male to raise his motherless nestlings may then have the opportunity to mate with the male and raise her own offspring.

Mechanisms other than kin selection and reciprocal altruism have been proposed by other sociobiologists to explain human altruism. For example, it is possible that altruistic persons have higher prestige and are better accepted by others than are less altruistic persons, and therefore are more likely to survive and reproduce (Hill, 1984). According to this explanation, altruism increases the individual's own fitness (i.e., the likelihood of reproducing), not that of the individual's kin. Alternatively, cultural factors and learning may interact with genetic predispositions in a manner that produces a level of altruism that is adaptive in a given culture (MacDonald, 1984). For example, altruistic behavior may be especially adaptive in nonindustrial societies with extended families because helping is likely to be directed toward relatives (who share the altruist's genes) or others who may reciprocate. However, in an economically stratified society, low levels of altruism and high levels of competitiveness, aggressiveness, and the ability to manipulate others may be advantageous, resulting in upward mobility and control of resources (including desirable mates and prosperity for one's offspring).

Wilson's *Sociobiology* (1975b) is a fascinating account of social behavior among many groups of animals, and it provides a lucid account of evolutionary principles that may account for such behavior. It has generated a great deal of controversy, most of it centered on the author's speculation that human social behavior, including altruistic behavior, may also be under genetic control. Wilson reasons this way: Altruistic acts in animal societies can be plausibly explained as outcomes of kin selection. Humans also perform altruistic acts; so these are also likely to have a genetic basis. But, as critics point out, similarity of results does not imply identity of causes.

There is no doubt that humans have a biological *potential* for altruistic actions – otherwise they could not perform them. Furthermore, human altruism is often adaptive. Some researchers suggest that it is the capacity for empathy (the tendency to vicariously experience emotional states consistent with those of another; see chapter 9) that has evolved in humans and is the basis for biologically based altruism (Hoffman, 1981; MacLean, 1982). This capability to empathize may have evolved from the capacity of mammals to provide nurturant parenting to their young (MacLean, 1982; Panksepp, 1986). Animals who empathize are more likely to be sensitive to their offsprings' needs and thus assure their survival; consequently, the capacity for empathy will be enhanced through natural selection.

The fact that humans have the biological potential for altruistic actions is not, however, sufficient evidence that *individual differences* in altruism result from evolution or are genetically controlled. Yet recent research (much of it from studies of twins or studies of biological and adopted children) suggests that personality differences between people, involving characteristics such as activity level, dominance, extraversion and sociability, temperament, and vocational preferences, are in part due to genetic factors (Goldsmith, 1983; Mednick, Gabrielli, & Hutchings, 1984; Scarr & Kidd, 1983).

Moreover, some initial empirical evidence is consistent with the notion that predispositions toward prosocial behavior may have some genetic basis. Rushton and his colleagues (Rushton, Fulker, Neale, Nias, & Eysenck, 1986; Rushton, Littlefield, & Lumsdem 1986) administered questionnaires designed to assess altruism, empathy, nurturance, and aggressiveness to adult identical twins and fraternal (nonidentical) twins. They found that identical twins (who have the same genes) were much more alike in these characteristics than were fraternal twins. According to their estimates, genetic factors accounted for 50% to 70% of the variability in participants' scores, and similar findings were reported in another study of adults' self-reported empathy (Matthews, Batson, Horn, & Rosenman, 1981). However, it is difficult to interpret these findings because the measures were all self-reports. It is quite possible that the similarity between identical twins is partially due to genetically based personality traits that influence how individuals wish to appear to themselves and others. Further research, using other measures of prosocial behavior, will be required to establish the extent to which genetic factors influence altruism in humans.

Even if genes play some role in determining human prosocial behavior, their impact may be less than that of environmental factors. Wilson maintains that humans genes "have given away most of their sovereignty"; he believes that perhaps 10% of human social behavior has a genetic basis.

Stephen J. Gould, a biologist and historian of science, has admired Wilson's empirical observation work, but has criticized his extrapolation of the concept of genetic determinism to human social behavior. In an account of an argument he had with an eminent anthropologist, he underscores the fallacy of unquestioning acceptance of genetic explanation for human altruism:

My colleague insisted that the classic story of Eskimo on ice floes provides adequate proof for the existence of specific altruist genes maintained by kin selection. Apparently, among some Eskimo peoples, social units are arranged as family groups. If food resources dwindle and the family must move to survive, aged grandparents willingly remain behind (to die) rather than endanger the survival of the entire family by slowing an arduous and dangerous migration. Family groups with no altruist genes have succumbed to natural selection as migrations hindered by the old and sick lead to the death of entire families. Grandparents with altruist genes increase their own fitness by their sacrifice, for they insure the survival of close relatives sharing their genes.

The explanation by my colleague is plausible, to be sure, but scarcely con-clusive since an eminently simple, nongenetic explanation also exists: there are no altruist genes at all, in fact, no important genetic differences among Eskimo families whatsoever. The sacrifice of grandparents is an adaptive, but nongenetic trait. Families with no tradition for sacrifice do not survive for many generations. In other families, sacrifice is celebrated in song and story; aged grandparents who stay behind become the greatest heroes of the clan. Children are socialized from their earliest memories to the glory and honor of such sacrifice.

I cannot prove my scenario, any more than my colleague can demonstrate his. But in the current context of no evidence, they are at least equally plausible. Likewise, reciprocal altruism undeniably exists in human societies, but this provides no evidence whatever for its genetic basis. As Benjamin Franklin said: "We must all hang together, or assuredly we shall all hang separately." Func-tioning societies may require reciprocal altruism. But these acts need not be coded into our being by genes; they may be inculcated equally well by learning. [Gould, 1976, p. 20]

Gould's viewpoint is consistent with that of Campbell (1982, 1983), who has suggested that altruism may have evolved through social rather than genetic evolution:

Through the social mechanisms of child socialization, reward and punishment, social restricted learning opportunities, identification, imitation, emulation, in-doctrination into tribal ideologies, language and linguistic meaning systems, conformity pressures, social authority systems, and the like...sufficient reten-tion machinery exists for a social evolution of adaptive social belief systems and organizational principles to have taken place. [Campbell, 1975, p. 1107]

These two apparently different views – that altruism is the product of genetic factors or of cultural evolution – may not be as discrepant as they initially appear. In recent work, ecologists and biologists (including sociobiologists) have started to outline ways in which cultural and genetic factors may influence one another (e.g., Boyd & Richardson, 1985; Lumsden & Wilson, 1981). For example, Lumsden and Wilson (the same Wilson who wrote *Sociobiology*) have discussed a theory of genetic and cultural coevolution, or what they call *gene-culture theory*. In brief, they propose that genes prescribe a set of biological processes, called epigenetic rules, that control the development of the brain. These processes are dependent in part on the individual's cultural context, that is, on the information derived from the individual's culture and physical environment. Such information is then used to develop cognitive schemata (cognitive organizations that affect ways of processing and interpreting information), which influence thought patterns and decisions. In other words, the development of epigenetic rules is influenced by both genetic and cultural factors. In addition, these rules control what the individual attends to, encodes, and learns, and thus they regulate individuals' learning of specific culturally based behaviors or patterns of thinking (called *culturgenes*), which will be taught to their children. The avoidance of sibling incest is an example of epigenetic rules in action:

This epigenetic rule is not directed precisely at biological siblings. It will respond to any child with whom the young individual lives in close association, an arrangement that is likely to generate sibling incest avoidance when it operates within the context of the human family structure....The well-documented result of brother–sister mating is a higher frequency of genetic deformation in the offspring....Thus, the possession of an epigenetic rule innately biasing human behavior away from incestuous activity is expected to confer enhanced reproductive success. [Lumsdem, 1988, pp. 247–248]

What theorists such as Lumsden and Wilson are suggesting is that genetic and cultural factors cannot be totally differentiated; they are interdependent. It is likely that this is true. However, the degree to which genetic and cultural factors coevolve is as yet unknown.

Based on the limited available evidence, we concur with the view that both genetic and cultural factors influence the development of social behavior, including prosocial actions. What humankind inherits is the potential for learning a wide variety of social behavior and certain temperamental personality characteristics. What is actually acquired depends very much on the social situation, which may affect our cognitive processing and learning. Moreover, *individual differences* in socially adaptive cooperative and altruistic behaviors probably are in large part the products of social evolution and social learning. Indeed, as is discussed in later chapters, there is abundant evidence that both the social experiences and situational factors of childhood influence individuals' tendencies to behave in prosocial ways.

4   Culture and prosocial behavior

Anthropologists describe the norms of behavior (including cognitions, beliefs, ideals, and values) that are traditional, typical (or modal), and "expected" of people in particular cultures or subcultures. The array of cultural variation is enormous. As Margaret Mead concluded, "human nature is almost unbelievably malleable, responding accurately and contrastingly to contrasting cultural conditions" (Mead, 1935, p. 191).

In many cultures, prosocial conduct predominates, whereas in others, egoistic and selfish qualities are the norm. Recall the sharp contrast between the self-seeking, hostile Ik and the gentle, humane Hopi described earlier. Turnbull (1972) compared the Ik to members of other hunting societies who "frequently display those characteristics that we find so admirable in man, kindness, generosity, consideration, affection, honesty, hospitality, compassion, charity. For them, in their tiny close-knit society these are necessities for survival." Turnbull hypothesized that the Ik lost these qualities when their established culture and traditions disintegrated completely because of a combination of disastrous historical, political, and technological events.

Societies and cultures can be maintained only if their members have at least some concern about each other, but the degree of social concern varies greatly from culture to culture. Cooperation and social responsibility are outstanding features of some cultures, but these qualities are not highly valued in others. Margaret Mead (1935) found two tribes on the same island, New Guinea, with strikingly different patterns of personality and behavior. Members of one, the Arapesh, were gentle, loving, cooperative, generous, unaggressive people who were highly responsive to the needs and feelings of others and unconcerned about personal property. Mundugamor men and women, in contrast, displayed opposite characteristics; they were ruthless, aggressive, quarrelsome, undisciplined, and uncooperative.

42

The traditional societies of the Polynesian people on the island of Aitutaki (Graves & Graves, 1983), the Papago Indians in Arizona (Rohner, 1975), and the Maisin in Papua, New Guinea (Tietjen, 1986), like the Arapesh, are described as cooperative, helpful, and harmonious. In these societies, a strong group orientation is encouraged from infancy and is highly valued:

Individuals must cooperate with each other in order to survive. Good interpersonal relationships are necessary and of great importance to the Maisin villagers. They believe that the best way to maintain good relations with others is to help them, always when asked for help, and even when there is no request for assistance. Children are taught early to help and to be aware of others' needs. [Eisenberg et al., 1986, p. 172]

Societies in developed countries also differ radically from each other in social orientations and interactions. For example, Israeli kibbutz culture

can survive only if the members of the kibbutz are highly motivated to work for the welfare of the entire society. The Sabras [native-born Israelis] seem to have acquired this drive. They have learned...that prestige is attained primarily by behavior which benefits others. For the youngest children, who are in the process of learning the cultural norms the most frequent response to the question [What are the things you could do for which others would praise you?] is "generosity" with either assistance or goods. For the oldest group [of children questioned] which presumably has already learned the cultural norms, the most frequent category of response is "social responsibility," i.e., doing those things from which the group as a whole will benefit. [Spiro, 1965, p. 478]

In contemporary Soviet society, cooperation and social responsibility, consideration of others, and the needs and welfare of the collective (rather than of oneself) are also highly valued personal qualities (Bronfenbrenner, 1970). As we shall see, these are emphasized and inculcated by parents and all other agents of socialization, including the school and youth groups, from early infancy on.

Studies of cultures that differ from our own help illuminate the wide spectrum of norms, of "typical" or "modal" behaviors, that exists. A demonstration of that range can broaden our perspective and keep us from concluding that any particular trait or motive prevalent in one culture reflects a significant fact about universal or "raw" properties of human nature.

It is unfortunate from our point of view that few researchers using ethnographic techniques have focused on prosocial behaviors such as

generosity, consideration, and helping. Some anthropologists have provided excellent descriptions of average or modal forms of prosocial
conduct in particular cultures and have offered suggestions about possible antecedents of such conduct, but they have not ordinarily collected
information about the underlying psychological dynamics or processes.
The fact that two phenomena occur together in one culture (e.g., a high
level of social responsibility and strong peer-group pressure, as in the
kibbutz, or, for the Arapesh, consideration of others and tender care in
infancy) is not evidence that one is the antecedent of the other. Testing
hypotheses about the role of cultural differences in the development of
particular traits or behaviors requires that data from many cultures be
collected and analyzed in the same ways, and then compared. Unfortunately, there have been relatively few cross-cultural studies that have
tested hypotheses about prosocial behavior in this way; the most
relevant studies are reviewed next.

Cooperation, competition, and sharing

Cultural variations in children's tendencies to cooperate or compete have
been investigated systematically by Millard Madsen, Spencer Kagan,
George Knight, and their associates. Their data are particularly appropriate for cross-cultural comparisons because they used comparable
research methods with different groups.

A number of specially devised situational tests of cooperation and
competition have been used in this research. One of these tests or
"games" makes use of an object called a cooperation board. The board
is 18 inches square, and it has an eyelet at each corner. A string passes
through each of the eyelets and is attached to a metal weight, which
serves as a holder for a ball-point pen. A sheet of paper is placed on the
board for each trial so that the movement of the pen as the children pull
their string is automatically recorded.

Four children sit around the board, one at each corner, and each
controls one of the four strings. They play the game together, and the
object is to draw lines through target circles, one at each side of the
square. The string and eyelets are arranged so that each child can pull
the pen in only one direction, toward himself or herself. It is therefore
practically impossible to cross a circle if any child tries to prevent it by
pulling his or her own string. Children must cooperate in order to draw

the lines through the circles and thus win prizes. Competition is maladaptive, because no one can win if the children oppose each other in pulling the strings.

Instructions can be varied to heighten cooperation and group orientation by having only *group* rewards. The following introduction to the game accomplishes this:

As you can see, when we pull the string the pen draws lines. In this game we are going to pull the strings and draw the lines, but in a special way. The aim of the game is for you to draw a line over the four circles within one minute.... If you cover the four circles twice, everyone will get two prizes and so on. But if you cover less than four circles no one will get a prize. You may talk to each other but are not allowed to touch another child's string. [Shapira & Madsen, 1969, pp. 612–613]

The introduction can be modified to raise the level of competition in playing the game, as in these instructions:

Now the game is going to be somewhat different. Now everyone gets his own circle. This is David's circle (E writes name on a circle to the right of David). This is Ron's circle. [Etc.] Now, when the pen draws a line across one of the circles, the child whose name is in the circle gets a prize. When it crosses David's circle, David gets a prize; when it crosses Ron's circle, Ron gets a prize, and so on. You will have one minute to play before I stop you. [p. 613]

Under these conditions, only one child can win a reward at a time; rewards are *individual*. However, because any child can prevent another from crossing his or her own circle, the adaptive strategy is to cooperate, so that all the circles can be crossed quickly and all players can thus receive prizes.

Cooperation in these studies differs in one very important respect from the forms of prosocial behavior with which we are principally concerned. In these situational tests, cooperation is self-serving, as well as helpful to others; the actor benefits as much as fellow players do. A critical component of our definition of altruistic behavior (specifically, the absence of direct reward for an action) is missing in this situation.

To appraise the extent of cultural differences in tendencies to cooperate or compete, investigators have administered this and similar games to children in many cultural settings – children in the rural traditional (generally agricultural) or communal cultures in which the way of life has been relatively unchanged over very long periods of time, as well as children from industrialized cities in which modern Western European orientations prevail. Data from a number of studies reveal a consistent pattern. Children of all cultures cooperate with others if cooperation is rewarded directly, that is, when there are *group* rewards to be shared by all. However, when the instructions are changed and only *individual* rewards are available, cultural differences become manifest. Children reared in traditional rural subcultures and small, semiagricultural communal settlements cooperate more readily than do children reared in modern urban subcultures. For example, schoolchildren in Mexican villages and small towns are far less competitive and are more likely to avoid conflict than are their urban middle-class Mexican, Mexican-American, Afro-American, or Anglo-American peers (Kagan, Knight, & Martinez-Romero, 1982; Knight, Kagan, & Buriel, 1982; Madsen, 1967, 1971; Madsen & Shapira, 1970). Similarly, children from kibbutzim and Arab villages in Israel are more cooperative than urban Israeli children (Shapira & Lomranz, 1972; Shapira & Madsen, 1969, 1974), rural Colombian children of school age cooperate more than do urban children in that country (Marin, Mejia, & DeOberle, 1975), and rural Korean children are more cooperative than urban Korean children (Madsen & Yi, 1975). Children from a semitraditional village in Kenya are more cooperative than American children (Munroe & Munroe, 1977), Australian Aboriginal children are more cooperative than Australian children of European origin (Sommerlad & Bellingham, 1972), and New Zealand Maori children from a traditional rural culture are more cooperative than European and urban Maori children in New Zealand (Thomas, 1975). Similarly, traditionally raised Aitutaki children from one of the Cook Islands are more cooperative than are urban, Westernized Aitutaki children from New Zealand (Graves & Graves, 1983). Indeed, children from all urban areas, whether in Zambia (Bethleheim, 1973), Japan (Toda, Shinotsuka, McClintock, & Stech, 1978), Greece (Toda et al., 1978), or the United States (e.g., Kagan, Zahn, & Gealy, 1977; Toda et al., 1978), tend to be competitive and rivalrous in their game behavior.

Effects of living in two cultures

Those who move from the traditional cultures in which they were raised to urban settings may adopt two different cultural orientations. Under these circumstances, the individual's motivations are apt to change in the direction of the new, dominant group's standards, that is, toward less cooperation and more competition. Thus, studies of Mexican, Mexican-American, and Anglo-American children 7 to 9 years old showed the Mexicans to be most cooperative, and the Anglo-Americans the most competitive. The Mexican-American children who participated in both Mexican and American cultures fell between the other two groups (Kagan & Madsen, 1971).

Analogously, Australian Aborigines who live in traditional Aboriginal ways tend to be more cooperative than Australians of European background, but Aborigines with high educational goals, and therefore a stronger orientation toward a European way of life, are less cooperative (more competitive) than those with lower educational objectives (Sommerlad & Bellingham, 1972). In general, Canadian Indian children, particularly males, show more cooperative behavior than do urban Canadians (Miller, 1973; Miller & Thomas, 1972). But Indians attending an integrated school, acculturated to white standards, are more competitive than Indians who have maintained their contacts with traditional Indian ways. Interestingly, the white Canadians at the integrated school seem to take on some of their Indian peers' cooperative orientation and tendencies. Similar findings were reported in research with the Aitutaki. At a young age, they were very cooperative and generous; however, those exposed to Westernized schools became more competitive and rivalrous (Graves & Graves, 1983).

The effects of exposure to the values and life-style of industrialized societies can also be studied by examining the process of acculturation across generations. Among second- and third-generation Mexican-American children, the second-generation Americans distributed more chips won in a game to peers with whom they were playing than did third-generation Americans; however, both of these groups distributed their winnings more altruistically than did Anglo-American children.

Explanations of cultural variations in prosocial behavior

Clearly, the culture in which a child is reared is a major force in shaping the child's disposition toward competition or cooperation and prosocial behavior. To understand the processes underlying these cultural differences, we need accurate descriptions of the socialization techniques that stimulate or restrict the development of these tendencies. Unfortunately, we know relatively few details of child-rearing practices in other cultures. Cross-cultural investigators usually make only very general references to socialization practices, assuming that children acquire the norms, values, and behavior of their own culture by imitation, identification, or reinforcement.

For instance, Mead (1935) hypothesized that the gentle characteristics of the Arapesh stem, in large part, from the "cherishing" and tender attention Arapesh parents give their children. Other researchers have speculated that the dramatic differences in cooperation between rural and urban Mexican children are rooted in different patterns of family functioning in the two settings. In poor agricultural communities, children must cooperate in working with other members of their families to raise enough food for the family's survival. Such cooperation is rewarded because it benefits the whole family, whereas competitive and aggressive tendencies are punished because they threaten family unity (Madsen, 1967). In addition, investigators have suggested that children from traditional cultures often are trained to conform and to be compliant, rather than to do only that which pleases themselves (Munroe & Munroe, 1977). On the other hand, middle-class urban parents may regard competitiveness as necessary and desirable because it is advantageous in the economic struggle for survival. They may be models of competitiveness themselves, repeatedly reinforcing their children's competitive responses. Teachers in middle-class urban schools also reward competition more than do teachers in rural schools.

Kibbutz parents and teachers reinforce each other in inculcating cooperative values and orientations and in discouraging competition among children (Devereux et al., 1974; Nadler, Romek, & Shapira-Friedman, 1979).

In the kibbutz. . .children are prepared from an early age to cooperate and work as a group, in keeping with the objectives of communal living. . . .Generosity and cooperation were the most frequently rewarded behaviors, while selfishness and failure to cooperate were among the behaviors most frequently punished.

The formal teaching methods in the kibbutz are also noted for their minimal emphasis on competitive goals and techniques. . . .Competition, with all its punitive aspects, is far less intense in the classroom of the kibbutz than in that of the city. Not only do the agents of socialization avoid inducing a favorable set toward competition, but also the children themselves develop an attitude against competition. . . . By far the majority of the students said that their desire was primarily to become equal to their peers or . . . to raise the achievement level of their group as a whole. [Shapira & Madsen, 1969, p. 610]

This is in sharp contrast to what is stressed by their Israeli counterparts in the cities, who encourage their children to achieve and succeed through competition. It is hardly surprising that kibbutz children exhibit higher levels of both social responsibility and generosity (Nadler et al., 1979).

Analogously, the cooperativeness of Blackfoot Indian children has been attributed to the tradition of sharing all material wealth, as well as child-rearing and housekeeping duties, with other members of the family. The sharply contrasting level of competition among their Canadian, non-Indian peers is alleged to result from their being raised "within the general North American cultural milieu with its support of individual competition and achievement" (Miller & Thomas, 1972, p. 1105).

These explanations of cultural variations in children's tendencies to compete or cooperate, conceptualized as consequences of the norms and values of different cultures, seem plausible. However, the hypothesized links between aspects of the cultural milieu and children's prosocial conduct seldom have been spelled out in detail and sometimes have not been supported empirically. For example, one possible explanation for the tendency of traditional groups to cooperate is that traditional cultures, in which face-to-face contacts are very frequent, enhance the need to affiliate with and please other people. However, Anglo-American and Mexican-American children who differ in competitiveness do not differ in their reports of the need to affiliate with others (Kagan & Knight, 1981).

More research on the psychological mediators of cultural differences in cooperation and competitiveness is obviously necessary. As Kluckhohn pointed out long ago, "historical accident, environmental pressures, and seeming immanent causation, though all important, are not adequate to explain fully the observed facts of cultural differentiation. Unless we are to assume that each distinct culture was divinely revealed to its carriers, we must have recourse to psychology as part of the process" (1954, p. 961). What is needed is detailed and focused examination of precisely how the norms and approved responses are communicated and inculcated, how children learn them, and how they are generalized to new circumstances.

Socialization in the Soviet Union

One exceptional study of the socialization of prosocial orientations is worthy of special note – Urie Bronfenbrenner's (1970) multifaceted analysis of how predominant tendencies toward altruism and orientations toward the group (or collective) were (and still may be) inculcated in children in the Soviet Union. That investigation showed clearly that the process is started in the early phases of childhood:

From the very beginning stress is placed on teaching children to share and to engage in joint activity. Frequent reference is made to common ownership: "Moe eto nashe; nashe moe" [mine is ours; ours is mine]. Collective play is emphasized. Not only group games, but special complex toys are designed which require the cooperation of two or three children to make them work. [Bronfenbrenner, 1970, p. 21]

All agents of socialization (parents, workers in child-care centers, teachers, peers, the mass media) reinforce and support each other's deliberate efforts to inculcate "Communist ideals," cooperation, and orientation toward collective living. With increasing age, children are expected to take on more communal responsibilities, such as helping others and sharing in the work of the school and the broader community. The schools emphasize not only subject matter but also "character development," which includes cooperation, sharing, altruism, and consideration of the group. Youth groups and collectives of children formed within the classroom help maintain discipline and further encourage a collective orientation. "In Communist schools, a deliberate effort is made – through appropriate models, reinforcements, and group experiences – to teach the child the values and *behaviors* consistent with Communist ideals" (Bronfenbrenner, 1970, p. 158).

Bronfenbrenner's study is unique in describing in detail the techniques and pressures used in one complex culture to inculcate a definite pattern of values, attitudes, and responses. In this sense the study is a model of the procedures to be used in attempts to understand fully the agents and processes of socialization in any culture. However, although Bronfenbrenner draws comparisons between Soviet and American cultures, it is difficult to make any generalizations from these findings, interesting as they are. Valid cross-cultural generalizations about socialization require comparable data as well as multidimensional analyses of child-rearing practices and techniques of socialization in many cultures.

Pooling data from many cultures

Data from ethnographic studies of diverse cultures can be used to test the relations between personality or behavioral properties characteristic of members of different cultures and dimensions of family structure (such as complexity and distribution of authority) or functioning (such as decision making, or working as a unit). Such studies, "which collect data on a limited set of topics from many cultural units [may be] advocated not as a substitute for the intensive ethnography of single people, but rather as a needed additional mode of data collection, particularly for those correlational types of analyses in which dozens of cultures are needed" (Campbell, 1961, p. 343).

For example, suppose it is hypothesized that early participation in the family's economy and sustenance promotes strong tendencies to help others and to share possessions. The fact that in one particular culture children contribute substantially to the family's work and are also very helpful and generous to others outside the family is not by itself convincing evidence that the hypothesis is valid. The association between the variables may be explainable in many possible ways, and few of them can be ruled out if we are looking at only one culture. But the hypothesis could be tested by examining data on the relevant variables (children's participation in work, and assessments of their generosity) from many cultures. We could then determine whether, as the hypothesis predicts, helpfulness and generosity are more common among children from cultures in which children contribute to the family's economy than among those from cultures in which they do not.

The work of Harvard University's Beatrice and John Whiting and their colleagues (Whiting & Whiting, 1973, 1975) represents a notable step in the direction of systematic pooling of data from several cultures to investigate the correlations between cultural variables and the individual's personality and behavior. For example, in studying the association between cultural variables and children's altruism, they used naturalistic observations of 134 boys and girls between 3 and 11 years of age in six cultures – in Kenya, Mexico, the Philippines, Okinawa, India, and a Yankee community in New England. Each child was observed for an average of 17 periods of 5 min each, in a variety of social interactions – in courtyards near their homes, in the fields, on school grounds; with adults present or absent; during group work, play, or casual social activities. Every interaction was recorded and categorized into classes such as the following: shows symbolic aggression, offers help, reprimands, offers support, seeks dominance, seeks attention, suggests responsibly. These categories were reduced statistically by factor analysis to three major dimensions, one of which was *altruism versus egoistic behavior*. The behaviors most closely related to the altruistic extreme of this dimension were "offers help" (including food, toys, and helping information), "offers support," and "suggests responsibly" (making helpful suggestions) – interactions that benefit another individual. In contrast, the behaviors loading most heavily on the egoistic end of the dimension ("seeks dominance," "seeks attention," and "seeks help") benefited the actors themselves.

Most of the children in Kenyan, Mexican, and Philippine cultures were high above the median of the total six-culture sample in altruism, whereas most of the children in the other three cultures (the Okinawan, Yankee, and Indian) scored relatively low in altruism. The three altruism-inducing cultures were then compared with the egoism-producing cultures on a number of cultural factors. In the altruistic cultures, people tend to live together in extended family groups, and the female role is an important one; women in these societies make major contributions to the economy and food supply. In cultures in which independent, nuclear family units (consisting only of father, mother, and children) predominate, there are more egoistic children. Children in complex societies characterized by occupational specialization, a caste or class system, and centralized governments were less altruistic than those in simpler societies. Apparently,

in...simpler kin-oriented societies, with economies based upon subsistence gardening, altruistic behavior is highly valued and individual egoistic achievement frowned upon. Women must work in the fields, and the children must help in order for the family to subsist. To offer help, to support others, and to be responsible are taught both by precept and practice....

On the other hand, in the more complex societies, where no child knows what he is going to be when he grows up, individual achievement and success must be positively valued. To help a friend sitting next to you in an examination is defined as cheating. To ask for help from specialists such as mechanics, dressmakers, shopkeepers, psychotherapists, priests, or servants is expected and paid for in cash rather than in reciprocal services. [Whiting & Whiting, 1973, p. 64]

The cultural variable most closely associated with altruism was early task assignment or taking on responsibility (the extent to which children performed household tasks or chores related to the family's economic security and the welfare of family members) (Whiting & Whiting, 1975). This finding has been replicated in the laboratory setting; children induced to assist others on one occasion are more likely to assist others at a subsequent time than are children who were not provided with the first prosocial experience (Eisenberg, Cialdini, McCreath, & Shell, 1987; Staub, 1979).

Some of the findings of Bronfenbrenner's study in the Soviet Union add further evidence supportive of this hypothesis (Bronfenbrenner, 1970). One component of the Soviet school curriculum, designed to instill a sense of social responsibility, is that early in school, children are given an assignment of responsibility for younger schoolmates whom they are expected to help with problems, particularly schoolwork. This assignment of responsibility to Soviet children appears to achieve its objective; the children develop a strong sense of consideration and responsibility for others.

Similarly, Graves and Graves (1983) observed that Polynesian children from Aitutaki who lived in an urban setting performed fewer chores and were less altruistic than were children raised in traditional extended families. These researchers assessed altruism with observational procedures similar to those used by the Whitings. Less assignment of chores to urban children apparently resulted in less responsibility, low maternal expectations, and fewer adult-direction learning experiences. Moreover, children from urban families engaged in fewer social interactions than did rural children. These differences in socialization experiences undoubtedly contributed to the observed differences between urban and rural children's prosocial behaviors.

Synthesizing the findings from many studies, we can draw some tentative conclusions about the features of cultures that seem to affect prosocial development. Children apparently are likely to develop high levels of prosocial behavior if they are raised in cultures characterized by (1) parental and peer stress on consideration for others, sharing, and orientation toward the group, (2) a simple social organization and/or a traditional, rural setting, (3) assignment to women of important economic functions, (4) living in an extended family, and (5) early assignment of tasks and responsibility to children.

Children in different cultures differ not only in their frequency of prosocial and cooperative behavior but also in the reasons they give when they explain why someone should assist or not assist another in hypothetical situations. As chapter 8 demonstrates, children from various Western, urban areas, such as Germany and the United States, do not seem to differ much from each other in their moral reasoning, but children from cultures and subcultures that differ in ideology or degree of industrialization reason somewhat differently (Eisenberg, 1986; Eisenberg, Boehnke, Schuhler, & Silbereisen, 1985). For example, in their moral reasoning, children from an Israeli kibbutz focused more on internalized norms or values related to helping and on the importance of human beings than did urban Israeli and American children (Fuchs, Eisenberg, Hertz-Lazarowitz, & Sharabany, 1986). Such reasoning is consistent with the ideology of the kibbutz.

As noted earlier, most studies of cultural differences in prosocial behavior have involved measures of cooperation (when cooperation benefits the actor as well as the other person) or of prosocial actions that have been low in cost to the benefactor. In the Whitings' and Graves' studies, the rural children's prosocial behaviors were primarily directed toward family members or others in their own community and therefore may have been motivated by concern with social evaluation or with reciprocity from others. Thus, it is possible that children in rural and nonindustrial societies are cooperative and prosocial primarily when there is little cost for such behavior or when the recipient of their assistance is someone they know. They may not be more altruistic toward strangers than are children in industrialized settings.

The most convincing, fine-grained data on the processes underlying socialization come from studies of child-rearing practices in the family, most of them conducted in American settings by American researchers. We shall proceed to discuss the findings of these studies shortly (see chapter 6). However, before proceeding to that discussion, we shall digress briefly to discuss some "person" variables, attributes of individuals (such as age, sex, social class, personal qualities) that are associated with a strong or weak predisposition to prosocial behavior.

5   "Person" variables and prosocial behavior

A number of characteristics of individuals that may be correlated with prosocial tendencies do not fit neatly into any of our major categories of *determinants*. We refer to variables such as sex, class membership, age, ordinal position, and some personal attributes, such as sociability, self-esteem, and emotional adjustment. In general, these cannot be considered *process* variables; they do not refer to mechanisms, actions, or operations that in themselves influence prosocial responses or predispositions, nor can they directly promote or diminish these.

However, characteristics such as age, gender, and socioeconomic class may be functionally connected with *process* variables (such as socialization practices or cognitive factors) that do influence or regulate prosocial behavior. To cite one example, the disciplinary practices parents use in rearing their daughters can differ considerably from those applied in rearing their sons. Therefore, if we discover that there are sex differences in prosocial predispositions, we might attribute these, at least in part, to the differential socialization of boys and girls. Similarly, as we shall see, age is significantly correlated with level of donating. This correlation may simply reflect a link between age and two classes of determinants of prosocial behavior: socialization practices and cognitive processes. Parents of older children, compared with parents of younger ones, may more frequently use socialization techniques conducive to the development of helping and sharing. An alternative explanation of the observed correlation involves cognitive maturity: Older children have attained higher levels of cognitive functioning and moral reasoning than younger ones, resulting in higher levels of prosocial behavior among the older ones. Finally, prosocial action may be associated with personal qualities such as sociability, although this characteristic per se may not be an antecedent of prosocial behavior; rather, sociability and strong

55

prosocial tendencies may both be consequents of similar socialization experiences.

Age, sex, and social class sometimes act as "moderator variables," influencing the relations between antecedents and prosocial actions. For example, sex would be a moderator variable if a cognitive measure, say role-taking ability, were found to be correlated with helping behavior in boys but not in girls. Analogously, age would be considered a moderator variable if identification with parents were correlated with helping or sharing among preschool children but not among 7-year-olds.

Age and prosocial development

It is clear from studies conducted in the last decade that even 1- and 2-year-old children share objects and help other people (e.g., Easterbrooks & Lamb, 1979; Levitt, Weber, Clark, & McDonnell, 1985; Rheingold, 1982; Rheingold, Hay, & West, 1976). For example, Rheingold (1982) found that all the sample of 18-, 24-, and 30-month-olds she studied not only assisted their parents with tasks such as sweeping and setting the table, but did so to a considerable extent. Moreover, most of the children assisted adults who were strangers:

> . . . the children spontaneously and promptly assisted the adults in a majority of the tasks they performed. Furthermore, the children accompanied their assistance by relevant verbalizations and by evidence that they knew the goals of the tasks, even adding appropriate behaviors not modeled by the adults. Their efforts were construed as prosocial not only because they contributed to the completion of the tasks but also because the children showed an awareness of themselves as actors working with others to a common end. [Rheingold, 1982, p. 114]

Both the number and complexity of early helping and sharing behaviors appeared to increase with the age of the child (Dunn & Munn, 1986; Rheingold, 1982).

Children 1 to 2 years old are also likely to respond to others' emotional and physical distress (e.g., Dunn & Kendrick, 1979; Radke-Yarrow & Zahn-Waxler, 1984; Weston & Main, 1980; Zahn-Waxler & Radke-Yarrow, 1982). Although infants 6 to 12 months old show little reaction to the distress of others (Hay, Nash, & Pedersen, 1981; Zahn-Waxler & Radke-Yarrow, 1982), children who are 12 to 18 months old frequently react with agitation or sustained attention (Kiselica & Levin,

1987; Radke-Yarrow & Zahn-Waxler, 1984). By 18 months of age, children often attempt to comfort others who are suffering, and by age 24 months they frequently respond by bringing objects to the distressed person, verbally sympathizing, and making suggestions (Radke-Yarrow, Zahn-Waxler, & Chapman, 1983).

It is difficult to assess the degree to which various prosocial behaviors increase or decrease from the preschool years to the later school years. Age trends vary depending on the type of prosocial behavior. The amount that children give anonymously to needy others (e.g., donating money or valued objects to a charity or to less privileged peers) generally increases with age (see Radke-Yarrow et al., 1983, and Underwood & Moore, 1982a, for reviews). In comparison with younger children, older children are likely to share more generously with peers who are actually present than with the unseen (such as needy children in another country), but the difference is not very large (Radke-Yarrow et al., 1983).

Helping behavior seems to increase only slightly with age (Radke-Yarrow et al., 1983; Underwood & Moore, 1982a). Helping in emergencies, such as assisting someone who has fallen and been injured, appears to increase in the mid-elementary school years, decline later in elementary school or early in high school, and then increase again in the high school years (Midlarsky & Hannah, 1985; Staub, 1970b). Interview data from children have suggested that young children often are inhibited from helping because they feel unable to assist. In contrast, young adolescents and older preadolescents are inhibited by fear of social disapproval for helping (e.g., if their help is not wanted) or fear of embarrassing the potential recipient of help (Midlarsky & Hannah, 1985), as well as fear of being incompetent as a helper.

Some investigators have found that caregiving and comforting behaviors increase with age (e.g., Bar-Tal, Raviv, & Goldberg, 1982; Berman, 1987; Whiting & Whiting, 1973, 1975), but others have not (e.g., Gottman & Parkhurst, 1980; Yarrow, Scott, & Waxler, 1973). However, there have been relatively few studies of this issue.

In general, then, prosocial behavior increases with age, although the increase may be small for some types of prosocial behaviors. However, the motive underlying children's prosocial behaviors clearly change with age. Older children are more likely than younger children to help or share when they will not be rewarded for doing so (e.g., Bar-Tal, 1982). Moreover, older children are more likely to justify prosocial behaviors with altruistic (e.g., other-oriented) as opposed to nonaltruistic, self-related considerations (Bar-Tal, 1982; Eisenberg, 1986). In addition, older children, as compared with younger children, are better able to assist in an appropriate manner (e.g., Burleson, 1982; Radke-Yarrow & Zahn-Waxler, 1984; Rheingold, 1982). Some of the probable reasons for these age trends include the enrichment of role taking and empathic capabilities with greater maturity (see chapter 8 and 9), higher levels of moral reasoning (see chapter 8), increased skill in helping (Peterson, 1983a, 1983b), and more frequent repeated exposures to socialization experiences that enhance prosocial responding.

Gender differences in prosocial development

On theoretical grounds, we might expect to find that boys and girls would differ in prosocial activities, as they do in many personality and social characteristics. Nevertheless, in the majority of studies, no consistent gender differences have been found (Bar-Tal et al., 1982; Dunn & Munn, 1986; Yarrow & Waxler, 1976; see Radke-Yarrow et al., 1983, for a review). Where gender differences have been observed, they have been somewhat more likely to favor girls (Radke-Yarrow et al., 1983; Underwood & Moore, 1982a). This pattern is especially evident in studies of prosocial behavior among siblings (Summers, 1987).

It is likely that, to some extent, the results favoring females are artifactual; the gender-role stereotype that females are more altruistic than males is widely accepted, and girls tend to be viewed as more prosocial than boys by peers and teachers (Berman, 1980; Block, 1973; Eisenberg & Lennon, 1983; Shigetomi, Hartmann, & Gelfand, 1981). In addition, some research techniques include ratings of behaviors or traits that are more characteristic of girls than of boys (such as comforting a younger, injured child), and girls therefore are rated higher (Zarabatany, Hartmann, Gelfand, & Viciguerra, 1985). Indeed, in research concerning adults' actual helping behaviors in laboratory or natural settings, males have been found to be more helpful than females (Eagly & Crowley, 1986), probably because the indices used often have been based on instrumental, rescuing actions (e.g., helping to change a tire) or have involved potential danger (e.g., picking up a hitchhiker) or chivalrous behavior. In contrast, in situations involving psychological assistance and helping friends and acquaintances, women may be more likely to assist.

In summary, there is no clear and consistent evidence of gender differences in prosocial responding, although girls may perform some types of prosocial behaviors more frequently than do boys. Gender differences may be due to several different factors. For example, child-rearing techniques used with girls (greater affection from their mothers, and more inductive and less power-assertive discipline) have generally been found to be conducive to the development of prosocial behavior (Hoffman, 1975a,c) (see chapter 6). Furthermore, in many cultures, helpfulness and nurturance of others are considered more appropriate for girls than for boys; girls are therefore more frequently and more strongly rewarded for such behavior by socializers (Fagot, 1978; Power & Parke, 1986). However, boys are more likely to be reinforced for helping behaviors that involve some risk or involve helping females.

Social class and prosocial behavior

Family socioeconomic status does not appear to have any consistent effect on children's predispositions to prosocial behavior. In some studies, researchers have found no social class differences in helping, sharing, or cooperative behaviors (e.g., DePalma, 1974; Nelson & Madsen, 1969; Yarrow et al., 1973); in other studies, differences favoring children of higher social-class status have been reported (e.g., Berkowitz, 1968; Doland & Adelberg, 1967; Payne, 1980; Raviv & Bar-Tal, 1981); still other findings favor children lower in family socioeconomic status (Friedrich & Stein, 1973; Knight & Kagan, 1977; Madsen, 1971; Ugurel-Semin, 1952).

Family size and ordinal position

No clear-cut or easily interpreted patterns of relations between family size or ordinal position and prosocial behavior have been discovered. Some investigators have found that family size and sharing behavior are unrelated (Dreman & Greenbaum, 1973; Gelfand et al., 1975; Handlon & Gross, 1959), whereas others have found that growing up in a large family promotes generosity (Benson et al., 1980; Ribal, 1963; Sawyer, 1966; Ugurel-Semin, 1952) and less emphasis on reciprocity as a reason for sharing (Dreman & Greenbaum, 1973). In contrast, according to the data from two other studies, small family size is positively correlated with helping in emergency situations (Staub, 1971a,b). The reasons for this positive correlation are unclear, although Staub speculated that children from small families may have a great deal of self-assurance and initiative and consequently may be more willing to act spontaneously to help another child.

Studies of the influence of ordinal position on prosocial behavior have also yielded inconsistent results. Thus, among Israeli sixth graders, secondborns were more altruistic than firstborns, as judged by sociometric nominations and willingness to volunteer time to assist others (Raviv, Bar-Tal, Ayalon, & Raviv, 1980). However, firstborn or older siblings in American families were more likely than middle or younger children to help a peer in distress and to share (or donate) generously (Staub, 1971b). According to naturalistic observations in six cultures, an only child or the youngest child in a family tends to be more egoistic than others, seeking more help and attention, but offering less help and support to peers (Whiting & Whiting, 1975).

A recent meta-analysis of data from a number of studies indicates that older siblings generally are much more likely to assist their younger siblings than vice versa, and more prosocial behavior occurs in sibling dyads characterized by large age differences (Summers, 1987). The greater helpfulness of older children may be most parsimoniously explained in terms of social learning theory; older children are expected to help with their younger siblings and frequently are rewarded for being helpful and nurturant to them. These responses thus might become strong and habitual and might generalize to interactions with others.

Personality characteristics and prosocial behavior

A few landmark studies in social psychology and the psychology of personality (e.g., Adorno, Frenkel-Brunswick, Levinson, & Sanford, 1950) have clearly demonstrated that certain forms of negative behavior (e.g., juvenile delinquency, and fascist and racist attitudes) are linked to specific personality traits and motives, such as emotional insecurity, rigidity, suspiciousness, and hostility. It therefore seems intuitively reasonable to hypothesize that prosocial dispositions also are associated with specific personality characteristics. However, as we show in the following review of relevant studies, the data provide only partial support for this hypothesis.

Expressiveness, sociability, aggression, and assertiveness

Apparently, young children who feel free to express their own emotions are more apt than other children to approach and assist others. Among toddlers, preschoolers, and school-age children, expressiveness of feeling – especially of positive rather than sad affects – is associated with spontaneous prosocial actions in the preschool classroom and in other settings (Bergin, 1987; Chapman, Zahn-Waxler, Cooperman, & Iannotti, 1987; Denham, 1986; Eisenberg et al., 1981; Lennon & Eisenberg, 1987; Strayer, 1980), as well as with cooperation (Marcus, 1986).

Sociability and gregariousness are also associated with toddlers' and children's tendencies to perform prosocial actions, especially outside of the home (e.g., Bergin, 1987; Eisenberg et al., 1981; Stanhope, Bell, & Parker-Cohen, 1987). Sociable preschool children are more likely than less sociable peers to help or share spontaneously (without being asked to) (Eisenberg et al., 1981; Eisenberg, Pasternack, Cameron, & Tryon, 1984). In contrast, the frequency of compliance with requests for assistance from peers is uncorrelated or negatively correlated with sociability, perhaps because less social children often find it difficult to refuse their peers' requests (Eisenberg et al., 1981; Eisenberg, Pasternack, Cameron, & Tryon, 1984).

In one study, sixth graders were exposed to a contrived (faked) emergency situation in which a child in another room apparently had been injured. If the "emergency" occurred in a social situation – that is, when the child was with another child – an extroverted child was more likely to go to the aid of the "injured" peer than was an introverted child. There were no differences in the helping responses of introverts and extroverts if they are alone at the time of the emergency. In general, extroverted children engaged in more active helping, whereas introverts tended to prefer passive modes of helping that did not require social interaction (e.g., giving information to an adult and getting the adult experimenter to assist) (Suda & Fouts, 1980).

The relation between aggression and prosocial responses in nursery-school children is complex. In a pioneering study, Murphy (1937) found that 2-to-4-year-old children's sympathetic behavior was positively correlated with their aggressiveness, leadership, and resistance (based on teachers' ratings), but these findings were replicated only for nursery-school boys (not for girls) in a later naturalistic study (Friedrich & Stein, 1973).

A more complex relationship among aggression, sharing, comforting, and helping was discovered in another interesting study of preschoolers. Aggression and being the victim of aggression were positively correlated with sharing and comforting for boys relatively low in aggression (below the mean), but there was a *negative* association between overt aggression and prosocial behavior for the more aggressive boys (those above the mean in aggression) (Yarrow & Waxler, 1976). Perhaps, as the investigators suggested, relatively infrequent manifestations of aggression are an indication of assertiveness, rather than of hostility, and assertiveness may be associated with greater likelihood of intervention to help others. This may not be true for elementary-school-age boys; among this group, boys who were either quite high or low in aggressiveness were low in prosocial responding (Barrett, 1979).

Assertiveness is, in fact, related to the performance of some forms of prosocial behavior, including elementary-school children's spontaneously emitted prosocial behaviors (Larrieu, 1984b), overall frequency of prosocial actions (Barrett, 1979; Larrieu & Mussen, 1986), and prosocial behavior as indexed by peers' sociometric nominations (Larrieu & Mussen, 1986). Moreover, assertive preschoolers – that is, children likely to defend objects in their possession and to grab objects from peers – show relatively high levels of spontaneously emitted prosocial behavior (Eisenberg et al., 1981; Eisenberg, Pasternack, Cameron, & Tryon, 1984; also see Romer, Gruder, & Lizzardo, 1986). In contrast, prosocial behavior in response to requests has been associated with low rates of preschoolers' defending objects or taking others' toys (Eisenberg et al., 1981; Eisenberg, Pasternack, Cameron, & Tryon, 1984), with low dominance in preschoolers' peer interactions (Eisenberg & Giallanza, 1984), and with nonassertiveness among elementary-school children (Larrieu, 1984b). A certain level of assertiveness may be necessary for many children to approach others needing assistance spontaneously (Midlarsky & Hannah, 1985), but on the other hand, children low in assertiveness are likely to be frequent targets of peers' requests for assistance and may be less inclined to refuse such requests.

On the surface, then, there seem to be some inconsistencies in the empirical findings. Emotional expressivity and assertiveness are associated with high levels of spontaneous prosocial behaviors, but not high levels of helping or sharing in response to requests. Moreover, young children who are prosocial are also more likely to manifest some aggression, but not high levels of aggression. Moderate levels of aggression probably reflect outgoingness, emotional responsiveness, and assertiveness, and such qualities may facilitate young children's tendencies to engage in positive, prosocial interactions with others. Indeed, a certain level of sociability and assertiveness may be necessary for children who wish to spontaneously offer their services or possessions. Unsociable, unresponsive, and nonassertive children would not be expected to approach others spontaneously or to initiate prosocial interactions frequently; rather, they seem to be viewed by peers as easy targets for requests (Eisenberg, McCreath, & Ahn, 1988). Such children frequently comply with requests for sharing or helping because they are unable to assert themselves and want to avoid conflict.

In summary, different personality characteristics are associated with different forms of prosocial behavior. Apparently, different forms of prosocial behaviors have different psychological meanings for different persons and are likely to be performed for different reasons (Gergen, Gergen, & Meter, 1972; Hampson, 1984). The ease with which a particular prosocial act such as helping is performed may depend on the child's ability to approach others, on the child's assertiveness, or on other aspects of personality.

Social and emotional adjustment

Preschool and elementary-school children with strong prosocial predispositions tend to be well adjusted, good at coping, and self-controlled. Among the preschool children in one longitudinal study, those who were rated high in the characteristics "helpful and cooperative," "concerned with moral issues," and "considerate of other children" scored high on an index of ego resiliency (ability to recover after stressful experiences) and were appropriately self-controlled. Adequate personal adjustment and ego strength (coping ability) at the age of 4 years also predicted generosity (sharing and distributing rewards) at the age of 5 years. Those who were generous at 5 years had been described by their nursery-school teachers a year earlier as bright, reasonable, generous, cooperative, considerate, planful, reflective, attentive, creative, dependable and responsible, calm, relaxed, and tending to recover readily after stressful experiences. In contrast, children low in generosity at the age of 5 years had been judged, at the age of 4 years, to be aggressive, unable to delay gratification, active, emotionally labile, restless and fidgety, afraid of being deprived, tending to overreact to frustrations, and behaving in immature and rattled ways to stress (Block & Block, 1973).

Fourth-grade children in another study were deliberately overpaid for their work and then given a chance to donate some of their undeserved earnings anonymously to poor orphans. Those high in ability to delay gratification (to forgo an immediate reward in order to receive a more desirable reward later on) – an index of ego strength or self-control – donated more than did their peers who showed less ability to delay gratification (Long & Lerner, 1974). In another study of fourth graders, positive self-concepts were positively correlated with peer nominations for prosocial behavior, but were not associated with levels of observed sharing, caring, and helping behavior (Larrieu & Mussen, 1986). In addition, children's helping, consideration, and donating have been shown to be associated with teachers' ratings of children's competence in peer interactions (Larrieu, 1984a), popularity (Gottman, Gonso, & Rasmussen, 1975; Raviv, Bar-Tal, Ayalon, & Raviv, 1980), and having close friends (McGuire & Weisz, 1982).

Among preadolescents, the most altruistic (as assessed by peer nominations) have been found to score higher than their less altruistic peers on self-report measures of ego strength and self-esteem. The altruists were more self-confident and self-assured and were more satisfied with their relationships with peers (Mussen et al., 1970). Similarly, eighth graders viewed as unpopular by peers engaged in less prosocial behavior (Hampson, 1984).

Overall, the data derived from a variety of studies, using diverse research methods and involving participants of a wide range of ages, are fairly consistent and hence permit some tentative conclusions about the correlations between personality structure and prosocial behavior.

Compared with their peers, children with strong prosocial dispositions appear to be better adjusted, socially skilled, more expressive, more gregarious, and somewhat aggressive or assertive.

The associations discovered are somewhat fragile, however. Some results have been replicated, and some have not; moreover, not all existing findings are consistent (e.g., Cox, 1974; O'Connor, Dollinger, Kennedy, & Pelletier-Smetko, 1979). This is unfortunate, for the discovery of clear-cut and direct connections between personality characteristics and prosocial behavior would have many theoretical and practical implications. If, for example, self-esteem in children were closely associated with helping behavior, we might infer that high self-esteem and strong predispositions to altruism are both consequences of the same family socialization experiences, or that certain socialization practices result in high self-esteem, which, in turn, enhances prosocial behavior. If the socialization antecedents of self-esteem were understood, this knowledge could be applied to raise children's self-esteem, and children's prosocial tendencies would probably increase automatically. Unfortunately, however, the correlations between self-esteem and prosocial conduct were not high, nor were they replicated in many studies. In fact, only a few correlations between children's personality characteristics and prosocial dispositions are well established and reliable; so we cannot yet make valid inferences about the family socialization practices or other factors that shape prosocial conduct from these correlations. The impact of child-rearing techniques on children's dispositions toward prosocial action must be studied directly. Indeed, that is the central topic of the next chapter.

6   Socialization in the family

As we have seen, children generally acquire the patterns of behavior, motives, personal characteristics, predispositions, values, and social responses that are adaptive and expected in their own cultures. Most children reared in Mexican villages, Hopi children on reservations in the Southwest, and youngsters on Israeli kibbutzim are more considerate, kind, and cooperative than their "typical" middle-class American counterparts.

Nevertheless, cultural factors alone cannot account for the wide range of prosocial actions within each culture; some children are consistently cooperative and generous, but others are not. These individual differences are attributable primarily to variations in the ways children are socialized in their own families, where they acquire many of their personal attributes, motives, and values.

Many agents contribute to the child's socialization and to the development of prosocial tendencies. In the early years, the family is the principal agent of socialization. In this chapter, attention is centered on how the family promotes (or inhibits) prosocial behavior and, most important, strengthens (or weakens) children's *internalized* motivations for altruism, helpfulness, generosity, and consideration of others.

Socialization involves many processes. Parents often self-consciously attempt to teach their children prosocial responses by praising and approving altruism and generosity and punishing selfish and uncooperative responses. They may instruct their children, reason with them, and explain rules or standards of prosocial behavior. But many of the child's prosocial actions and motivations are the products of more subtle processes, such as imitation or identification; these responses appear to emerge spontaneously, without direct training or reward – usually without anyone intending to "teach" and without the child intending to learn. In addition, as we shall see, the nature of the family milieu (e.g., permissive or strict), the quality of parent–child interactions (e.g., nurturant or aloof), and specific child-rearing practices (such as the use of punishment or reasoning as disciplinary techniques) appear to have direct bearing on the child's prosocial tendencies.

Unfortunately, we do not know the extent to which any particular class of prosocial responses, such as sharing or caring, is attributable to specific processes or experiences. We cannot determine whether generosity is primarily a product of identification with a generous parent or the result of previous rewards for acts of charity. Furthermore, the principal determinants of any response may vary from one child to another; one child's generosity may be the result of frequent observation of generous peers, whereas another child's generosity may stem from identification with a nurturant, generous father.

Although experts agree that prosocial responses are multiply determined, the consequents of many interacting factors, most investigations have concentrated on only one or a few critical factors at a time. The antecedents selected for study, and the way they are investigated, depend on the investigator's theoretical orientation, hypotheses, values, and methodological preferences. Some researchers prefer to study children in their natural settings, such as home or playground; others conduct experiments in a laboratory or school. Suppose, for example, an investigator wants to test the hypothesis that parental modeling of altruism increases children's generosity. An experimental test of the hypothesis might involve having a group of children observe an adult model playing a game, winning prizes, and then donating some of those winnings to charity. A control group of children would also observe the model playing the game and winning, but not sharing the winnings.

Afterward the children themselves play the game, collect prizes, and then have an opportunity to share their winnings. If the children who observed the model's sharing then share their prizes with others, whereas the controls do not, we might conclude, correctly, that adult modeling of sharing increases children's tendencies to share. Such an experiment would provide valuable information about imitation as a fundamental process in the development of sharing behavior. But further tests would be necessary to determine whether this prosocial behavior is temporary or lasting, restricted to this particular situation or generalized.

Can we generalize from the findings of experiments to the probable consequences of certain socialization practices in the family? That is, are the experimental situations really accurate representations of what occurs in the home? If children in a laboratory imitate a model's performance, can we conclude that they will ordinarily copy a parent's behavior at home? If manipulations in an experimental situation modify prosocial responses in discernible ways, it seems entirely reasonable to infer that many repetitions of comparable events in the real world would have similar – and perhaps more pronounced and more lasting – consequences. Yet we cannot be *certain* that such inferences are valid without testing them directly in family settings.

Experimental studies are extremely useful in clarifying the fundamental mechanisms underlying socialization, including the acquisition of prosocial responses. But the experiments are not, strictly speaking, investigations of socialization, because the contrived laboratory situations may be radically different from those the child encounters at home. In an experiment, the child usually observes the model's performance only once, or at most a few times, and the model is in most cases a stranger to the child. In the real world, the child's models are likely to be parents or others with whom there are frequent, close, and affectionate interactions. If an experiment does not accurately simulate real-life circumstances, we must be very cautious about generalizing its conclusions to the processes of socialization in the family.

Modeling and identification

Our review begins with research on those family determinants of prosocial behavior that are the most subtle, but among the most powerful, antecedents: modeling and identification.

In one typical experiment on the effects of modeling, children observed an adult model playing a miniature bowling game, winning tokens that could be exchanged for desirable prizes, and then donating half of her winnings to poor children. A control group observed the model playing the game and winning, but she was called out of the room before she could make any donations. The children were then left alone, and their behavior was observed through a one-way mirror. Those in the experimental group were generous in their donations, matching the model's behavior very closely, whereas the control children gave little (Rice & Grusec, 1975).

These findings have been replicated in other studies (e.g., Bryan & Walbek, 1970; Grusec, Kuczynski, Rushton, Simutis, 1978), although some investigations have yielded less clear-cut results (e.g., Lipscomb, Larrieu, McAllister, & Bregman, 1982). Thus, in one study, children in kindergarten and the sixth grade were randomly assigned to one of three kinds of modeling experiences: a model who, after playing a game, generously donated most of the money she won to a fund for crippled children, a model who selfishly kept all she won, or a neutral model who neither kept nor donated her winnings. As expected, the kindergarten children imitated the model they observed: Those exposed to the generous model donated the greatest amount, and those exposed to the selfish model donated the least. However, the sixth-graders' donations were not significantly affected by the behavior of the model, perhaps because these older children had already internalized "the norm of social responsibility which conveys the societal expectation that, generally speaking, people in a position to do so should help those in need" (Lipscomb et al., 1982, p. 280). Consequently, these children may not have needed to consider the model's behavior as an example of appropriate, expectable behavior.

The weight of the evidence, however, clearly indicates that children are likely to imitate the altruistic actions of models they observe and thus enhance their own prosocial behavior. Even relatively brief exposures to a generous model may have some generalized and lasting positive effects (Rice & Grusec, 1975; Rushton, 1975). Two to four months after they first observed a model playing a game and making generous donations to charity from her winnings, a group of 7-to-11-year-olds played the game again in another setting (a different room, a different experimenter, and a different potential beneficiary of their donations). These children donated significantly more generously from their winnings than did a control group who had not witnessed the model donating to charity (Rushton, 1975). Furthermore, exposure to displays of great generosity by models may amplify such increases in children's altruism, and these effects are maintained, at least for a few weeks (Rushton & Littlefield, 1979).

Do the effects of modeling and imitation of one class of prosocial responses (say generosity in donations) generalize to other classes, such as sharing or helping others in distress? In general, research indicates that generalization from the effects of brief exposures to models is limited, evident only in similar or slightly different situations, but not in situations that are different from the original one (Elliott & Vasta, 1970; Midlarsky & Bryan, 1972). For example, children who observed and imitated a model's generosity to poor children were no more likely than a control group to share pennies with classmates or to collect gifts for sick children (Grusec, Saas-Kortsaak, & Simutis, 1978). Apparently the effects of modeling and imitation "do not generalize to situations... discrepant from the original training situation" (Grusec, 1981, p. 73); see also Moore and Eisenberg (1984) and Radke-Yarrow et al. (1983).

Effects of the model's power and nurturance

Not all models are equally successful in inducing imitation of prosocial acts. There is at least partial support for the hypothesis that models who are powerful (i.e., in direct control of resources or rewards of value to the child), competent, and nurturant (warm and friendly) are more effective than models lacking these characteristics (Radke-Yarrow et al., 1983). Children between 7 and 11 years old in one study more frequently emulated the sharing responses of a powerful model (someone in a position to select the winner of a special prize) than the responses of a model who was not perceived as powerful (Grusec, 1971; Moore & Eisenberg, 1984).

Similarly, although not all studies have yielded the same findings (e.g., Grusec, 1971; Weissbrod, 1976), nurturant (warm, friendly, and responsive) models may be more likely to be imitated frequently than are non-nurturant (aloof, matter-of-fact, and unresponsive) models. Compared with children who observed a non-nurturant model helping a child in distress, a group of children who witnessed a nurturant model performing the same acts were, on subsequent occasions, more likely to offer help (Radke-Yarrow et al., 1983; Staub, 1971b). However, children are not as likely to emulate the generosity of a nurturant model if their exposure to that model is only brief. If the model dispenses nurturance in noncontingent ways, or if the cost of the prosocial behavior for the children is high (Grusec, 1971; Grusec & Skubiski, 1970; Rosenhan & White, 1967; Weissbrod, 1976). Perhaps "noncontingent nurturance is interpreted by children as indicating permissiveness and consequently children do as they please after contact with noncontingent nurturant models.... However, when adult nurturance is part of an ongoing relationship and is not entirely unconditional (which is generally the case in real life), it appears that nurturance increases the effectiveness of a prosocial model" (Moore & Eisenberg, 1984, p. 148).

Generalizations from the findings of these experimental studies must be drawn cautiously, because the situations and experimental manipulations were quite different from what children ordinarily encounter. In the experiments, the model was a stranger, and the nurturance experiences were few (often only one) and of brief duration, whereas in the actual world the child experiences nurturance frequently and over extended periods of time from models such as parents, peers, and teachers. Under these latter circumstances, nurturance may well be expected to have more profound and lasting effects on imitation.

Compelling evidence of this was found in an experimental study of preschoolers (ages 3.5 to 5.5 years) that more adequately duplicated a real-life situation (Yarrow et al., 1973). Children's initial dispositions toward helping were assessed by observing their reactions to pictures of people or animals in distress (e.g., a picture of a child falling off a bike and getting hurt) and their reactions to actual instances of distress (encountering a kitten tangled in yarn, struggling toward its mother). The model, an assistant teacher at the nursery school for 2 weeks before the modeling sessions began, was a significant, familiar figure to the children. During the pretraining period, the model was consistently nurturant with one-half of the children, initiating friendly interactions, offering help and support freely, sympathizing and protecting, and praising them frequently. With the other half of the participants she was generally non-nurturant, aloof, reserved, and only minimally helpful.

Each child participated in two individual modeling sessions separated by an interval of 2 days. With one group of children – half of them from the high-nurturance group and half from the low-nurturance group – the model demonstrated *symbolic* helping behavior in play situations, using miniature reproductions of distress situations involving children, families, and animals. Duplicates of these reproductions, one for the model and one for the child, were arranged on a table in a playroom. When the child arrived, the model greeted her and explained the procedure: "Here are some animals that need someone to take care of them. I'll have the first turn and the next turn will be yours." Then, turning to the first reproduction, a monkey trying to reach a banana, she said, "Oh, Mr. Monkey, you must be hungry. You can't reach your food. I'll help you. Here's your banana. Now you won't be hungry." The child then took his turn, using his matched set of toys. If the child retrieved the banana for the monkey, the adult said, "I think the monkey feels better because you gave him his food. He isn't hungry now." If the child did not help, the adult went on the next set of reproductions, repeating the procedures. The modeling always included verbalized awareness of the distress, sympathy and help for the victim, pleasure or relief at the comfort or well-being that resulted, and use of the word "help" to summarize what had been done.

The children in another group – half had high nurturance by the model and half did not – were exposed to two types of modeling: the same *symbolic* altruism the first group observed, and *actual* help to an individual in distress. The latter consisted in the model's showing concern and giving aid to a woman who entered the playroom during the training session and "accidentally" banged her head against a table, winced, and held her head. The model responded sympathetically, putting her hand on the confederate's shoulder and saying, "I hope you aren't hurt. Do you want to sit down a minute?" The victim responded appreciatively.

Two days after the training sessions, the altruistic responses of the children were tested with a series of pictures, sets of toys, and behavioral incidents. Then, to evaluate the durability and generalization of the effects of training, 2 weeks later the children were taken individually to a neighboring house to visit a mother and her baby. While there, they had an opportunity to help the mother by picking up a basket of spools or buttons that had spilled or by retrieving toys that had dropped out of the crib.

The two types of modeling had vastly different effects on children's helpfulness. Symbolic modeling alone produced less increment in altruistic responses than did the combination of symbolic modeling and actual helping. Two days after the end of the training, those exposed exclusively to symbolic modeling showed increases only in symbolic altruism, that is, in play situations; their altruism did not generalize to pictured situations or to real-life incidents. However, observing a model helping someone enhanced children's helping behavior. Although nurturance from the model in itself had no significant influence on children's helpfulness, nurturance together with specific modeling of helpfulness to others, accompanied by the model's verbal communications, resulted in a significant increase in the probability that helping actions would be imitated and generalized to other situations. Two weeks after the training, 84% of those who had experienced the combination of the model's nurturance and extensive (live) modeling expressed sympathy and helped the mother and baby, although only 24% of them had helped in the original (pretraining) situations. The investigators therefore concluded that "the optimal condition for the development of sympathetic helpful behavior was one in which children observed an adult manifesting altruism at every level – in principle and in practice, both toward the child and toward others in distress" (Yarrow et al., 1973, p. 251).

Parental modeling, identification, and prosocial behavior

Identification, which shares some of the features of imitation, is a major concept of psychoanalytic theory referring to the child's attempts to incorporate the behavior and characteristics of another person. "Identification endeavors to mold a person's own ego after the fashion of one that has been taken as model" (Freud, 1921/1960, p. 47). Whereas imitiation refers simply to copying another's response, identification generally denotes a more subtle process of incorporating broad *patterns* of behavior, motivation, and thought. Furthermore, identification is presumably based on strong emotional ties to the model whose behavior is adopted, whereas imitation is not. For the child, the most salient models are parents, and according to psychoanalytic theory, parental characteristics such as warmth, competence, and control of resources lead to strong identification.

The powerful role of identification in promoting the development of prosocial tendencies has been amply demonstrated in a number of studies dealing with different forms of prosocial behavior. The generous preschool boys in the one study (judged by their willingness to share prizes with friends) frequently portrayed their fathers in projective doll play as nurturant and warm, as well as generous, sympathetic, and compassionate, whereas boys low in generosity seldom perceived their fathers in these ways (Rutherford & Mussen, 1968). The findings are consistent with the notion that the father's warmth resulted in strong identification with him and consequently led to adoption of his patterns of generosity and sympathy.

Among children in the fifth grade, altruism and consideration for others, assessed by classmates' sociometric nominations, are correlated with the personal value of altruism in the value hierarchy of the same-sex parent. The fathers of altruistic and considerate boys and the mothers of girls who ranked high in these characteristics judged values like "showing consideration of others' feelings" and "going out of one's way to help other people" as very important to them. Presumably, parents who value altruism provide good models of caring, helping, and consideration to their children, and at this age, children are particularly likely to identify strongly with the parent of their own sex, incorporating and imitating that parent's behavior, attitudes, values, and motives (Hoffman, 1975a).

Studies of adult altruists

The lasting consequences of identification with altruistic parents are dramatically illustrated in several studies of the life histories of unusually altruistic adults. During World War II, large numbers of gentiles in Europe risked their lives to rescue Jews from the Nazis. Intensive clinical interviews with 27 such rescuers revealed that they had strong identifications with parental models of strong moral convictions who acted in accordance with their convictions, serving as excellent models for their children's later self-sacrifice and altruism (London, 1970).

In a related but much more extensive international study, 406 rescuers of Jews and a matched sample of nonresuers – matched on age, sex, education, and geographic location during the years of the war – were interviewed in depth. Although the investigators found no one developmental course that inevitably produced such altruism, they were able to delineate a "composite portrait" of rescuers that highlights the critical influence of child-rearing practices, parental modeling, and identification. The findings, highly consistent with the findings of other studies of altruists, were summarized in this way by the investigators:

It begins in close family relationships in which parents model caring behavior and communicate caring values. Parental discipline tends toward leniency; children frequently experience it as almost imperceptible. It includes a heavy dose of reasoning – explanations of why behaviors are inappropriate, often with reference to their consequences for others. Physical punishment is rare....
    ...parents set high standards they expect their children to meet, particularly with regard to caring for others. They implicitly or explicitly communicate the

obligation to help others in a spirit of generosity, without concern for external rewards or reciprocity. Parents themselves model such behaviors, not only in relation to their children but also toward other family members and neighbors. Because they are expected to care for and about others while simultaneously being cared for, children are encouraged to develop qualities associated with caring. Dependability, responsibility, and self-reliance are valued because they facilitate taking care of oneself as well as others. . . .

Because of their solid family relationships, such children tend to internalize their parents' values, increasingly incorporating standards for personal integrity and care within their own value systems. While they may articulate such standards as cognitive principles, they experience them viscerally. They provide an organizing framework for their life activities and assessments of right and wrong. Even minor infractions distress them, and fundamental violations threaten them with a sense of chaos.

It is no accident that when the lives of outsiders are threatened, individuals with this orientation are more likely to initiate, or be asked for, help. More sensitive than others to violations that threaten their moral values, they may seek out opportunities to help. Personal relationships with the victims themselves encourage early awareness and empathic reactions. If such relationships do not exist, their social groups, which already embrace norms of inclusive caring, will alert them. Already more accustomed to view social relationships in terms of generosity and care rather than reciprocity, they are less inclined to assess costs in times of grave crisis. Already more deeply and widely attached to others, they find it difficult to refrain from action. Already more inclined to include outsiders in their sphere of concern, they find no reason to exclude them in an emergency. Unable to comprehend or tolerate brutality as anything but destructive of the very fabric that gives their lives order and meaning, they react in much the same way as if caught in a flood – holding back the tide through whatever means possible. Hence, their actions appear impulsive, without due consideration of consequences. In fact, however, they are merely the extension of a characteristic style of relating developed over the years. [Oliner & Oliner, 1988, pp. 249–251]

The civil rights movement in the United States in the late 1950s and 1960s generated some highly altruistic activity. For example, a group of white young adults, called "freedom riders," participated in marches, protested, picketed, and gave speeches on behalf of equal rights and opportunities for blacks. These activities entailed tremendous expenditures of effort and money; in addition, they were carried out at the risk of encountering a great deal of hostility, including physical assault (and even murder), from racists.

Some of the freedom riders were *fully committed*, guided by what has been labeled internalized or *autonomous altruism*, active for a year or longer, often sacrificing their homes, leaving their jobs, and postponing their education to engage in the civil rights movement. Others were *partially committed* (*normative* altruists), participating in one or two freedom rides or marches, and making relatively few personal sacrifices.

Intensive clinical interviews showed clearly that the members of the two groups were equally strong advocates of equality of whites and blacks, but they had experienced different kinds of parental modeling, identification, and nurturance in their early years. When the fully committed had been children, their parents had been excellent models of prosocial behavior and concern with the welfare of others, working for altruistic causes, protesting Nazi atrocities and other injustices, and discussing their altruism with their children. By contrast, the parents of the partially committed generally had been supporters of prosocial morality, but, as they reported, "their parents preached one thing and practiced another." These parents apparently provided symbolic, but not actual, modeling of prosocial behavior (Rosenhan, 1972).

In addition, the fully committed freedom riders reported nurturant, respecting, and loving relationships with their parents during childhood and continuing through early adulthood, interactions that are conducive to forming strong identifications and consequently adoption of parental standards and patterns of behavior. The partially committed, on the other hand, described their relationships with their parents much less positively – as ambivalent or avoidant, often involving feelings of anxiety, hostility, and guilt – and much less likely to promote close identification.

An ingenious recent naturalistic study of volunteers at a crisis counseling center replicates and extends the findings of the study of freedom riders. The participants were men and women between the ages of 17 and 49 who had to complete a difficult and extensive training period before beginning their counseling work, work that often is emotionally draining and requires great expenditures of time and effort. Those who completed the training were expected to work 4 hours per week for 6 months; the criterion for sustained helpfulness was whether or not they fulfilled this commitment.

It was hypothesized that volunteers who had had warm, identification-fostering relationships with altrusitic parents during childhood would become "autonomous altruists" – comparable to the fully committed freedom riders – who would fulfill their commitments, whether or not external reward were offered, because they were intrinsically motivated to care for and help others. However, those who had not had identification-fostering relationships with their parents – like the partially committed freedom riders – were not expected to maintain long-term helpfulness *unless* they were rewarded for it. Indeed, some of the volunteers did find external rewards in the situation because their training group was highly cohesive, offering good times, friendship, and esprit de corps; volunteers in other training groups did not experience these external rewards.

The underlying hypotheses were confirmed. As predicted, for the autonomous (fully committed) altruists, the training-group experience had no significant effect. The majority (approximately 60%) of them fulfilled their commitment regardless of whether or not their training group was highly cohesive. However, the majority of the other volunteers (normative or partially committed altruists) showed sustained helpfulness only if they had been trained in highly cohesive, rewarding groups (Clary & Miller, 1986).

Apparently, extrinsic rewards for altruistic responses – at least in some situations – can result in sustained prosocial action even among those who have not had the kind of early relationships that generate intrinsic altruistic motivation and spontaneous, enduring prosocial behavior.

Parent-child relationships and prosocial behavior

Many authorities believe that children's prosocial inclinations are governed primarily by the quality of their relationships with their parents, by their child-rearing practices, and by broad features of the family environment. As a result, numerous studies have been focused directly on general dimensions of parent-child relations – such as attachment, warmth, harsh treatment – whereas others have been centered on the prosocial consequences of specific disciplinary practices such as the use of rewards or reasoning. Relevant investigations with both kinds of emphases are reviewed here, beginning with studies of infants and toddlers.

Attachment

The most systematically investigated dimension of mother-infant relationships is the infant's attachment, generally assessed by observing the infant at 12, 15, or 18 months of age in the Ainsworth Strange Situation test. This procedure consists of a series of eight brief episodes in which the infant is introduced to an unfamiliar room, a set of toys, an unfamiliar adult, and two brief separations from the caregiver and reunions with her (Ainsworth, Blehar, Waters, & Wall, 1978). The infant's behavior in the reunion situation is used to assess attachment: Securely attached infants seek proximity to, and contact with, the caregiver when she returns; insecurely attached infants are ambivalent or avoid contact with her. The mothers of the securely attached infants are sensitive and appropriately responsive to their infants' needs and signals (cries, glances, smiles, and vocalizations) and are generally warm, supportive, and gentle, whereas mothers of insecurely attached infants do not manifest these characteristics (Ainsworth, 1979).

Secure maternal attachment during infancy appears to facilitate the development of prosocial behavior, both concurrently and long afterward. Eighteen-month-olds who are securely attached to their mothers are more sociable with peers and strangers, readily obey their mothers, and, in addition, show more concern with a crying adult than do children who are insecurely attached (Londerville & Main, 1981; Weston & Main, 1980). As preschoolers, children who had been securely attached to their mothers as infants were social leaders, generally sensitive to their peers' needs and feelings, and sympathetic with others in distress (Waters, Wippman, & Sroufe, 1979). In contrast, children who had been insecurely attached at 12 and 18 months tended to be hostile and socially isolated (Sroufe, 1983). In brief, early maternal warmth, sensitivity, and responsiveness are conducive to the development of enduring concern with others. Perhaps secure children, whose early caregivers are responsive and trustworthy, acquire positive social orientations and motivations as well as lasting sensitivity to others' feelings.

Abusive treatment

In marked contrast, harsh and abusive treatment by caregivers in the early years can inhibit the development of prosocial responses. Abused, economically disadvantaged toddlers between 1 and 3 years of age and a comparable group of children from families under stress, but not abusive, were carefully observed in a day-care center. More than half of the nonabused children expressed concern, sadness, or empathy when a peer was distressed, but no abused child ever showed these responses.

In fact, abused children often reacted to a peer's distress with fear, aggression, or anger, responses that were very rare among the non-abused controls (Main & George, 1985).

Nurturance

Nurturance is generally defined as warmth and involvement in caregiving, sensitivity and responsiveness to the child's needs, and expression of affection – qualities that may evoke strong maternal attachment and parental identification, which in turn are associated with high levels of prosocial motivations. Furthermore, parental nurturance, which entails consideration, kindness, generosity, helpfulness, and sympathy for others, may serve as a model of prosocial responses for the child. The findings of many studies offer substantial support for the hypothesis that parental nurturance fosters the development of prosocial predispositions, although not all investigations have yielded consistent results.

In one study, for example, mothers of toddlers under 2 years of age were observed taking care of them at home, and records were kept of the youngsters' helpfulness and altruism. The toddlers whose mothers were rated high in empathy and nurturance – warmth, anticipation of difficulties or dangers the child might encounter, sensitivity and responsiveness to the child's needs, hurts, and distress – expressed greater concern with others' distress and were more altruistic than were toddlers whose mothers were less empathic and nurturant (Zahn-Waxler, Radke-Yarrow & King, 1979); the study is more fully described later in this chapter.

Other studies have yielded mixed results, however. Thus, maternal, but not paternal, affection was associated with middle-class preadolescent boys' and girls' consideration for others in one study, but both maternal affection and paternal affection were related to lower-class boys', but not girls', consideration of others (Hoffman & Saltzstein, 1967). In at least two studies, maternal affection has been found to be positively correlated with boys', but not girls', consideration of others, helpfulness, and generosity (Feshbach, 1973; Hoffman, 1975a). The findings on paternal affection are less clear; sometimes it is linked with prosocial tendencies, and sometimes not (Radke-Yarrow et al., 1983).

Given these mixed findings, we cannot make any definitive generalizations about the influence of parental nurturance per se on children's prosocial actions or motivations. Perhaps it is most appropriate to regard nurturance as a "codeterminant" caregiver variable that interacts with, and reinforces, other determinants such as modeling.

Authoritative parenting

No single dimension of child rearing can account for all, or most, of the variability in personality, motivation, or social behavior. Consequently, a number of outstanding researchers have been investigating styles or *patterns* of child-rearing practices, relating them to children's social behavior, including prosocial dispositions, and adjustment. The focus is on *organizations* or *patterns* of parenting dimensions; for example, nurturance is considered in combination with other significant dimensions such as control, demandingness, punishment, and quality of parent–child communication.

In her extensive in-depth longitudinal study, Baumrind used an array of procedures, including home visits, observations, and interviews, to assess four aspects of parent behavior: *parental nurturance* (warmth and involvement); *control*, that is, discipline to influence the child to conform with parental standards; *maturity demands*, pressures on the child to perform at a high level intellectually, socially, or emotionally; and *clarity of parent-child communication*, giving reasons for demands and asking about the child's opinions and feelings.

By combining or clustering parental ratings on these four dimensions, Baumrind derived three major types or patterns of child rearing: *authoritative, authoritarian*, and *permissive*. Authoritative parents are warm, loving, responsive, and supportive. They respect their children's independence, personality characteristics, point of view, interests, and motives; they communicate well with their children, encouraging give and take in discussions, and being clear about the reasons for directives. At the same time, they are controlling and demand mature behavior, guiding their children's activities firmly and requiring them to contribute to family functioning by helping with household tasks. Authoritarian parents are highly controlling, rely heavily on coercive discipline, and provide relatively little warmth. They attempt to instill conventional values such as respect for authority, work, and tradition, and they do not discuss their decisions or rules. Permissive parents are nurturant, but lax in disciplining and rewarding their children. They are not controlling and make few maturity demands, allowing their children to regulate their own activities as much as possible (Baumrind, 1967, 1973).

Intensive observations, teachers' ratings, interviews, and psychological tests were used to evaluate the children when they were preschoolers and again when they were 9 years old. At both periods, those with authoritative parents were more competent intellectually, more achievement-oriented, more planful, and more socially competent (showing greater social assertiveness and social ascendance). In addition, and most important from the point of view of prosocial development, they were more socially responsible, friendly, and cooperative than were children reared by the other types of parents. If both parents were authoritarian and punitive, their children manifested little socially responsible behavior. These results clearly indicate that the development of children's prosocial behavior tendencies is regulated by *patterns* of parent behavior, rather than by single dimensions like warmth or control. Summarizing her findings, Baumrind concluded that "authoritative childrearing is the only pattern that consistently (and significantly) produced competent children (that is, children high in social competence *and* social responsibility) and failed to produce incompetent children (those low in both social competence and social responsibility) in the preschool years and in middle childhood. . . and this was true for both boys and girls" (Baumrind, 1988).

Disciplinary techniques

We shift our attention now from the broad features of family milieu and parent–child relations that contribute to, or inhibit, the development of prosocial motivations and actions to more specific disciplinary practices. Among these specific techniques are rewards (praise or approval) for prosocial acts, punishment of selfish and uncooperative responses, reasoning and explaining rules or norms of prosocial behavior, lecturing or preaching. Of course, broadly defined dimensions of child rearing and specific disciplinary techniques are not independent of one another, for the latter are embedded in, and strongly influenced by, the general nature of parent–child interactions. For example, authoritative parents are more likely to use reasoning to motivate the child to behave in prosocial ways, whereas rejecting or authoritarian parents are more likely to use punitive techniques.

What follows is a brief survey of some relevant studies, both natural-istic and experimental, in which the consequences of using particular disciplinary techniques on prosocial behavior were assessed; in most of these studies, the techniques themselves, rather than the context in which they were used, were the major independent variables.

Explanations and reasoning

When caregivers react to their children's transgressions by reasoning with them, pointing out the consequences of their actions for themselves and for others, they inevitably model consideration and concern for others and a rational, controlled orientation toward social interac-tions. At the same time, they inform their children about acceptable standards of behavior, arouse empathic feelings, stimulate role taking, and communicate that the children are responsible for their behavior, thus promoting the internalization of motivation for prosocial behavior. For all these reasons, it has been hypothesized that the use of reasoning or induction as a disciplinary technique enhances the development of children's prosocial behavior. There is substantial support for this hypothesis.

An ingenious naturalistic study demonstrates that explanations, especially if they are emotionally toned, can raise the level of the prosocial behavior of toddlers (ages 15–29 months).The principal data of the study were records made by the toddlers' mothers, each of whom was trained (and modestly paid) to observe and report all the child's reactions to expressions of distress in others (sorrow, pain, discomfort, anger, fatigue) and the mother's responses, as well as the preceding and following events. The records included instances in which the child was the cause of distress (e.g., grabbing a toy from another child) and in-stances in which the child was only a witness or bystander. The following is a mother's report of an incident involving her 22-month-old son, John, and a guest, Jerry:

Today Jerry was kind of cranky; he just started completely bawling and he wouldn't stop. John kept coming over and handing Jerry toys, trying to cheer him up so to speak. He'd say things like, "Here, Jerry," and I said to John, "Jerry's sad; he doesn't feel good; he had a shot today." John would look at me with his eyebrows kind of wrinkled together, like he really understood that Jerry was crying because he was unhappy, not that he was just being a crybaby. He went over and rubbed Jerry's arm and said, "Nice Jerry," and continued to give him toys. [Zahn-Waxler et al., 1979, p. 322]

On the average, these youngsters made prosocial responses to one-third of the distress incidents they caused or witnessed, but there was a wide range of individual differences; some children made virtually no prosocial responses, whereas others frequently displayed altruism.

Mothers' frequent use of explanations with emotional loading (e.g., "Look what you did! Don't you see you hurt Amy! Don't *ever* pull hair!") was linked with high levels of reparations and altruism. By contrast, verbal prohibitions alone ("Stop that!"), physical restraint, and physical punishment were associated with relatively low rates of altruism, and simple explanations of cause and effect ("Tom's crying because you pushed him.") had no effect on altruistic expression. "The effective induction is not calmly-dispensed reasoning, carefully designed to enlighten the child; it is emotionally imposed, sometimes harshly and often forcefully" (Zahn-Waxler et al., 1979, p. 327).

In pioneering work, Martin Hoffman and his associates contrasted the effects of induction and power assertion (control by physical power or material resources, such as physical punishment, deprivation of objects or privileges, force or threats) on the prosocial tendencies of older children. In one of their studies, seventh-grade students' consideration of others was measured by classmates' nominations of "the most likely to care about other children's feelings" and "most likely to defend a child being made fun of by the group." Parental disciplinary techniques were evaluated by asking parents how they would react to four hypothetical situations, such as the child's being careless and destroying something of value that belonged to another child. Reports of frequent use of induction by mothers were positively associated with their daughters' consideration of others, whereas reports of frequent use of power-assertive discipline were associated with low levels of consideration. In short, the pattern of frequent induction and infrequent power assertion facilitated the development of prosocial behavior in girls, but not in boys (Hoffman & Saltzstein, 1967).

Studies of different classes of prosocial behavior in children of various ages have yielded similar findings. For example, frequent maternal use of induction, together with little use of power assertion, was found to be associated with high levels of preschoolers' helpfulness and sensitivity to the needs of others (Hoffman, 1963). That pattern of maternal discipline also promotes the development of generosity in boys between 6 and 8 years of age (Feshbach, 1973); among children in the fifth and eighth grades, those whose parents frequently used reasoning in discipline were more kind and considerate (sociometric nominations), expressed more prosocial values (such as concern for others), and made more generous donations to charity (Dlugokinski & Firestone, 1974).

The consistency of these findings leads us to conclude that the extensive use of inductive techniques is generally conducive to the development of prosocial tendencies. Hoffman and others have suggested that this is largely attributable to the fact that induction is "most capable of eliciting the child's natural proclivities for empathy" (Hoffman & Saltzstein, 1967, p. 553). If that is the case, inductive reasoning that is victim-centered, directing the child to consider the victim's feelings and encouraging the child to make reparations or to apologize, may have especially strong consequences for prosocial behavior: "Techniques that point up the harmful consequences of the child's behavior for the victim or encourage him to imagine himself in the other person's place may help put the feelings and thoughts of the victim into the child's consciousness and thus help guide his future actions in an altruistic direction" (Hoffman, 1975a, p. 938). This proved to be the case among fifth-grade pupils; their mothers' use of victim-centered inductive techniques was significantly correlated with boys' considerateness and helpfulness, and the fathers' use of this technique was associated with prosocial tendencies among the girls (Hoffman, 1975a). Furthermore, induction that stresses the consequences of the child's behavior for others (rather than for the child) has proved more powerful than other kinds of reasoning in fostering self-control and compliance with the requests of authorities, attributes linked with prosocial tendencies (Kuczynski, 1982).

Reward and punishment

As we have seen, the use of power assertion as a principal disciplinary technique typically results in relatively low levels of prosocial behavior in children. Yet, according to social learning theory, punishment can serve to weaken or extinguish undesirable responses, whereas reward or reinforcement can strengthen prosocial responses such as generosity and helpfulness. Caregivers often seem to apply social learning theory intuitively; if they observe their children acting in a prosocial way – for example, assisting another child – they are likely to reward their children by praise or in some other way (Grusec, 1982). Or seeing a child transgressing or acting in disapproved ways (failing to share toys with others) a mother may scold the child or administer punishment in other ways. Do reward and punishment produce the results predicted by social learning theory? The issue has been tested in many studies, most of them experimental, and the answer is qualified affirmative.

Simple social rewards, such as getting attention, may lead to increments in the prosocial responses of preschool children. The nursery-school teachers in one study were instructed to call attention to a child's cooperative and prosocial statements simply by repeating what the child said. For example, a teacher hearing a child say, "I'll help you," would respond, "Liz, you said, 'I'll help you'." Children rewarded in this way made more prosocial statements and ordinarily followed these with helpful and cooperative acts (Slaby & Crowley, 1977). However, there was no information about whether or not these positive effects persisted over time or generalized to other settings.

In another pertinent study, kindergarten and first-grade children played a marble game, and earned pennies that could be exchanged for prizes, and were given repeated opportunities to donate to a peer who had poor luck in the game. Those who did not donate were prompted to do so and were then praised by the examiner. After this, the rewarded children's generosity increased markedly, but the effect was short-lived; most of the children stopped donating when the praise were discontinued (Gelfand et al., 1975).

After children between 7 and 11 years of age were praised for sharing the prizes they won in a game, they shared more of their winnings on subsequent trials, when the experimenter was not present, than did a control group that had not been rewarded or punished. Children who had been punished for sharing ("That was silly for you to do") shared even less than the controls. These effects of reward and punishment were still apparent 2 weeks later when the children played the same game again, but there was no evidence of generalization to sharing in a different situation (Rushton & Teachman, 1978).

Outside the laboratory, punishment is not usually given for prosocial acts; rather, punishment is used by caregivers to reduce or extinguish negative behaviors such as selfishness or failure to assist others. In an experimental analog of this, 8-to-10-year-olds playing a game were fined if they did not donate some of their winnings to a charity when they were given an opportunity to do so. These children became much more generous in later trials, but they became less generous as soon as they were told that they would no longer be fined for failure to donate (Hartmann et al., 1976).

The results of these experiments confirm the hypothesis that rewards and punishments influence children's generosity and helpfulness, at least in these settings. However, the experiments provide little evidence that praise and punishment produce enduring changes or that the effects extend (generalize) to other domains of prosocial behavior or influence the child's intrinsic prosocial motivation (Moore & Eisenberg, 1984). Naturalistic studies are needed to obtain accurate, useful information about rewards and punishments in home, school, and community. In these real-life settings, the effects of reward and punishment undoubtedly vary with such factors as amount, intensity, frequency, timing, and the context in which they are administered. For instance, mild punishment by a nurturant caregiver, accompanied by verbal explanation of the reason for it, should have different consequences than the same amount of punishment given without explanation by an authoritarian parent.

Providing cognitive mediators: effectiveness of verbal persuasion, instruction, and preaching

Obviously, rewards and punishments are not the only mechanisms of learning; knowledge is also acquired through verbal instruction, guidance, advice, discussion, lecture, and suggestion. In their efforts to augment children's prosocial development, parents, teachers, and clergy are likely to lecture ("preach," "exhort") children about the virtues of kindness, consideration, sharing, helping, and caring. Are these verbal techniques effective? This question has been tested in a number of experimental investigations, typically conducted in laboratories or schools, most of them contrasting "preaching" with modeling. (The term "preaching" has considerable surplus meaning, and most caregivers and other agents of socialization probably would protest that they do not "preach"; rather, they discuss, suggest, point out, guide, persuade, or give good advice. Avoiding the semantic argument, we shall discuss a variety of verbal techniques in this section.)

Some early investigations seemed to indicate that it was what a model *did*, rather than what she *said*, that influenced the child's subsequent behavior. If, for example, a model behaved generously in donating prizes to poor children, but preached greed (making statements such as "I don't think we should give to poor children. . . ." – or if she preached charity but acted selfishly – children were more likely to emulate her *behavior* than to follow her verbal suggestions) (Bryan & Walbek, 1970). However, according to more recent research, direct suggestions and instruction may have as much immediate influence as modeling and may perhaps, in the long run, have more marked and enduring effects. In one well-designed experimental study, children between 7 and 11 years of age observed a model playing a game, winning prizes, responding to an appeal for donations to charity, and commenting about charity. For some of the children, what the model said matched what she did – for example, she donated generously and advocated generosity, or she failed to donate and made negative statements about charity. Other participants observed modeling behavior that was inconsistent with the model's statements. Immediately after modeling, the model left the room, leaving the child to play the game and to donate (or not to donate) to the charity. At this time, the model's actions had a more powerful impact than the model's words on the children's reactions; that is, the children emulated the model's generosity or selfishness, but were not influenced by her comments. However, 2 months later, when the participants played the game again, the verbal message had more marked effects on children's generosity: Those exposed to a generous model who advocated selfishness acted selfishly, donating relatively little of their winnings to charity, whereas those who observed a selfish model who preached generosity made generous contributions (Rushton, 1975).

The positive long-term consequences of verbal persuasion were also demonstrated in a study of 8-to-10-year-olds who played a game, won prizes, and were urged to share, either by a specific statement ("It's good to donate to poor children to make them happy") or by a general statement ("It's good to help people in any way one can"). Some of the children only heard one of these statements, but others heard a statement and also observed a model donating some of the prizes she had won. Again the powerful effects of modeling were apparent immediately – those who observed the model donated more to charity than did those who simply heard the statements – but these effects were short-lived. Three weeks later, in the same setting, those exposed to the model and those exposed only to verbalization donated equally. However, the statements themselves produced some other interesting generalized effects. Immediately after training, boys who heard the specific statement about the virtues of donating were more willing than were those who heard the general statement to share a reward for participation with a peer who was unable to take part in the study. A month later, boys and girls who had been exposed to general statements about helping those in need complied more generously with an adult's request to do some work for hospitalized sick children than did those in other groups (Grusec, Saas-Kortsaak, & Simutis, 1978).

It may be inferred that clear verbal communications serve as cognitive mediators – knowledge encoded as general rules, principles, or norms – that are recalled and applied later and in other situations. Such mediators would function in a variety of ways, making the child conscious of the needs of others, enabling the child to label the situation, eliciting empathy, and, perhaps most important, providing knowledge of expectations and rules about what ought to be done. Consequently, these messages – given by preaching, persuasion, or instruction – may produce lasting and generalized effects, reflected in a broader spectrum of actions.

Not all types of verbal instructions or persuasions are equally effective in modifying children's behavior. For young children, direct instructions appear to be more powerful than suggestions in raising the level of generosity in sharing prizes with others. After participating in an experiment, children in the first, second, third, and fourth grades were rewarded tokens that could be traded for prizes. Half the children in each grade were given directive instructions; that is, they were told that before trading tokens they *would have to* share some of them with children at another school who did not have a chance to earn any. The other children in each grade received permissive instructions ("You *might want to* share some of your earnings, but you *don't have to*"). The directive instructions elicited greater generosity and sharing than did the permissive instructions in the first three grades, but the two types of instructions did not have a differential impact on boys in the fourth grade. For the younger children, the stronger influence of directive instructions was still evident a month later when the children were tested again in the same setting. Perhaps young children, at Piaget's heteronomous phase of moral development, accept the instructions given by authorities, store them in memory, and apply them inflexibly when they encounter the same situation again (Piaget, 1932/1965). Older children, however, may interpret and evaluate instructions differently (Israel & Brown, 1979; Israel & Raskin, 1979), or, perhaps, having internalized a norm of responsibility, they are more likely to act in accordance with that norm and are less influenced by the experimenter's instructions. Generalizations and interpretations from these findings must be made very cautiously.

In another study, 8- and 9-year-olds who were urged to share prizes with poor children responded with significantly greater generosity to an experiment's empathy-arousing statements about how happy and excited the beneficiaries would be than to statements about norms emphasizing that people ought to share their possessions with others (Eisenberg-Berg & Geisheker, 1979).

As attribution theorists would predict, children's prosocial tendencies are more likely to be strengthened if they believe that their prosocial acts are intrinsically motivated than if their helpfulness and kindness are attributed to external incentives. After children between 7 and 10 years of age donated some of their winnings in a game to charity, the experimenter-model told some of them, "I guess you shared because you're the kind of person who likes to help other people." To another group she said, "I guess you shared because you thought I expected you to.... When I'm here with people playing the game I expect them to give while I'm watching." And to a third, control group, she simply said, "You shared quite a bit." Later, when they were left alone to play the game, children who were told they were intrinsically motived donated more to a charity than did those in the external attribution and control groups. In addition, the positive effects of internal attribution were durable and generalized to other prosocial acts, such as sharing pennies with other children (Grusec, Kuczynski, Rushton, & Simutis, 1978).

In another experiment, the effects of simply social reinforcement (praise) for donating to charity were contrasted with the effects of a self-attribution comment by the experimenter. The two treatments were equally effective in motivating children to increase their donations immediately following training, but self-attribution resulted in greater generalization to other classes of responses, including sharing and helping adults and children, immediately and 3 weeks later. Clearly, "prosocial attributions are not just a variant of social reinforcement...but they have clear special characteristics, one of which appears to be the ability to affect not only the behavior they follow..." (Grusec & Redler, 1980, p. 633).

Early assignment of responsibility

Taking on responsibility for others can enhance children's prosocial tendencies. Parental pressures on their children to behave in mature ways, including doing household chores appropriate to the child's abilities, are associated with preschoolers' manifestations of social responsibility, altruism, and nurturance toward others (Baumrind, 1971, 1988).

Cross-cultural research also indicates that early assignment of responsibility stimulates prosocial development. Children reared in cultures in which they are assigned responsibilities for taking care of younger siblings or contributing to the family economy are more helpful and supportive of peers and family members than are children in other cultures (Whiting & Whiting, 1975).

The findings of several experimental studies are entirely consistent with the findings in these naturalistic investigations (Eisenberg, Cialdini, McCreath, & Shell, 1987; Staub, 1970a). In one study, some children were taught to make puzzles so that they could later teach younger children to construct similar puzzles for hospitalized children, whereas others also learned to make these puzzles, but were not given any responsibility for teaching others. Several days later, and again several weeks later, the participants were asked to donate some of the gift certificates they had earned to needy children and to indicate how many puzzles they were willing to make for sick children. Boys and girls who had been assigned teaching responsibilities during the training period responded more generously to both requests than did children in the control group (Staub, 1979).

In an ingenious experimental field study, groups of children trick-or-treating on Halloween night were asked to donate some of the candy they received to hospitalized children. In some groups, no one was designated as responsible for getting donations; in others, one child was arbitrarily selected by the experimenter as responsible; in a third condition, every child was made responsible (pointing to each child in turn, the experimenter said, "I will be counting on you and you and you...."). As predicted, assignment of responsibility to everyone elicited the most generous contributions, and the smallest donations came from the groups in which no one was given responsibility for collecting donations (Maruyama, Fraser, & Miller, 1982).

In their homes, schools, and communities, children who take responsibility often are rewarded for prosocial acts (by praise or feelings of self-competence or maturity), which strengthens prosocial tendencies. In addition, being assigned responsibility may evoke greater empathy for others, heighten the child's sense of importance, or add to the child's self-concept as a "helpful person," intrinsically motivated. Any of these factors, or any combination of them, may help to raise the level of children's prosocial predispositions.

The association between responsibility assignment and prosocial behavior has been applied in the Soviet Union, where, as part of the elementary-school curriculum, children assist younger children with their schoolwork and with their problems. The program is designed to strengthen prosocial predispositions, and it is apparently successful, for Soviet children in fact are helpful and considerate and demonstrate a strong sense of responsibility for others (Bronfenbrenner, 1970) (see also chapter 3).

Sibling influences

More than 80% of American children have one or more sisters or brothers who are likely to be significant agents of socialization. By the time they are in kindergarten, children spend over twice as much time in the company of their siblings as with their parents (Bank & Kahn, 1975). Furthermore, sibling relationships are more egalitarian than parent–child relationships, and therefore they provide rich opportunities for learning patterns of loyalty, helpfulness, and consideration, as well as conflict, domination, and competition. Siblings can teach, reinforce or punish each other's responses, advise, "set and maintain standards, provide models to emulate... and serve as confidants and sources of social support in times of emotional stress" (Lamb, 1982, p. 6).

Although rivalry or aggression often can characterize their relationships, young siblings spend a great deal of time playing together, cooperating in games, expressing affection, and attempting to help each other (Dunn, 1983; Dunn & Kendrick, 1982; Pepler, Corter, & Abramovitch, 1982). Even very young children, sometimes as young as 14 months, show concern for their older brothers or sisters and seem to understand their feelings and know how to comfort them (Dunn & Kendrick, 1979). The frequency of positive social responses from younger siblings to older ones increases with age, and younger siblings are likely to imitate older ones, especially those of the same sex, more often than older ones imitate younger ones (Dunn & Kendrick, 1982; Pepler et al., 1982).

The most relevant information about siblings as socializers comes from systematic observations in homes or other naturalistic settings. In one longitudinal investigation, toddlers were observed at 18 months and again 6 months later as they interacted with their siblings, who were, on the average, 26 months older. The older siblings exhibited more prosocial behavior each time, and, on the average, both siblings showed significant increases in prosocial actions over the 6-month interval. The correlations between the younger and older siblings' cooperative behavior were significant at both periods; toddlers whose older siblings were frequently "giving" were most likely to behave cooperatively. The younger child undoubtedly emulates the older's behavior, but the data suggest reciprocal effects; if the younger siblings manifested high levels of sharing, helping, comforting, and cooperating at 18 months, their older siblings were more likely to be more cooperative 6 months later. Apparently, "children who grow up with a sibling who joins them in a cooperative way in a high proportion of their interactions become themselves more cooperative than children whose siblings have not acted in this way" (Dunn & Munn, 1986, p. 282). Furthermore, "individual differences in friendly behavior by the older sibling. . . are linked with the development of relatively mature behavior by the second born in conflict incidents and in cooperative exchanges and similarly differences in friendly behavior by the younger. . . are linked to the frequency of prosocial behavior by the older sibling" (Dunn & Munn, 1986, p. 282).

Sibling relationships are embedded in the family constellation, and "interactions between any two family members are influenced by the larger family interactional system" (Cicirelli, 1976, p. 594). The mother's interactions with each child have a marked impact on the quality of the relationship between the siblings, as evidenced by the findings in a longitudinal study that began with newborns, their mothers, and their older siblings: If the mother discussed the newborn's feelings and needs with an older child, the latter was subsequently much more likely to show more affectionate interest in the baby, offering to help, entertain, and cuddle the baby. Friendly interest in the younger sibling persisted: Compared with older siblings who had not demonstrated early interest in their baby siblings, those who were friendly in the first 3 weeks showed significantly more positive social behavior toward their younger siblings when those younger siblings were 14 months old and, 3 years later, were significantly more likely to share toys or candy and to respond to the younger siblings' distress by comforting them. Furthermore, the influence was reciprocal; when the younger siblings of friendly children were 14 months old, they showed more positive social behavior toward their older siblings than did babies in other families (Dunn & Kendrick, 1982).

Maternal influences on sibling relationships often are complex. Many aspects of mother–daughter and sister–sister interactions were evaluated in a seminaturalistic study of girl siblings in the fourth and fifth grades, their mothers, and their sisters who were 2 or 3 years younger. The data revealed that mothers who were highly responsive to their children's needs had children who were likely to make frequent prosocial responses – and relatively few antisocial responses – toward each other. Youngsters who experienced sensitive mothering often comforted their older siblings and shared with them.

These investigators expected that the mother's ignoring the child's requests for help or attention would elicit negative reactions, but they found that for the older siblings, ignoring was actually associated with both antisocial (disparaging, discomforting, and rule stating) *and* prosocial (comforting, sharing, and helping) actions. If the mother gave preferential treatment to one of her daughters, meeting one's needs to a high degree and ignoring the other's, each daughter was likely to be hostile toward her sister. But ignoring by the mother may also create greater opportunities for prosocial interaction between the siblings. If the child did not get a response from her mother, she often would turn to her sibling for help, and often she got it (Bryant & Crockenberg, 1980).

Concluding statement

The research findings reviewed in this chapter, derived from both experimental and naturalistic studies, provide abundant evidence that many aspects of family interaction contribute to the development of prosocial behavior. The experimental studies have confirmed that the fundamental mechanisms underlying socialization – modeling, reward and punishment, reasoning, lecturing, explaining – *can* influence the acquisition and enhancement of prosocial behavior. In these experiments, the independent (socialization) variables usually have been operationally defined in restricted ways – for example, a short exposure to a model, a few rewarded trials, low-key "preaching" – and the dependent (prosocial) variables have been isolated bits of behavior, such as responding to an appeal for donations for poor children, or sharing prizes. With few exceptions, most experimental studies have not examined interaction effects – such as the consequences of a joint operation of modeling and explanation – generalization, or duration of the effects. [The Yarrow et al. (1973) study of the interaction between nurturance and modeling in promoting prosocial behavior, as reviewed earlier, is one of the few exceptions.]

But in the family, these fundamental mechanisms operate and interact in intricate and complex ways – conditions that cannot be simulated realistically in experiments. More naturalistic studies are urgently needed to provide in-depth information about the family's contribution to socialization of prosocial tendencies and intrinsic prosocial motives. Socialization antecedents, such as the general characteristics of the home environment, the family system or organization (including siblings and other family members), and disciplinary practices, must be defined in meaningful ways and investigated by means of multiple methods such as direct observations, interviews, and structured tests. Similarly, prosocial consequents must be gauged by multiple, global methods, based on extensive observations and/or composite indices such as those used in the studies of Baumrind (1971, 1988), and Zahn-Waxler, Iannotti, and Chapman (1982).

Studies of this kind are very difficult to conduct and are extremely costly and time-consuming. Yet, judged in terms of the salience, richness, and social utility of the findings such studies may yield, the potential payoff is enormous.

7   Socialization by agents outside the family

Although caregivers and the immediate family generally are the primary agents of socialization in the child's earliest years, other agents become increasingly important as children grow older. Among these are peers, schools, and media that socialize, as caregivers do, by direct instruction, modeling, administering rewards and punishments, and providing contacts and experiences from which children acquire knowledge of the social world, its norms and expectations. Yet, until recently, there had been surprisingly little systematic investigation of the actual influences of these socializing agents on prosocial behavior. As we shall see, relevant studies of the impact of television far outnumber investigations of the influences of peers and schools programs.

Peer influences

Common sense, folk wisdom, and casual observation all attest to the truth of the statement that "peer interaction is a socializing context" (Hartup, 1983, p. 164). Parents try to discourage their children from associating with certain peers because they are afraid that their children may acquire those peers' undesirable characteristics. On the other hand, friendships with children with desirable characteristics are encouraged in the hope that their own children will emulate these characteristics. These hopes and fears may be well founded, for abundant research evidence demonstrates that peers can play critical roles in shaping children's behavior patterns in either positive or negative ways. If peers reinforce preschoolers' gender-typed activities by approval and attention, these activites are continued; gender-inappropriate activities are likely to be criticized and hence discontinued (Fagot, 1977; Lamb & Roopnarine, 1979). Peer reinforcement of aggressive behavior strengthens a child's

95

aggressive tendencies (Patterson, Littman, & Bricker, 1967), and peer models' aggressive actions often are imitated (Bandura, 1973). Positive peer influences have been found in studies in which severely withdrawn nursery-school children, when exposed to televised models of peer interaction, became markedly more sociable (O'Connor, 1969), and children with an intense fear of dogs approached and petted dogs after they observed peer models happily playing with a dog (Bandura, Grusec, & Menlove, 1967).

Given findings such as these, it is not surprising to learn that interactions with peers can facilitate the acquisition and modification of a variety of prosocial activities. Thus, in one study, withdrawn children, each of whom was paired in a series of play sessions with another child, became more sociable, and their prosocial behavior (helping, giving, sharing, and participating in cooperative play) increased significantly. Although the mechanisms producing these changes are not fully understood, these investigators believed that "the play sessions must have provided the isolates with experiences [one-on-one play sessions] that occurred infrequently in the classroom" (Furman, Rahe, & Hartup, 1979, p. 921).

Peers can be effective agents of reinforcement that facilitate the acquisition and modification of prosocial behavior. Children respond positively to peers' prosocial actions quite often. According to the data of one observational study, 30% of preschoolers' spontaneous prosocial actions and 48% of their helping and sharing responses to requests brought reactions such as continuing with conversation or play, thanks, approval, and smiles from their peers (Eisenberg et al., 1981).

The potential of peer reinforcement for raising the level of youngsters' prosocial behavior is seen most clearly in experimental studies. Thus, when kindergarten children were encouraged to report instances of cooperative or friendly behaviors (such as helping and sharing) to the class during "sharing time," cooperative classroom play increased, and aggressive acts decreased. Although generalization of these effects was not systematically tested, the kindergarten teachers reported that during this period, the children shared their materials more eagerly and were more concerned about the needs of others (Grieger, Kauffman, & Grieger, 1976).

Modeling is one of the principal means by which peers influence prosocial tendencies. Abundant evidence from many studies shows that children are likely to imitate the prosocial responses of peer models, live or televised, especially if those models are rewarded for those responses (Strain, Cooke, & Apolloni, 1976). Children, particularly boys, who witness peers donating to charity, expressing sympathy, or helping someone in distress are likely to make these responses themselves in similar situations on later occasions (Bryan & Walbek, 1970; Elliott & Vasta, 1970; Hartup & Coates, 1967). Televised peer models exhibiting cooperation or helping are most likely to be imitated if their behavior is discussed afterward (DeVoe, Render, & Colins, 1979). Unfortunately, peers' selfish (nonsharing) responses are also likely to be imitated. After observing a peer model whose selfishness was not rewarded or punished, 7- and 8-year-olds were inhibited in sharing (Ascione & Sanok, 1982). (For further discussion of television modeling and prosocial behavior, see later sections in this chapter.)

Clearly, peers can be powerful models in the acquisition and modification of prosocial responses. But further research is needed to clarify such issues as the possible effects of repeated exposure to prosocial models, the relative effectiveness of peer versus adult models, and the influences of friendship and familiarity on imitation (Zahn-Waxler et al., 1982).

School and teacher influences

As we learned earlier, nursery-school teachers can relatively easily strengthen children's prosocial response tendencies simply by calling attention to the children's own prosocial statements, which are generally followed by prosocial behavior. In the course of their interactions with the youngsters, nursery-school teachers frequently give explicit instructions about helping, sharing, and consideration; they can instigate these behaviors, and reward them when they occur. Furthermore, they inevitably serve as models of nurturance, consideration, and kindness, eliciting imitative prosocial responses. However, teacher modeling of prosocial conduct in naturalistic classroom settings has not been systematically investigated – a problem for future research. (See the discussion of adult modeling in chapter 6.)

American educators have traditionally claimed that "moral education" is one of their prime objectives, but in fact the teaching of morality in schools usually has been restricted to preaching on virtues such as kindness, consideration, and generosity, and inculcating prohibitions against stealing, lying, and cheating. From the moral educators' point of view, the teacher's function was to "impart the society's traditions, respect for authority, and a sense of duty through inculcation and even indoctrination...morality is not fostered by reflection, critical thought, or understandings formed by individuals" (Turiel, in press). There have been very few concerted efforts to integrate prosocial values, ideals, and behavior into the curriculum in American elementary schools.

In this respect, America has lagged behind the Soviet Union and China, where, from the earliest years, children are taught – by reward, example, and instruction – to share, cooperate, and consider others' needs and feelings; common ownership of toys and materials, as well as collective play, is emphasized. Responsibility for others, "socialist humanism," good manners, and high standards of behavior are important educational goals (Bronfenbrenner, 1970; Rushton, 1980). Teachers in China repeatedly tell their pupils stories about altruistic heroes, instructing youngsters to take these heroes as models. When a child acts in a prosocial way, such as helping another child who has had an accident, the teacher calls the attention of the class to this exemplary behavior and praises the child who helped. The other pupils applaud in response.

It appears that since the 1970s, American and European attitudes toward moral education in the schools have been changing. Alarmed by growing rates of juvenile delinquency, juvenile gang terrorism, drug abuse, and teenage pregnancies, many people, including public officials, have been pressuring the schools to give more attention to moral values and behavior. As a result, a number of experimental training programs designed to promote prosocial tendencies have been initiated. Some of them have yielded very promising results.

The Empathy Training Program, for third- and fourth-graders, has two goals: regulation of children's aggression, and promotion of prosocial behavior (Feshbach, 1979: Feshbach & Feshbach, 1982, 1983). The program consists of a number of classroom exercises that enhance one or more of the essential components of empathy – recognition and discrimination of the feelings of others, role taking, and emotional responsiveness (the ability to experience and be aware of one's own emotions). Underlying the training is the assumption that higher levels of empathy will lead to stronger tendencies toward prosocial behavior.

To evaluate the outcome of participation in the program, these investigators assigned children to groups of six, who met with a trainer and followed the prescribed empathy exercises for 1-hour sessions, three times a week for 10 weeks. Control groups engaged in academic problem solving or did not participate in any training activities during these 10 weeks. Ratings of aggressive and prosocial behaviors (helping, generosity, sympathy, and sharing) were made by teachers, peers, and the children themselves, and social understanding and role-taking skills were tested. In the groups that received empathy training, prosocial actions increased, and both self-concepts and social understanding improved. Neither of the control groups showed these positive effects. The empathy training was effective for children who were average in aggression as well as for those who were initially highly aggressive (Feshbach & Feshbach, 1983).

A number of programs concentrate on "cooperative learning," in which children participate in learning tasks that reduce competition and facilitate "interdependence, coordination, cooperation, exchange, and helping" (Hertz-Lazarowitz & Sharan, 1984, p. 424). In a program involving the jigsaw technique, children in a class are divided into groups of six students, and each one is assigned a segment of a lesson, for example, the biography of a past president. Each one learns a part of the necessary information, and the parts must then be put together like pieces of a jigsaw puzzle. Thus, the students are dependent on each other, for each must learn all the parts of the lesson (Aronson, Blaney, Stephan, Sikes, & Snapp, 1978).

In a systematic evaluation of this technique, students in several sixth-grade classes met in jigsaw groups for about 45 min per day, 3 days per week, for 6 weeks, whereas control groups did not participate in such projects. Compared with the controls, the children in the jigsaw learning groups were more helpful, considerate of others, and cooperative. They also expressed greater self-esteem and increased liking for other children of their own and other ethnic groups, as well as more positive attitudes toward school and learning (Blaney, Stephan, Rosenfield, Aronson, & Sikes, 1977).

A more comprehensive, cooperative learning program, the Small Group Teaching (SGT) project, has proved very effective in fostering children's prosocial behavior. Classrooms in some lower-socioeconomic-class schools in Israel were experimentally restructured into a "group of groups" with "communication and cooperation in each of several (up to eight) small groups in the class. There is also coordination among the groups so that the class remains an integral social unit. Thus the classroom operates as a peer society organized into subunits, each concentrated on some aspect of a broad learning task. These subunits provide its members with mutual help and support, collaboration on task related activities, exchange of ideas and other resources, and mutual acceptance" (Hertz-Lazarowitz & Sharan, 1984, p.429).

Compared with a control group of comparable children in traditional schools, those in the cooperative learning program performed better in academic tasks and scored higher in tests of thinking skills and creativity. Most important from the point of view of enhancement of prosocial behavior, tension and conflict were significantly reduced in the SGT classrooms, compared with the controls, and helping behavior and motivation increased significantly, as did cooperation in experimental game situations. Judges who observed groups of children working together to construct new words from the letters in an anagram found that "the groups from the Small Group classroom emerged as significantly more helpful, less competitive, and less tense than did groups from traditional classrooms. Furthermore...groups from the Small Group classes produced more new words than did their peers from the control classes, indicating that greater helpfulness in the groups led to superior products" (Hertz-Lazarowitz & Sharan, p. 439). These findings "support the contention that school experience can enhance prosocial behavior among children in all grades of elementary school" (Hertz-Lazarowitz & Sharan, 1984, p. 439).

An ongoing comprehensive longitudinal field-experimental study of the school's role in the socialization of prosocial behavior, being conducted in a suburban middle-class community in the San Francisco Bay area, was initiated when the participants were in kindergarten and has continued until the fourth grade. Children in three schools are participating in a multifaceted program whose goal is to strengthen children's prosocial orientation, defined as "an attitude of concern for others, commitment to the values of fairness and social responsibility, and the ability and inclination to act on these values in everyday life" (Solomon, Watson, Schaps, Battistich, & Solomon, in press). The control or comparison group consists of children in three equivalent schools in the same community that do not use the program.

The program has five basic components, "some focusing directly on promoting prosocial behavior, others emphasizing the motives, values, knowledge, and competencies assumed to underlie it" (Solomon, Watson, Battistich, & Schaps, 1986): *cooperative activities* (joint interdependent activities with common goals, giving children experience at working together, negotiating, stating positions, and compromising); *developmental discipline* (classroom management designed to develop children's intrinsic motivations for academic excellence, as well as prosocial values, including self-control and commitment to rules and values; warm teacher–child relationships, discussion of general moral principles, and student participation in decision making are emphasized); *promoting social understanding* (making use of opportunities to enhance interpersonal sensitivity and understanding of others through discussions of events in school and of characters in stories, exploring their perspectives, motives, feelings, needs, and perceptions); *modeling and highlighting prosocial values* (observation and discussion of prosocial acts by other students and adults, as well as extensive use of literature and other media in which values such as kindness, responsibility, and sharing are central elements); *helping activities* (encouraging helpfulness within the school, e.g., doing chores and assisting classmates and younger children, and outside, e.g., collecting supplies for victims of disasters). Each year, teachers in the three program schools are trained to implement the program.

The outcomes of the program are assessed by means of frequent and extensive observations in classrooms, on playgrounds, and in structured small-group tasks (e.g., constructing a tower with materials that have to be shared); the observers are unaware whether or not the school has a program. In addition, the children are interviewed and respond to questionnaires.

The program has had some impressive results. During the first 5 years of school, children in the program show significantly more prosocial behavior than do those in the comparison classrooms, and the differences are maintained consistently across the years. Specifically, children in the program schools are more supportive of each other, more spontaneously helpful and cooperative, and more concerned about others. In addition, when presented with hypothetical interpersonal conflict situations and other social problem-solving tasks in interviews, the program-school children offer more prosocial strategies for resolution, that is, strategies involving less aggression, more compromise, more planful-ness, and more attention to the needs of all individuals in the conflict. Their responses to questionnaires reveal that these children are more concerned with democratic values and with stating their positions in a group even if they are unlikely to prevail (Solomon et al., 1986, 1987, in press).

Clearly, "the program is having some effect beyond the classroom – that is, it is producing real differences in the children's perceptions, attitudes, and behaviors" (Solomon, Watson, Battistich, & Schaps, 1986). Furthermore, achievement tests have revealed no significant differences between children in the program and those in comparison schools. Apparently "pursuit of the . . . program did not impede academ-ic progress" (Solomon et al., in press).

The success of these experimental programs is compelling evidence that schools and teachers can, with some effort and with minimal inter-ference with the regular curriculum, help raise the level of their students' prosocial behavior and values. Teachers can model kindness and con-sideration, use the techniques of developmental discipline, stimulate discussions of moral values and behavior, devise cooperative learning projects, highlight prosocial actions in literature and in everyday life, and augment pupils' empathy through discussions of needs and feelings. Most of these techniques can be readily integrated into the ordinary school curriculum. Given the potential social benefits of applying these procedures, schools administrators and teachers should be encouraged to learn more about them and to try to apply them in the course of their everyday activities.

Influence of television

By the time the average American reaches age 18, he or she has spent over 15,000 hours watching television, more time than in any other activity except sleep. Children begin watching television on a regular basis 3 or 4 years before entering elementary school, and most children watch some television every day. Inevitably, children will be influenced by what they see and hear on television, for television arouses emotions, communicates values, norms, and standards, and provides models whose actions will be imitated – all factors that may modify a child's behavior (Rushton, 1979, 1981). In the words of a former commissioner of the

Federal Communications Commission, "all television is educational television. The only question is, what is it teaching?" (Nicholas Johnson, quoted in Liebert, Neale, & Davidson, 1973).

Television's potential for producing harmful effects has been the theme of a tremendous amount of controversy, protest, and, fortunately, research, most of it centered on the impact of the pervasive violence and aggression in television programs. Evidence from a wide variety of studies indicates that "television violence has a causal effect on aggressive behavior for children and adolescents" (Friedrich-Cofer & Huston, 1986). In this interactions with peers, 8-year-olds who were frequent viewers of violent television programs were more aggressive than were their peers who watched violent programs less, and 22 years later, they were still highly aggressive and more likely to be convicted of serious crimes (Eron, 1987; Eron, Lefkowitz, Huesmann, & Walder, 1972).

If observational learning from television has such striking and lasting antisocial consequences, it is reasonable to expect that the medium also has potential for modifying behavior in desirable, prosocial directions. Recent studies in laboratory and naturalistic settings have provided evidence supportive of this hypothesis, although the correlations are not generally as strong or as clear as those between viewing TV violence and subsequent aggressive behavior.

In a pioneering study, preschool children between 3 and 5 years of age were randomly assigned to one of three groups that, each day for 4 weeks, viewed aggressive cartoon programs ("Batman" and "Superman"), prosocial programs ("Mr. Rogers' Neighborhood," a program that stresses cooperation, sympathy, sharing, friendship, understanding, and consideration of others' feelings), or programs with neutral content. The children exposed to prosocial television programs displayed more positive behavior, such as more obedience to school rules, greater persistence at tasks, and greater self-control (ability to tolerate delays), than did children in the other two groups. Among children of lower socioeconomic status, those who viewed the prosocial programs became more cooperative, nurturant, and sympathetic and better at verbalizing their own and others' feelings. These effects were still discernible 2 weeks after the training was completed (Friedrich & Stein, 1973).

The socially desirable effects of exposure to prosocial television can be amplified by combining viewing prosocial programs with other experiences, such as role playing (manipulating puppets and enacting events and dialogue similar to those in the program) and verbal labeling (discussion of the events portrayed in the program and of the feelings and actions of the characters). The kindergarten children in another study were assigned to one of five treatments for four sessions: (1) prosocial television programs and verbal labeling; (2) prosocial television programs and role playing; (3) prosocial television programs plus verbal labeling *and* role playing; (4) prosocial television programs plus irrelevant activity (playing games); (5) neutral television programs and irrelevant activity.

To evaluate the effects of these treatments, the investigators tested the children's learning of the content of the programs, generalization of the learning to other situations, and actual helping behavior (assisting in repairing another child's collage that had been damaged). As predicted, exposure to prosocial programs had positive effects. The children exposed to prosocial television made more prosocial responses in the generalization tests than did those who saw neutral films, but simply watching prosocial television did not produce gains in helping behavior. However, the combination of exposure to prosocial television and role playing of the behavior portrayed in the television programs significantly enhanced helping behavior. Verbal labeling itself did not increase boys' helping behavior, but verbal labeling plus role playing further augmented girls' tendencies to assist others.

The clear effects of television and training...suggest that this type of prosocial television can have a strong impact on children who watch it in naturalistic contexts where viewing can occur over a much longer period of time than one week. These results appear to be readily applicable to naturalistic settings because the children generalized both learning and behavior to situations quite different from those to which they were exposed in the television and training, and because this generalization occurred in measures administered 2 or 3 days after the television viewing. [Friedrich & Stein, 1975, p. 37]

In a test of the effects of repeated exposures to prosocial television, a group of preschool children was shown 20 half-hour episodes of television, over a 4-week period, consisting of portions of standard broadcast programs (such as "Lassie," "I Love Lucy", and "The Brady Bunch") that were low in aggression and high in prosocial content and expression of concern for others, empathy, and sympathy. Another group was exposed to the same number of programs, drawn from the same television series, but containing few instances of prosocial behavior. To establish baselines, the children were tested on a variety of measures of helpfulness and cooperation 1 week prior to beginning their television viewing and again 1 week after the end of the 4-week period. Both boys and girls who viewed prosocial television gained more in cooperativeness than did those in the other group, and the boys in this group became more helpful than those in the control group.

In the same study, other children participated in several types of role-taking activities, but were not exposed to either prosocial or neutral television programs. These role-taking experiences proved to be more effective than exposure to prosocial programs in increasing children's sharing and helping. Nevertheless, the positive influences of exposure to prosocial programs were clearly established, and these effects carried over (generalized) to situations quite different from the ones portrayed in television (Ahammer & Murray, 1979).

It can be concluded that for young children, viewing prosocial television programs per se facilitates acquisition or enhancement of prosocial behavior. However, the influences of such experiences are not as powerful or as direct as are the influences of specially designed school programs, training in role taking, or the combination of prosocial television programs, role playing, and verbal labeling. Perhaps the prosocial actions in television programs are not as salient or as attention-getting for young children as is active participation in discussion and role playing; hence, the children are less likely to think about or remember the messages of the programs or to make inferences or generalizations from them. Therefore, "prosocial television might be used as an adjunct to other training procedures when attempting to teach or enhance prosocial tendencies in children" (Rushton, 1981, p. 95). Caregivers and teachers can make the messages of prosocial television more effective if they engage the children in discussions, and possibly role playing, of the program and its lessons.

Studies of older children have yielded findings that essentially substantiate the findings for younger children. In one study, a group of first-graders was shown an episode from the "Lassie" series in which a boy risked his life to save a dog, whereas control groups were shown either a "Lassie" episode without such altruism or a family situation comedy. Subsequently, each child had an opportunity to come to the aid of some distressed puppies, but only at some cost – helping the puppies meant withdrawing from a game in which the child could win a valuable prize. The children who had seen the altruistic "Lassie" episode gave substantially more help to the puppies in distress than did the children exposed to the other programs (Sprafkin, Liebert, & Poulos, 1975).

In another study, some 9-, 12-, and 15-year-olds watched a commercial television program in which the hero reacted constructively to interpersonal conflict and intimidation, whereas others of the same age viewed an edited version in which he responded aggressively; a third group was shown a wildlife documentary. Subsequently, they were all given an opportunity to help or hurt an absent peer, who was having difficulty completing a task, by pressing either a "Help" button, which decreased a distracting noise, or a "Hurt" button, which intensified it. Those who had seen examples of constructive, coping behavior were more likely to make prosocial, "Help" responses than were those who viewed either the aggressive version or the documentary (Collins & Getz, 1976).

The participants in another naturalistic study were older children who were members of Little League baseball teams, lacrosse teams, or ice hockey teams. Observations of their behavior during the games were made before and after the teams saw videotapes of people playing the viewers' own sport. In some videotapes, the players were antisocial (unnecessarily rough or cheating); in others, the players showed prosocial behavior (helping, encouraging, being sympathetic, displaying respect, apologizing for a wrong, expressing positive feelings) or manifested neither antisocial nor prosocial behavior. "The results indicated that exposure to such prosocial media increased the level of prosocial behavior for the hockey and lacrosse players, but not for the baseball players. In addition, the survey data indicated a tendency for those who played in the most prosocial manner...to prefer watching prosocial television at home" (Moriarty & McCabe, 1977, cited in Rushton, 1980, p. 149).

These studies suggest that for older children, exposure to prosocial television may help foster prosocial development, at least in certain areas. Perhaps being at a more advanced stage of cognitive development, older children pay more attention and formulate generalizations from their observational learning. These generalizations may be stored in memory and subsequently serve as mediators between the child's perception of other people's needs and the child's response (help, sharing, cooperation) to those needs.

Perhaps if prosocial programs could be made more attractive to children – by incorporating more action and appealing music – their potential for modifying children's prosocial behavior might be expanded. Further research is needed to test this possibility and to determine the social circumstances and personal backgrounds that may moderate the potential effectiveness of prosocial television. It is also important to discover other ways to combine prosocial television with other experiences to increase children's prosocial orientations and activities.

8 Cognition, role taking, interpersonal problem solving, and moral judgment

Before we help others, act considerately, or donate to charity, we have to perceive and interpret a situation and make inferences about others' feelings. We also evaluate their needs and desires and decide which actions will be most effective and beneficial to them. Finally, we must formulate and execute a plan for prosocial action. In short, mature prosocial action involves several fundamental cognitive processes: perception, reasoning, problem solving, and decision making.

The roles of cognitive processes in the genesis, development, and execution of prosocial behavior are not fully understood. At the earliest stages of cognitive development, children probably are not able to perceive and interpret another individual's needs or distress accurately, nor do they know what to do to help relieve someone else's distress. Hence, they cannot act altruistically. What are the cognitive prerequisites of showing consideration or kindness, of sharing or helping? At what stage of cognitive development does the child become capable of accurate perceptions of someone else's feelings? Are intelligent children more likely than unintelligent children to sympathize with victims of oppression? Does more mature reasoning ability or greater sophistication in resolving moral and social problems lead to stronger tendencies toward prosocial responses? These are the kinds of questions that are examined in this chapter. As we shall see, there have been many relevant investigations, but we do not have many definitive answers.

Most of the pertinent research pertains to six interrelated topics: general intelligence, perception of others' needs, role taking, interpersonal problem solving, attributional inferences (inferences about others' motives and behavior), and moral reasoning or moral judgment.

Intelligence and prosocial behavior

There appears to be a modest correlation between performance on intelligence tests, the most widely used measures of general cognitive ability, and predispositions to prosocial behavior. Many different criteria of prosocial behavior and a wide variety of intelligence tests have been used in pertinent studies. Substantial correlations (about .40) between intelligence test scores and prosocial behavior were reported in three studies, two involving naturalistic observations of altruism (Kiselica & Levin, 1987; Krebs & Sturrup, 1982), and one involving sociometric criteria (peer nominations for "most considerate" and "most likely to help") (Mussen et al., 1970). In a fourth study, one measure of general intelligence was moderately correlated (.34) with reporting of altruistic motives for helping, but not with the degree to which fifth-graders helped in an experimental situation, whereas a measure of verbal intelligence was significantly, but only modestly, related (.20) to quality of helping (i.e., whether the person assisted voluntarily or only after adult pressure or the promise of a reward) (Bar-Tal, Korenfeld, & Raviv, 1985). The correlations reported in most other studies generally have been positive, but low, or have been significant for some, but not other, indices of prosocial behavior (Friedrich & Stein, 1973; Grant, Weiner, & Rushton, 1976; Hansen, Goldman, & Baldwin, 1975; Harris, Mussen, & Rutherford, 1976; Hartshorne et al., 1929; Payne, 1980; Rubin & Schneider, 1973; Rushton & Wiener, 1975). It thus seems reasonable to conclude that the level of general intelligence or general cognitive ability has some relation to children's predispositions toward prosocial behavior. The association may be stronger in contexts in which the cues related to the other's need are subtle; in such situations, more intelligent children may be better able to detect the other's need, role take, and figure out a way to assist.

Perception of others' needs

It is logical to assume that young children are less able to perceive others' needs accurately than are older children. Very young children sometimes have difficulty differentiating their own needs from others' needs (Hoffman, 1982), and this inability may affect their ability to respond prosocially. Among girls (but not boys) 18 to 24 months old, the ability to recognize themselves in the mirror – a measure of the ability to differentiate perceptually between oneself and others, and an index of self-awareness – was associated with attempts to help or comfort their mothers when they feigned distress (Johnson, 1982). Moreover, several researchers have noted that young children sometimes seem uncertain who is experiencing distress – themselves or another – when they view another person in distress (Zahn-Waxler & Radke-Yarrow, 1982). For example, an 11-month-old who saw another child fall "first stared at the victim, looking as though she were about to cry herself, and then put her thumb in her mouth and buried her head in her mother's lap," which is what she typically did when she hurt herself (Hoffman, 1982, p. 287).

Even when children are old enough to clearly differentiate between their own and another's distress, they may have difficulty interpreting subtle cues that are indicative of another's distress (Barnett & Thompson, 1985). In one study, some preschoolers and third-graders viewed videotaped vignettes in which a distressed child's needs and the cause of the problem were explicit (e.g., the story protagonist looks sadly at the cookie jar that he cannot open, gives up trying, and says "Rats!"); others saw tapes in which these were not explicit (e.g., the story protagonist gives up, but does not say "Rats!"). Explicitness had little effect on the third-graders' recognition of the problem; however, when the cues were explicit, preschoolers' awareness of the problem was greater, as was the likelihood that they would suggest a helpful response (Pearl, 1985). Apparently, most third-graders were able to infer another's need or the cause of the problem on the basis of subtle cues, whereas the preschoolers could not. This is evidence that the abilities to recognize and process cues related to another's distress increase with age and that these abilities enhance prosocial responding.

Role taking

Many theorists have argued that role taking, the ability to understand and infer another's feelings and emotional reactions, thoughts, perspectives, motives, and intentions, is a prerequisite to the ability and willingness to act altruistically.

Piaget maintained that young children do not have sufficient cognitive maturity to take another's point of view. In his view, children who have not yet reached the period of concrete operations (before the age of 7, approximately) cannot readily "decenter"; they attend to only one dimension of a situation at a time and cannot consider several aspects of a problem or multiple perspectives simultaneously. At this stage, children are egocentric and capable of considering only their own points of view. In later childhood, during the stage of concrete operations (about 7 to 12 years of age), the child can attend to several aspects of a problem at a time and, in addition, can consider reciprocal relationships and the viewpoints of others.

Research findings support Piaget's idea that role-taking abilities increase with age in the early years and during childhood (Flavell, Botkin, Fry, Wright, & Jarvis, 1968; Kurdek, 1977; Selman, 1971, 1980; Shantz, 1983). However, it is also clear that children have some ability to infer others' feelings, perspectives, and cognitions long before age 6 or 7 (Borke, 1975; Liben, 1978; Shantz, 1983). Indeed, even 1- to 2-year-olds sometimes understand another person's emotions (Radke-Yarrow et al., 1983). Hoffman described an incident illustrating early role taking by Michael, aged 15 months, who was fighting with his friend Paul over a toy. Paul started to cry.

Michael appeared disturbed and let go, but Paul still cried. Michael paused, then brought his teddy bear to Paul but to no avail. Michael paused again, and then finally succeeded in stopping Paul's crying by fetching Paul's security blanket from an adjoining room. [Hoffman, 1975b, p. 621]

Apparently, Michael could assess the "specific needs of another person which differed from his own" (p. 612).

The assertion that role taking is a mediator of prosocial actions has been systematically tested and amply supported. Although role taking probably is irrelevant to prosocial actions that are habitual or are performed without analyzing another individual's thoughts or feelings, it does seem to facilitate prosocial behaviors that are motivated by concern for others.

A variety of tests have been devised to measure children's understanding of others' feelings and cognitions. The simplest tests are concerned with the ability to discriminate and label emotions. For example, a child is told a brief story (such as one about a happy child at a birthday party) and then is asked to identify the emotions of a story character by selecting one of several pictures of faces expressing happiness, anger, and fear. Such tests tap only rudimentary cognitive aspects of role taking – essentially social comprehension – and by the age of 3, most children differentiate between happy and unhappy reactions, whereas fear and anger are accurately identified a little later (Borke, 1971). This simple type of perspective taking has been associated with prosocial behavior in some studies (Buckley, Siegel, & Ness, 1979; Denham, 1986; see Underwood & Moore, 1982b), but not others (Iannotti, 1975).

Performance on tests of cognitive role taking (the ability to understand others' thoughts) is positively related to prosocial behavior, however. Second- and third-graders in one highly relevant study of altruism were administered two role-taking tasks. In the first (Flavell et al., 1968), the child was presented with two boxes; "5 cents" was printed on a box containing a nickel, and "10 cents" was printed on the other, which held a dime. The child was told that in a few minutes he or she would be asked to outwit another child in a simple game in which the opponent would be permitted to choose one of the boxes for himself or herself. The object of the game was to prevent the opponent from winning either of the two coins by guessing which of the two boxes would be chosen and removing the money from it. (The children were told that the opponents would know that an attempt would be made to trick them.) The participant was questioned about how to go about tricking the opponent. The score for role-taking ability was based on the child's skill in taking the perspective of the opponent.

In the second test of role-taking ability, the child was presented with a series of seven pictures and asked to make up a story about them. Then three pictures were removed, and the child was asked to make up a story that another child would tell about the remaining four pictures. Responses to questions that followed each task revealed the child's ability to assume the perspective of another child. The children were also frequently observed in school and on the playground over a 2-month period, and interactions were coded according to a preplanned set of categories. Each child's altruism score was the proportion of his or her responses that were in the categories "offers help," "offers support," and "suggests responsibly" (Krebs & Sturrup, 1982).

As predicted, the measures of role taking were significantly correlated with the behavioral indices of altruism and with teachers' independent ratings of prosocial behavior, patience, and cooperativeness. This study is notable because the major criterion of altruism was based on repeated observations of children in their natural settings over an extended period.

In another confirming study, second-graders were classified as high or low in role-taking ability on the basis of three tests assessing the abilities to make inferences about the intentions of a character in a story, to label and explain story characters' affective states (e.g., if a wife and husband in the story were angry or bored), and to tell a cartoon story from the perspective of a person who had less information about the story than the children themselves did. Then the children were videotaped while they were teaching two kindergarteners to make caterpillars with construction paper, scissors, glue, and crayons. Those high in role-taking ability were more responsive to the kindergarteners' questions and were more likely to offer to assist than were children low in role taking. The high role takers were especially likely to respond to indirect requests for help, which suggests that they were more attuned to the younger children's needs (Hudson, Forman, & Brion-Meisels, 1982).

When the results of a number of studies have been combined and examined with appropriate statistical procedures (i.e., with meta-analytic techniques), role taking has been positively and significantly related to prosocial behavior (Underwood & Moore, 1982b). Moreover, when multiple measures of role taking and prosocial behavior are used as indices, the association between the two is stronger than when only one index of each construct is used (Elder, 1983). A battery of measures aggregated together may provide a more reliable and more accurate index of the behavior or ability in question than can a single measure (Epstein, 1979; Rushton, Brainerd, & Pressley, 1983).

It is important to realize that role-taking capability per se is insufficient to instigate prosocial action. A child with high role-taking ability may act prosocially only if he or she is assertive enough to approach the person in need (Barrett & Yarrow, 1977), is motivated to assist, and is confident of possessing the skills required to assist (Peterson, 1983a,b).

Interpersonal problem-solving skills

The concept of interpersonal problem-solving skills encompasses sensitivity to interpersonal problems, generating a variety of possible solutions to such problems, articulating steps that may be necessary in order to carry out solutions to interpersonal problems, and consideration of the consequences of social acts for others as well as oneself (Shure, 1982; Spivack, Platt, & Shure, 1976).

As would be expected, interpersonal problem-solving skills increase with age. Older elementary-school children, in comparison with younger school-age children, define interpersonal problems more thoroughly, generate more alternative ways of responding and more consequences, and select solutions that reflect an understanding of the perspectives of others (Marsh, 1982). Kindergarteners are less likely than older children to realize that different modes of helping should be used for different problems and to recognize the role of the beneficiary's characteristics (e.g., cooperativeness) when choosing effective helping strategies (Barnett, Darcie, Holland, & Kobasigawa, 1982).

Interpersonal problem-solving skills have been positively correlated with positive social interactions with peers, helpfulness, and concern for others (Marsh, Serafica, & Barenboim, 1981; Olson, Johnson, Belleau, Parks, & Barrett, 1983; Shure, 1980). In addition, training in interpersonal problem-solving skills has been shown to produce increases in fifth-graders' prosocial behaviors (broadly defined as including popularity as well as concern for others) (Spivack & Shure, 1974).

Attributions about others

As we observe others, we tend to make judgments or inferences about what motivates their activities, what "causes" them to act as they do. These attributions can influence whether or not we react altruistically. Suppose, for example, we encounter someone who appears to need some kind of help. We probably will ask ourselves why the individual needs help: Is the need due to internal factors (e.g., low intelligence, inability to walk, or laziness) or external factors (such as loss of a job because of the closing of a factory)? The problem may be attributable to factors within one's control (i.e., one's own effort or choices) or beyond one's control (e.g., inability to walk because of a genetically transmitted condition or trauma at birth) (Kelley, 1967; Heider, 1958; Weiner, 1986).

Adults are more willing to help people whose needs, distress, and problems are due to factors out of their control, rather than to factors they could have controlled. Students are more likely to lend classmates notes taken during a lecture if those classmates missed class because of illness, as compared with being careless or lazy or simply not wanting to attend class that day (Ickes & Kidd, 1976; Meyer & Mulherin, 1980; Reisenzein, 1986).

School-age children also are more likely to help those whose needs are due to factors beyond their control (Barnett, 1975; Braband & Lerner, 1975; Miller & Smith, 1977). Similarly, preschoolers appear more likely to empathize with a story character who had experienced sadness or happiness for an acceptable reason rather than for an inappropriate reason (e.g., when a story protagonist was sad because he could not continue playing with a kite he took from a smaller child) (Barnett & McMinimy, 1988).

The relation between attributions concerning the reasons for another's need and prosocial responses is mediated by the emotional reactions associated with an attribution. Adults experience more sympathy and pity and greater willingness to assist when another's need is uncontrollable. In contrast, they report less concern and pity and more negative response (e.g., anger or disgust) in reaction to distress that could be controlled (e.g., that due to drunkenness or failure to look for work) (Weiner, 1980, 1986).

Moral reasoning

Some types of prosocial behavior are based on moral principles or concern with others' needs, whereas others are not. By definition, altruistic conduct involves nonegoistic motives, judgments, or reasoning. Therefore, cognitions concerning intentions, motives, principles, and values are fundamental to an understanding of altruistic behavior.

Common experience and observation suggest that moral cognitions and moral behavior are not necessarily closely connected. People do not always behave in accordance with their moral judgments or values; almost all of us have encountered individuals who articulate the most noble moral principles, but act in self-serving ways.

The gap between moral reasoning and behavior may yawn wide even in history's moral heroes. Gore Vidal's *Burr* levels this charge against Thomas Jefferson: "Proclaiming the unalienable rights of man for everyone (except slaves, Indians, women and those entirely without property), Jefferson tried to seize the Floridas by force, dreamed of a conquest of Cuba, and after his illegal purchase of Louisiana sent a military governor to rule New Orleans against the will of its inhabitants....It was of course Jefferson's gift at one time or another to put with eloquence the 'right' answer to every moral question. In practice, however, he seldom deviated from an opportunistic course, calculated to bring him power." [Vidal, cited by Lickona, 1976, p. 357]

Unfortunately, investigators of prosocial *behavior* – even those concerned with the forces that shape such behavior – often do not examine the actors' cognitions and motivations. On the other hand, theorists and researchers in the field of moral *judgment* have focused almost exclusively on developmental (age) changes in the form and structure of moral concepts, that is, on the stages in the maturation of moral reasoning and judgment. Consequently, it is useful to sketch out the most influential theories of moral reasoning, those of Piaget and Kohlberg. Both of these theorists postulate that moral judgment develops through a specific sequence of stages. The individual's stage or level of moral judgment is assessed by means of interviews or questionnaires about moral dilemmas and decisions.

Piaget's theory of moral development

No one has had greater impact on research and theory in the field of cognitive development than Jean Piaget. Although his principal interests were in age changes in logic and thinking, some of his work was devoted to children's concepts of justice and morality. In one of his earliest books, *The Moral Judgment of the Child*, Piaget (1932/ 1965) described interviews in which children of different ages were told short stories and were questioned about rules of conduct, punishment, authority, transgressions, wrongdoing, equality, and reciprocity among people. Children were asked, for example, who was naughtier, a boy who unintentionally gave wrong directions to a man, so that he got lost, or a boy who mischievously gave wrong directions to a man, who then found his way despite the misinformation the boy gave him. Analyses of the responses led Piaget to conclude that there are two successive stages in the development of one's understanding of rules, moral judgment, and sense of justice, as well as a transitional, intermediate stage.

The first stage, variously labeled the stage of *heteronomous morality, moral realism* or *morality of constraint*, is characteristic of children who have not yet achieved the stage of concrete operations, that is, children below the age of 7 or 8 years. During this stage, the child is morally realistic, regarding duty as "self subsistent and independent of the mind, as imposing itself regardless of the circumstances in which the individual may find himself" (Piaget, 1932/1965, p. 111). Rules, obligations, and commands are regarded as "givens," external to the mind, inflexible, and unchangeable. Justice is whatever the ruling authority (adults) or the law commands, whatever reward or punishment authorities decree. The "good" is obedience, and wrongdoing is judged according to the letter, not the spirit, of the law.

The thinking of children at this stage is characterized by belief in immanent justice (that Nature will punish transgressions) and in the absoluteness of the values held (everything is totally right or totally wrong). Furthermore, acts are evaluated on the basis of their consequences, rather than on the basis of the actor's intentions or motivations. Severe, arbitrary punishments are favored; the more serious the consequences of an act, the greater the punishment the actor deserves.

According to Piaget, the sources of moral realism are the child's cognitive structures and experiences. The principal cognitive factors are general egocentrism, which is reflected in the child's belief that everyone shares the child's particular view of events, and realism of thought, that is, the tendency to reify psychological phenomena such as thoughts, rules, or dreams, to conceive of them as physical, thing-like entities. The environmental or experiential factors that Piaget suggested as the basis for moral realism are adult control and constraint, that is, the inherently unequal relationship between children and parents.

The intermediate period in the development of moral reasoning begins about the age of 7 or 8 years. At this age the child interacts more extensively with peers and has more egalitarian, give-and-take relationships with others. A sense of autonomy and egalitarianism becomes prominent; equality begins to take priority over authority in matters of distribution, and belief in immanent justice and severe punishment is superseded by belief in reciprocal punishment (punishment fitting the crime).

The most mature stage, called *autonomous morality, moral relativism*, or *morality of cooperation*, generally emerges at about 11 or 12 years of age. Equity dominates the child's thinking about justice; extenuating circumstances, motivations, and intentions weigh heavily in making moral judgments. Egalitarian concepts of justice prevail; arbitrary punishments, immanent justice, moral absolutism, and blind obedience to authority are rejected. Rules are considered to be products of social interaction and therefore to be modifiable.

In Piaget's view, the achievement of mature, autonomous concepts of justice is, to a large extent, the product of cooperation, reciprocity, and role taking among peers. Because there are no absolute authority figures in the peer group, children develop ideas of equality, cooperation, and group solidarity, and discussion and criticism among peers are commonplace. By interacting with peers, the child becomes more skilled in assuming others' views – that is, in taking roles. As a result, the child's egocentrism diminishes, and concern for the welfare and rights of others increases.

According to Piaget, all normal children progress through this hierarchical sequence of stages. Individual differences in rates of progress are due to variations in cognitive maturity, opportunities for peer cooperation and reciprocal role taking, moral education, home life, and other environmental factors.

Some aspects of Piaget's notions of the developmental sequence from heteronomous to autonomous conceptions of justice have been confirmed in empirical research. For example, with age, boys and girls of many nationalities and races, socioeconomic classes, and intelligence levels increasingly recognize the importance of intentions and motives when judging the morality of others' actions (Berg & Mussen, 1975; Lickona, 1976). Nevertheless, Piaget's methods have also been criticized. For example, he tended to confound motives for acting and consequences of action in his stories (see Grueneich, 1982; Karniol, 1978; and Keasey, 1978, for further disscussion of these issues). But, as would be predicted from Piaget's theory, there are developmental changes in children's abilities to evaluate positive and negative motives (Eisenberg, 1986; Keasey, 1978) and to evaluate intentionality (Keasey, 1978; Shantz, 1983). Although fairly young children may be able to assess intent, they are likely to weight the consequences of an action more heavily than the actor's intentions (Karniol, 1978; Surber, 1982).

Recent empirical work based on Piagetian notions

Piaget's work has stimulated many studies of children's ideas about the kindness or goodness of prosocial actions. In this research, children generally are presented with short stories about people who have helped, shared with, or comforted others (or have not done so), and then they are asked to evaluate these actions. The use of intentionality as a criterion for judging others increases dramatically from the pre-school years to elementary-school years (Baldwin & Baldwin, 1970; Baldwin, Baldwin, Castillo-Vales, & Seegmiller, 1971; Eisenberg, 1986). Moreover, although young elementary-school children often judge a prosocial act that is rewarded as kinder than the same act when unrewarded, by the middle elementary-school years, the pattern is reversed (Baldwin & Baldwin, 1970; Baldwin et al., 1971; Cohen, Gelfand, & Hartmann, 1981; DiVitto & McArthur, 1978; Leahy, 1979).

Indeed, with increasing age, individuals tend to view a prosocial act that reaps a social or material reward, that is coerced, that is based on reciprocity considerations (e.g., the expectation of help or a reward in the future from the individual who is assisted), or that fulfills a social obligation as being less kind than acts performed voluntarily and without reward (Baldwin & Baldwin, 1970; Benson, Hartmann, & Gelfand, 1981; Cohen et al., 1981; Peterson, 1980; Peterson & Gelfand, 1984). Moreover, from the elementary-school years into adulthood, there is an increase in the tendency to view as altruistic those prosocial acts performed at a cost to oneself, performed despite obstacles, or performed on behalf of someone who previously had refused to assist the actor (Leahy, 1979; Suls, Witenberg, & Gutkin, 1981).

It may be inferred that with age, children become better able to distinguish between egoistic and altruistic motives and to use their understanding of intentionality and others' motivations to evaluate prosocial actions. Prosocial acts based on altruistic motivations are increasingly judged as being more kind or moral than are prosocial actions that are based on egoistic motives or are performed for reasons other than concern and regard for others. Thus, we expect older children to value altruistic behavior more highly than do younger children and to be more likely to perform prosocial behaviors for altruistic reasons.

Kohlberg's theory of moral development

Lawrence Kohlberg (1969, 1976, 1981, 1984) of Harvard University presented another theory of the development of moral judgment that amplified Piaget's sequence of stages. Kohlberg's schema was based on analyses of interviews in which he presented people with a series of moral dilemmas in story form. In most of these dilemmas, obedience to laws or to authority conflicts with the welfare of the actor or other people. The subject is asked what the hero of the story should do, and this is followed by a series of questions (probes) about the thinking underlying the answers. Here is the best-known story and some of the probes that go with it:

In Europe, a woman was near death from a special kind of cancer. There was one drug that the doctors thought might save her. It was a form of radium that a druggist in the same town had recently discovered. The drug was expensive to make, but the druggist was charging 10 times what the drug cost him to make. He paid $200 for the radium and charged $2,000 for a small dose of the drug. The sick woman's husband, Heinz, went to everyone he knew to borrow the money, but he could only get together about $1,000, which is half of what it cost. He told the druggist his wife was dying, and asked him to sell it cheaper or let him pay later. But the druggist said, "No, I discovered the drug and I'm going to make money for it." So Heinz got desperate and broke into the man's store to steal the drug for his wife.

Should Heinz have done that? Was it actually wrong or right? Why? Is it a husband's duty to steal the drug for his wife if he can get it no other way? Would a good husband do it? Did the druggist have the right to charge that much where there was no law actually setting a limit to the price? Why?

Of central importance in assessing moral maturity is the quality of the judgment – the ways of perceiving the conflict situation, the individual's ways of conceptualizing moral issues, and the individual's application of moral principles to a number of different kinds of issues (e.g., civil liberties, punitive justice, personal conscience, and issues of authority). The "solutions" chosen by an individual (e.g., whether or not Heinz should have stolen the drug) are relatively unimportant (Kohlberg, 1969, 1981).

According to Kohlberg, children's moral development advances through a sequence of six stages, ordered into three levels of moral orientation. These are summarized in Table 8.1. The schema is more complex and extensive than that of Piaget, and it deals with changes that occur in middle childhood, adolescence, and adulthood. In fact, principled moral reasoning, the highest level, is characteristic of only a small proportion of mature adults.

The stages are said to be invariant or unchanging in sequence, hierarchical in their ordering, universal to all people, and intrinsic to the species, although any particular individual's development may cease at any stage. Each successive stage is seen as qualitatively different

Table 8.1. The six moral stages

Content of stage			
Level and stage	*What is right*	*Reasons for doing right*	*Social perspective of stage*
LEVEL 1 – PRECONVENTIONAL Stage 1 – Heteronomous Morality	To avoid breaking rules backed by punishment, obedience for its own sake, and avoiding physical damage to persons and property.	Avoidance of punishment, and the superior power of authorities.	*Egocentric point of view.* Doesn't consider the interests of others or recognize that they differ from the actor's; doesn't relate two points of view. Actions are considered physically rather than in terms of psychological interests of others. Confusion of authority's perspective with one's own.
Stage 2 – Individualism, Instrumental Purpose, and Exchange	Following rules only when it is to someone's immediate interest; acting to meet one's own interests and needs and letting others do the same. Right is also what's fair, what's an equal exchange, a deal, an agreement.	To serve one's own needs or interests in a world where you have to recognize that other people have their interests, too.	*Concrete individualistic perspective.* Aware that everybody has his/her own interest to pursue and these conflict, so that right is relative (in the concrete individualistic sense).
LEVEL II – CONVENTIONAL Stage 3 – Mutual Interpersonal Expectations, Relationships, and Interpersonal Conformity	Living up to what is expected by people close to you or what people generally expect of people in your role as son, brother, friend, etc. "Being good" is important and means having good motives, showing concern about others. It also means keeping mutual relationships, such as trust, loyalty, respect and gratitude.	The need to be a good person in your own eyes and those of others. Your caring for others. Belief in the Golden Rule. Desire to maintain rules and authority which support stereotypical good behavior.	*Perspective of the individual in relationships with other individuals.* Aware of shared feelings, agreements, and expectations which take primacy over individual interest. Relates points of view through the concrete Golden Rule, putting yourself in the other guy's shoes. Does not yet consider generalized system perspective.
Stage 4 – Social System and Conscience	Fulfilling the actual duties to which you have agreed. Laws are to be upheld except in extreme cases where they conflict with other fixed social duties. Right is also contributing to society, the group, or institution.	To keep the institution going as a whole, to avoid the breakdown in the system "if everyone did it," or the imperative of conscience to meet one's defined obligations (Easily confused with Stage 3 belief in rules and authority.)	*Differentiates societal point of view from interpersonal agreement or motives.* Takes the point of view of the system that defines roles and rules. Considers individual relations in terms of place in the system.

Table 8.1. *(continued)*

LEVEL III – POST-CONVENTIONAL, or PRINCIPLED Stage 5 – Social Contract or Utility and Individual Rights	Being aware that people hold a variety of values and opinions, that most values and rules are relative to your group. These relative rules should usually be upheld, however, in the interest of impartiality and because they are the social contract. Some nonrelative values and rights like *life* and *liberty*, however, must be upheld in any society and regardless of majority opinion.	A sense of obligation to law because of one's social contract to make and abide by laws for the welfare of all and for the protection of all people's rights. A feeling of contractual commitment, freely entered upon, to family, friendship, trust, and work obligations. Concern that laws and duties be based on rational calculation of overall utility, "the greatest good for the greatest number."	*Prior-to-society perspective.* Perspective of a rational individual aware of values and rights prior to social attachments and contracts. Integrates perspectives by formal mechanisms of agreement, contract, objective impartiality, and due process. Considers moral and legal points of view; recognizes that they sometimes conflict and finds it difficult to integrate them.
Stage 6 – Universal Ethical Principles	Following self-chosen ethical principles. Particular laws or social agreements are usually valid because they rest on such principles. When laws violate these principles, one acts in accordance with the principle. Principles are universal principles of justice: the equality of human rights and respect for the dignity of human beings as individual persons.	The belief as a rational person in the validity of universal moral principles, and a sense of personal commitment to them.	*Perspective of a moral point of view* from which social arrangements derive. Perspective is that of any rational individual recognizing the nature of morality or the fact that persons are ends in themselves and must be treated as such.

Reprinted with permission from Kohlberg (1976).

from the others, a more advanced "structured whole," embracing a new, more comprehensive, and more coherent cognitive organization of moral thinking (Kohlberg, 1981, 1984).

Like Piaget, Kohlberg asserted that progress from one moral stage to the next is the result of the interaction of the maturation of the organism and experience. The maturation of cognitive capacities is critical because judging and evaluating right and wrong are primarily active cognitive processes. Social role taking (called sociomoral perspective taking) is considered the most influential experiential factor in moral development. Role taking enhances the individual's ability to empathize with others and to perceive things from others' points of view. By taking roles, one becomes aware of conflicts or discrepancies between one's own and others' judgments and actions. The resolution of conflicts between differing points of view brings the individual to higher, more mature moral stages that are more stable than the lower ones.

The basic developmental concept underlying the revised stage sequence is level of sociomoral perspective, the characteristic point of view from which the individual formulates moral judgments. In regard to level of sociomoral perspective, we interpret the perspective-taking underlying the moral stages as intrinsically moral in nature rather than as a logical or social-cognitive structure applied to the moral domain....These levels provide a general organization of moral judgment and serve to inform and unite other more specific moral concepts, such as the nature of the morally right or good, moral reciprocity, rules, rights, obligation or duty, fairness, and welfare consequences, and moral values such as obedience to authority, preservation of human life, and maintenance of contracts and affectional relations. [Colby & Kohlberg, 1984, p. 43]

Some tenets of Kohlberg's theory have been tested empirically and have been found to be partially supported by the empirical evidence. Children from vastly different cultures such as Taiwan, Mexico, Israel, and Turkey advance through the first two or three stages in the same sequence as Americans do, thus partially supporting Kohlberg's hypothesis that the sequence of development is universal. Subjects in other cultures, particularly in British Honduras and in isolated villages of Yucatan and Turkey, move through the sequence more slowly, however, and very few of them use Stage 4 conventional reasoning or principled reasoning (e.g., Kohlberg, 1969; Nisan & Kohlberg, 1982; Turiel, Edwards, & Kohlberg, 1978; White, Bushnell, & Regnemer, 1978; see Snarey, 1985, for a review).

The idea that maturity of moral judgment depends on one's level of cognitive development is central to Kohlberg's theory. The attainment of a particular stage of thinking and reasoning is considered a necessary, although not sufficient, precondition for the achievement of a parallel stage of moral judgment. The empirical support for the notion that cognition is significantly correlated with moral reasoning is impressive; cognitive development, as assessed by I.Q. (Arbuthnot, 1973; Harris et al., 1976; Kohlberg, 1969; Kuhn, Langer, Kohlberg, & Haan, 1977) or performance on Piagetian logical tasks (Cauble, 1976; Kuhn et al., 1977; Tomlinson-Keasey & Keasey, 1974; Walker, 1980; Walker & Richards, 1979), has been associated with level of moral judgment. However, it is unclear whether or not certain cognitive prerequisites (such as attainment of a specific level of logical reasoning) are necessary for the attainment of each stage of moral judgment (Haan, Weiss, & Johnson,

1982; Krebs & Gillmore, 1982; Kuhn et al., 1977; Walker, 1980). Regardless, it is obvious that mature levels of moral reasoning reflect more sophisticated cognitive conceptualizations than do lower levels. Moreover, Kohlberg's hypothesis that role-taking opportunities contribute to the development of moral maturity has been confirmed in a number of experimental and correlational studies (Ambron & Irwin, 1975; Kurdek, 1978; Moir, 1974; Selman, 1980).

The theories of Piaget and Kohlberg have had enormous impact on research and thinking about the development of moral reasoning. Yet, in a sense, both deal with a circumscribed domain because the data base consists primarily of children's verbalizations about laws, rules, authority, responsibility, equality, and justice. The prosocial domain (thoughts, concepts, and judgments about issues such as personal sacrifice and conflict between one's own needs and those of others) is relatively neglected in Piaget's or Kohlberg's procedures. Consider the moral dilemma of a girl who has to decide between protecting herself and risking her own safety to help someone in distress. There is no a priori reason to believe that the same conceptions, judgments, and principles are applied in resolving this dilemma as in dealing with most of the dilemmas presented by Piaget and Kohlberg.

Prosocial moral reasoning

More recently, some investigators have devised moral dilemmas that focus on assisting others at a cost to oneself. For example, Eisenberg has presented preschool, elementary-school, and high-school children with several moral-judgment dilemmas concerning prosocial actions and conflicts between one's own and another's desires. One of the dilemmas (as worded for older children) follows:

Bob, a young man who was very good at swimming, was asked to help young crippled children who could not walk to learn to swim so that they could strengthen their legs for walking. Bob was the only one in his town who could do this job well because only he had had both life-saving and teaching experiences. But helping the crippled children would take much of Bob's free time left after work and school, and Bob had wanted to practice very hard as often as possible for a series of very important swimming contests coming up. If Bob did not practice swimming in all his free time, his chances of winning the contests, and also for receiving a paid college education or a sum of money, would be greatly lessened.

Should Bob agree to teach the crippled children? Why? [More probes follow; the dilemma is simplified for studies involving younger children.]

Careful analysis of children's and adolescents' responses to these stories has revealed five major age-related levels in the development of thinking about prosocial moral issues. These are summarized in Table 8.2 (Eisenberg, 1982, 1986; Eisenberg, Lennon, & Roth, 1983; Eisenberg,

Table 8.2. *Levels of prosocial reasoning*

Level 1: Hedonistic, self-focused orientation: The individual is concerned with self-oriented consequences rather than moral considerations. Reasons for assisting or not assisting another include consideration of direct gain to the self, future reciprocity, and concern for others because one needs and/or likes the others (because of the affectional tie). (Predominant mode primarily for preschoolers and younger elementary-school children.)

Level 2: Needs-oriented orientation: The individual expresses concern for the physical, material, and psychological needs of others even though the other's needs conflict with one's own needs. This concern is expressed in the simplest terms, without clear evidence of self-reflective role taking, verbal expressions of sympathy, or reference to internalized affect such as guilt. (Predominant mode for many preschoolers and many elementary-school children.)

Level 3: Approval and interpersonal orientation and/or stereotyped orientation: Stereotyped images of good and bad persons and behaviors and/or considerations of others' approval and acceptance are used in justifying prosocial or nonhelping behaviors. (Predominant mode for some elementary-school and high-school students.)

Level 4a: Self-reflective empathic orientation: The individual's judgments include evidence of self-reflective sympathetic responding or role taking, concern with the other's humanness, and/or guilt or positive affect related to the consequences of one's actions. (Predominant mode for a few older elementary-school children and many high-school students.)

Level 4b: Transitional level: The individual's justifications for helping or not helping involve internalized values, norms, duties, or responsibilities and concern for the condition of the larger society, or refer to the necessity of protecting the rights and dignity of other persons; these ideas, however, are not clearly and strongly stated. (Predominant mode for a minority of people of high-school age or older.)

Level 5: Strongly internalized stage: Justifications for helping or not helping are based on internalized values, norms, or responsibilities, the desire to maintain individual and societal contractual obligations or improve the condition of society, the belief in the dignity, rights, and equality of all individuals. Positive or negative affect related to the maintenance of self-respect for living up to one's own values and accepted norms also characterizes this stage. (Predominant mode for only a small minority of high-school students and no elementary-school children.)

Source: Adapted from Eisenberg (1986).

Shell, Pasternack, Lennon, Beller, & Mathy, 1987; Eisenberg-Berg, 1979; Eisenberg-Berg & Roth, 1980).

Level 1 reasoning, reflecting a hedonistic and self-oriented outlook, is predominant only in the responses of preschoolers and young elementary-school children. Young children also verbalize much reasoning in which they orient to the other's need (Level 2); such reasoning often may reflect primitive role taking or empathy. In elementary school, children's judgments begin to reflect approval-oriented considerations and the desire to behave in stereotypically "good" ways (Level 3). By high school, students often use Level 4, self-reflective empathic reasoning (e.g., "He'd know how she feels"); such reasoning is verbalized only occasionally by older elementary-school children. Adolescents, especially 11th- and 12th-graders, also occasionally make references to internalized values and norms (including duty, responsibility, and the need to protect society and the rights of others). In addition, adolescents frequently are concerned with issues related to guilt and feelings about living up to one's own values (Level 5).

In studies of elementary-school children in Germany and Israel, similar patterns of reasoning about prosocial moral dilemmas were noted (Eisenberg et al., 1985; Fuchs et al., 1986). There were some cross-cultural differences, however. For example, Israeli children living in a kibbutz expressed more reasoning concerning internalized laws and norms and the importance of human beings than did urban American or Israeli children (Fuchs et al., 1986). This difference is consistent with the ideological emphasis on prosocial norms in the kibbutz. Moreover, although young Maisin children from nonindustrial, non-Western villages in New Guinea express reasoning quite similar to that of American children, older children and adults in the Maisin village express relatively little higher-level reasoning (Tietjen, 1986). Tietjen (1986) has argued that the needs-oriented empathic and interpersonally oriented types of reasoning used by the Maisin are appropriate for their culture because they must cooperate with one another in a face-to-face fashion to survive.

The reasoning used in resolving prosocial dilemmas is similar in some respects to that underlying the proposed solutions to dilemmas involving constraints (laws, rules, and obligations) (Eisenberg, 1986; Eisenberg-Berg, 1979). But there are also some differences in children's thinking about these two domains. For example, in dealing with Kohlberg dilemmas, children of 10 years or younger usually resort to Kohlberg's

Stage 1 reasoning (oriented toward authority and punishment), but this kind of explanation is scarcely apparent among even preschoolers solving prosocial dilemmas. Global concepts of good and bad behavior seem to be invoked at an earlier age in solving prosocial dilemmas than in response to the Kohlberg stories, and empathy plays a more significant role in making judgments about prosocial issues. In contrast, adolescents' reasoning about Kohlberg's dilemmas is more advanced than their reasoning about prosocial dilemmas (Higgins, Power, & Kohlberg, 1984).

Kohlberg's, Piaget's, and Eisenberg's data clearly demonstrate that modes of thinking about moral issues, and conceptualizations of the motives underlying moral decisions, vary with age and cognitive maturity. Are there corresponding changes with age and cognitive maturity in the motivations and cognitions underlying prosocial conduct?

The answer is yes. In a series of studies, children were given opportunities to assist another child. When children assisted, they were questioned regarding their motives for doing so. For example, kindergarteners and second- and fourth-graders played a game with a peer, won candy as a prize, and then were provided with a number of opportunities to share the candy with the peer who had lost (the sequence of opportunities ended when the child shared) (Bar-Tal, Raviv, & Leiser, 1980). The conditions in which the children could share (in order of occurrence) were as follows: (1) altruistic condition (the child was left alone for 3 min with the loser); (2) normative condition (the child could share after the experimenter explicitly and at length referred to the norm of sharing); (3) internal initiative and concrete reward (the experimenter told the child that there would be a reward for sharing); (4) compliance (the experimenter told the winner to share with the loser, and moved aside for a couple of minutes); (5) compliance and concrete-defined reinforcement (the experimenter told the winner to share and promised a big prize for sharing). After children shared in any of these conditions, they were interviewed regarding their reasons for sharing.

The children's expressed motives for their prosocial behavior were coded into categories such as the following: (1) concrete reward (initiated because of a promised reward); (2) compliance (initiated because the experimenter told the child to do so); (3) internal initiative with concrete reward (initiated because the child believed that a concrete reward, other than a promised prize, would be received for performing the act); (4) normative (the child held the normative belief prescribing sharing with other children, and conformity with that norm would bring social approval, e.g., "It's nice to share"); (5) generalized reciprocity (the child believed in a generalized social rule that people who act prosocially will receive aid when they are in need); (6) personal willingness without expectation of an internal reward, but with expressions of self-satisfaction (e.g., "I like to share to give others satisfaction"); (7) personal willingness to act prosocially without any reward (e.g., "Candy should be shared to make the other children happy") (Bar-Tal et al., 1980; Raviv, Bar-Tal, & Lewise-Levin, 1980).

In general, with increasing age, children are more likely to exhibit "higher-quality" prosocial behavior, that is, to assist without being told to do so or before being offered concrete rewards (Bar-Tal et al., 1980; Raviv, Bar-Tal, & Lewis-Levin, 1980). Their self-reported motives for assisting also tend to become more sophisticated with age (Bar-Tal et al., 1980). Normative reasoning (references to norms and concern for the social approval that accompanies compliance with the norm) is used frequently by kindergarteners, school-age children, and young adolescents to justify their actions (Bar-Tal & Nissim, 1984; Bar-Tal et al., 1980). Younger children, especially kindergarteners, also often explain their actions with reference to concrete rewards when such rewards are offered (Guttman, Bar-Tal, & Leiser, 1979). Younger children report altruistic, internal, or clearly empathic motives relatively infrequently (Bar-Tal et al., 1980), but references to these motives increase with age (Bar-Tal & Nissim, 1984; Bar-Tal et al., 1980; Guttman et al., 1979).

Moral reasoning and prosocial behavior

It is reasonable to hypothesize that one's level of moral judgment is positively correlated with one's predisposition to prosocial behavior, and a number of studies have supported this hypothesis. Low levels of moral judgment, assessed by means of a variety of measures of moral reasoning, have been found to predict delinquency and dishonesty (e.g., Blasi, 1980; Malinowski & Smith, 1985; Nelsen, Grinder, & Biaggio, 1969). Moreover, children and adolescents with relatively mature moral judgment are likely to manifest more helping and generosity than are peers at lower levels of moral reasoning (see reviews by Blasi, 1980; Eisenberg, 1986; and Underwood & Moore, 1982b). Significant and positive, though moderate, correlations are typical. In addition, children who exhibit more altruistic behavior tend to provide higher-level justifications for their prosocial actions than do children who assist in situations requiring less altruism (Bar-Tal, 1982; Bar-Tal et al., 1980).

With regard to prosocial moral reasoning, Eisenberg and her colleagues have found that empathic, other-oriented preschoolers and school-age children are more likely to share or donate valuable objects to others than are children lower in prosocial moral reasoning (Eisenberg et al., 1985; Eisenberg, Shell, Pasternack, Lennon, Beller, & Mathy, 1987; Eisenberg & Shell, 1986; Eisenberg-Berg & Hand, 1979). Also, hedonistic reasoning is associated with children's failure to share costly possessions (e.g., stickers, toys) and with low levels of assisting others when doing so requires that the children sacrifice time that could be spent playing with attractive toys (Eisenberg & Shell, 1986; Eisenberg-Berg & Hand, 1979).

A positive association between moral reasoning and prosocial behavior cannot be expected in all situations. Lower-level reasoning may be positively correlated with prosocial action that is motivated by egoistic concerns (e.g., people may assist because they expect a monetary reward for doing so), whereas aggressive acts are sometimes motivated by higher-level moral principles (e.g., support for a "just" war) (see Romer et al., 1986). Moreover, in many circumstances, trivial prosocial behaviors may be enacted without much conscious processing (e.g., helping to pick up dropped objects). In such situations, situational cues, habitual patterns of behavior, or a variety of personal preferences may be more relevant to what individuals do than are their levels of moral reasoning. Prosocial acts that are not costly may be especially likely to be unrelated to moral reasoning because such behaviors are unlikely to evoke moral conflict and moral reasoning and are likely to be performed rather automatically (Eisenberg & Shell, 1986).

Based on the empirical evidence, we can conclude that one's level or mode of moral reasoning is a significant factor influencing one's propensity to behave prosocially. However, the correlation between moral reasoning and prosocial behavior is not high because prosocial behavior is affected by many other factors, including children's affective reactions and their competencies, needs, and wants at a given time. Some of the affective factors that influence prosocial behavior are examined in the next chapter.

Introspection will convince most people that more than cognition is involved in much prosocial behavior; often we engage in prosocial behavior because of what we *feel*, or what we think we shall feel, if we are kind or considerate (or what we might feel if we failed to help the needy). Feelings of concern or sadness for the needy or distressed ordinarily precede helping, sharing, or comforting, and pangs of guilt may follow a failure to act prosocially. Prosocial behavior is not usually based solely on logic, understanding, or reasoning; a number of emotions are critical antecedents of altruism.

Empathy and sympathy

Empathy and sympathy have been defined in many ways (Eisenberg & Strayer, 1987; Wispe, 1986). We define them primarily in affective or emotional terms. Empathy is defined as a vicarious affective state that stems from another's emotional state or condition and is congruent with the other's state or condition. If a girl who observes a distressed peer feels sad or distressed herself, she is empathizing. Although empathy is an emotional response, it also involves cognitive skills such as the ability to label another's emotional state or role taking (Feshbach, 1978; Hoffman, 1982, 1984).

Sympathy is an emotional response to someone else's emotional state or condition that consists of feelings of sorrow or concern for another, but does not refer to feeling the *same* emotion as the other person. Sympathy, which has often been called empathy, is the basis of much prosocial responding. However, because the two terms have not been differentiated in most research, we generally use the term "empathy" to signify both types of reactions.

130

Theories of empathy

Many writers consider empathy to be the chief motive for altruism (Aronfreed, 1970; Batson, 1987; Hoffman, 1982, 1984). In Aronfreed's detailed explanation, empathy is acquired early by conditioning or association, that is, by repeated pairing of the child's feelings of pleasure or pain with someone else's expression of those feelings (see chapter 2).

Some psychoanalytic theorists believe that empathy develops from early infant – caretaker interactions as the caretaker's moods are communicated to the infant by touch, tone of voice, and facial expressions (Ekstein, 1972; Olden, 1958; Sullivan, 1940). Others use the principles of conditioning to explain the significance of the infant–caretaker relationship in the genesis of empathy – especially if the infant is closely attached to the caretaker:

When baby and mother face a common cause of distress, or when emotional upset in the baby calls forth an empathic response in the mother, then from the baby's point of view, perception of the mother's distress will become conditioned to his own feelings of distress. As a consequence, the later perception of her distress will evoke a similar response in him. We may presume that a good deal of such conditioning goes on in the earlier years (and indeed throughout life). But it is also most likely to occur within a close mother–child attachment, since the devoted mother is constantly mirroring back to her child his own emotional states in an amplified and enriched form. In her efforts to get into tune with him she may well exaggerate her expressions of pleasure or distress in response to his .... It is difficult to overestimate the importance of this continual and intimate interaction of mother and child for the development of sensitive empathic responsiveness to others. [Wright, 1971, p. 135]

Martin Hoffman (1975b, 1982, 1984) has proposed an intriguing theory of growth and change in altruistic motivation in the early years that emphasizes both the cognitive and affective aspects of empathy:

The central idea of the theory. . . . is that since a fully developed empathic reaction is an internal response to cues about the affective states of someone else, the empathic reaction must depend heavily on the actor's cognitive sense of the other as distinct from himself which undergoes dramatic changes developmentally. The development of a sense of the other. . . interacts with the individual's early empathic responses to lay the basis for altruistic motivation. [Hoffman, 1975b, p. 610]

Empathic responses – particularly empathic distress, defined as "experiencing another's painful emotional state" – develop early in infancy as a consequence of either built-in (i.e., biologically determined) human tendencies toward empathy or early classical conditioning:

> ...cues of pain or displeasure from another or from his situation evoke associations with the observer's own past pain, resulting in an empathic affective reaction. A simple example is the child who cuts himself, feels the pain, and cries. Later, on seeing another child cut himself and cry, the sight of the blood, the sound of the cry, or any other distress cue or aspect of the situation having elements in common with his own prior pain experience can now elicit the unpleasant affect initially associated with that experience. [Hoffman, 1975b, p. 613]

Hoffman believes that infants are capable of experiencing empathic distress before they can differentiate themselves from others:

> For most of the first year, witnessing another person in distress may result in a global empathic distress response. Distress cues from the dimly perceived "other" are confounded with unpleasant feelings empathically aroused in the self. Since infants cannot differentiate themselves from the other, they may at times act as though what happened to the other happened to themselves. An 11-month-old girl, on seeing a child fall and cry, looked as if she were about to cry herself and then put her thumb in her mouth and buried her head in her mother's lap, which is what she does when she herself is hurt. [Hoffman, 1984, p. 285]

When babies cognitively differentiate themselves from others, at about 1 year of age or a little later, they distinguish between their own and others' distresses. Then the child's empathic distress "may be transformed at least in part into a reciprocal concern for the victim. That is, they may continue to respond in a purely empathic manner – to feel uncomfortable and highly distressed themselves – but they also experience a feeling of compassion for the victim, along with a conscious desire to help because they feel sorry for the victim and not just to relieve their own empathic distress" (Hoffman, 1984, p. 287).

However, for some time, although aware of others as separate individuals, toddlers see the world only from their own perspective and do not realize that others have their own traits and feelings. Instead, toddlers attribute their own feelings to others and may therefore use inappropriate means in attempting to relieve another's distress. For example, a 12-month-old brought his own mother to comfort a crying friend, even though the friend's mother was equally available, and another toddler offered his own favorite doll to cheer up an adult who looked sad.

At about the age of 2 or 3 years, children begin to consider others as distinct physical entities with their own feelings, thoughts, and emotions. Some children this age are capable of rudimentary role taking and are more highly motivated to put themselves in another's place and find the real source of another's distress. Hence, they can respond in ways that may relieve the other's distress rather than their own. With the development of language, which enables children to derive meaning from symbolic cues of affect such as a written or verbal communication, "they can empathize with an increasingly wide range of emotions including complex ones like disappointment and feelings of betrayal" (Hoffman, 1984, p. 286).

Until they are between 6 and 9 years of age, children's empathic responses are restricted to another's immediate, transitory, and situation-specific distress. With greater cognitive maturity and awareness of their own and others' continuing existence, children begin reacting to general conditions (including deprivation, oppression, illness, and incompetence) as well as to immediate distress. "With further cognitive development the person may also be able to comprehend the plight not only of an individual but also of an entire group or class of people – such as the economically impoverished, politically oppressed, socially outcast, victims of war, or mentally retarded" (Hoffman, 1975b, p. 617).

Hoffman's theory is appealing because it views empathy in a broad developmental perspective, changing with increasing age, with advancing cognitive capacities, and with maturation of affective processes. Some aspects of the theory are supported by research findings, such as the shift from helping behaviors based on an egocentric view of the world (e.g., confusion regarding helping that would make oneself, rather than another, feel better) to those based on an understanding of others' needs as well as one's own. However, some of the theory is speculative, and some postulates are extremely difficult to test empirically.

Research findings

A major tenet of a number of theories is that empathy and sympathetic concern are critical factors mediating prosocial actions. This idea has been tested systematically, and there is ample evidence to support it.

The clearest findings with regard to the role of empathy in prosocial behavior have come from studies with adults. One of the major investigators in this area, Batson, has made an important conceptual differentiation in his work – between empathy and personal distress. Personal distress is an affective reaction to another's emotional state or condition that is experienced as a personally aversive emotion such as anxiety, alarm, or worry. According to Batson, empathy results in altruistic, other-oriented motives (e.g., the desire to reduce another's distress), whereas personal distress leads to the egoistic motivation to reduce one's own distress. Thus, people who experience personal distress will sometimes assist others, but primarily when helping is an easy way to relieve their own distress. For example, individuals experiencing personal distress are likely to help if helping is an easy way to terminate exposure to the aversive cues emanating from the needy other. However, if it is possible to escape easily from the aversive stimulus (e.g., the needy other), they will tend to do so rather than assist.

In one study (Toi & Batson, 1982), college women were asked to evaluate pilot radio shows; only one person would evaluate each program. Half of the students were told to

imagine how the person in the news feels. Try to take the perspective of the person who is being interviewed, imagining how he or she feels about what has happened and how it has affected his or her life. Try not to concern yourself with attending to all the information presented. [Toi & Batson, 1982, p. 285]

This manipulation was designed to induce role taking and empathy. The remaining students were instructed in a manner designed to preclude sympathizing:

Try to be as objective as possible, carefully attending to all the information presented about the situation and about the person who is being interviewed. Try not to concern yourself with how the person being interviewed feels about what has happened. [Toi & Batson, 1982, p. 285]

The first radio show was an affectively neutral newscast (containing announcements of upcoming events at the university). After hearing it, students described their emotional reactions to the newscast. Some of the adjectives referred to feelings of personal distress (e.g., worried, alarmed, anxious), whereas others assessed empathy (e.g., empathic, soft-hearted). Then the students heard the next pilot radio show. It concerned another student (Jane) who had been in an automobile accident and had broken her legs. She discussed the troubles she was having with her psychology class and her fear that she would not graduate. After hearing this tape, the students again reported their emotional reactions after the experimenter left of the room.

When the experimenter returned, she told each subject that the professor in charge of the study had asked her to give the subject two letters, one from the injured student and one from the professor. The professor's letter said that the viewer might be able to help the injured student by sharing notes from the psychology course lectures Jane had missed. The second letter, ostensibly from Jane, described her need and said that any assistance would be welcomed, but indicated that it was okay not to help. For half the subjects, the letter indicated that Jane would not be coming back to class (labeled the easy escape condition, because subjects could escape from dealing with Jane); for the remainder, the letter indicated that Jane would return to class, and so the subject might have future contact with Jane (labeled the difficult escape condition).

The subject then was asked to indicate on a separate sheet of paper how many hours she could assist and to put this slip of paper in a sealed envelope to be mailed to Jane.

The results of this study (and similar studies) demonstrated that subjects who were in the empathy-inducing condition were more sympathetic than were the other subjects. Moreover, they helped approximately the same amount in the easy and difficult escape situations. However, persons instructed to remain objective helped less in the easy escape condition than in the difficult escape condition. Batson suggested that those instructed to listen objectively experienced personal distress because they were relatively unlikely to experience the needy other's emotional state, and therefore they helped only when doing so was the easiest way to relieve their feelings of personal distress. Batson also found that the amount of reported sympathy correlated positively with helping behavior in situations in which it was easy to escape from experiencing the other's distress (i.e., to escape empathizing), whereas the reported amount of personal distress was not correlated with helping (Batson, 1987).

In another study involving adults (Krebs, 1975), each of the 60 participants (the average age of the participants was 20 years) was paired with a confederate of the experimenter and watched him play a game of roulette. Physiological responses associated with emotional arousal (changes in galvanic skin response, blood pulse volume, and heart rate) were recorded as the participants observed his fate. Perception of similarities between oneself and someone else facilitates empathy arousal, and so half of the subjects were told that the performer had values and interests similar to their own; the other half were informed that they had been paired with the performer because they were different from him. In addition, half of the "similar" group and half of the "different" group were informed that the performer received a reward (money) when the roulette ball landed on an even number and a shock (punishment) whenever it landed on an odd number. The other half of the participants believed that they were observing the performer playing a game without receiving any rewards or punishments. When the performer was rewarded or punished, the psychophysiological reactions of those who believed they were like him showed that they empathized with him.

After the first series of trials was completed, additional trials were anounced. The participants were informed that for these trials they would regulate both the amount of money the performer won and the amount of shock he received. Furthermore, they themselves would win money or receive shocks on these extra trials, the amounts depending on what the performer received: The more favorable the outcome for the performer, the less favorable the outcome for the participant. If the performer received less money, the participant would receive more, and if the former received less shock, the latter was given more. In short, the participants had to choose between benefiting themselves at a cost to the performer and helping him at a cost to themselves. The results were clear-cut: The subjects who believed themselves to be similar to the performer (i.e., the group that was most empathic with the performer) were highly altruistic toward him, most willing to help him even though this entailed self-sacrifice.

Empathy and prosocial behavior also are correlated in real-life settings. Rescuers of Jews from Nazis during World War II were interviewed regarding their motives for their actions. More than half reported that they helped primarily because they felt empathy and sympathy for the victims they rescued (Oliner & Oliner, 1988).

The studies involving children have yielded somewhat less consistent findings than those involving adults, but nevertheless indicate that empathy is related to prosocial behavior. Some measures of empathy are associated with children's prosocial behavior, whereas others are not

(Eisenberg & Miller, 1987). Often, empathy has been assessed by tests in which children are exposed to stories and/or pictures containing information about another's affective state or situation (e.g., a child who lost his dog). Then they are asked to report, either verbally or by means of nonverbal responses (i.e., pointing to pictures of facial expressions), what they themselves are feeling. Children are scored as empathizing if they report experiencing the emotion the story protagonist would be expected to feel (Eisenberg & Lennon, 1983; Feshbach & Roe, 1968; Hoffman, 1982).

Such indices of empathy have not been positively related to prosocial behavior (Eisenberg & Miller, 1987), perhaps because these indices are not valid measures of emotional empathy. The stories used to evoke emotion may be too short to elicit an emotional response, and, in addition, children may try to give the expected or desired response even if they themselves feel nothing when they hear the stories (Eisenberg & Lennon, 1983; Hoffman, 1982). Also, children may not be able to shift their emotions as quickly as they are shifted from one scenario to another.

When children's observed emotional responses are the measures of empathy, the pattern of relations between measures of empathy and prosocial behavior is quite different. For example, 1-year-olds who exhibited sadness on their faces in response to viewing a sad adult were more likely to make active attempts to comfort other persons they witnessed crying by hugging, touching, or caressing them (according to parental report) (Weston & Main, 1980). Moreover, young children who exhibit emotional responsiveness to another's distress frequently try to comfort the distressed person (Radke-Yarrow & Zahn-Waxler, 1984; Radke-Yarrow et al., 1983).

In one study, preschoolers viewed two films on two occasions, 1 week apart (Lennon, Eisenberg, & Carroll, 1986). In each film, a boy and a girl who were playing on local playgrounds fell and hurt themselves. The actors in the two films were different pairs of children, and the children were told that the events in the film were real. The preschoolers' facial and gestural reactions to the films were videotaped and coded for affects such as sadness or distress. The preschoolers also were given an opportunity to assist the injured children in one film by helping to make a game for them to play in the hospital, but at a cost to themselves (the preschoolers could either help or play with attractive toys). Moreover, on another day, the children were given the opportunity to donate attractive stickers to needy children whom they did not know.

Among both boys and girls, facial and gestural indicators of empathy (reactions such as sadness and distress) were associated with prosocial behavior. Boys who exhibited more empathy were especially likely to assist the hospitalized children; empathic girls donated more than did less empathic girls. In a similar study (Eisenberg, McCreath, & Ahn, 1988), facial reactions indicating sadness or concern for injured others were related to preschoolers' spontaneous sharing and helping in play sessions with a peer. In addition, in a study in which second- and fifth-graders viewed a film of injured, hospitalized children, there were some positive correlations between facial evidence of sympathetic concern and willingness to assist the children, as well as some negative correlations between facial personal distress (anxiety in reaction to viewing the films) and prosocial actions (Eisenberg, Fabes, Miller, Fultz, Shell, Mathy, & Reno, in press). Thus, empathy and sympathy apparently mediate at least some instances of prosocial responding.

Not all prosocial behavior is motivated by empathic or sympathetic reactions. People may assist others for nonaltruistic motives, for example, to attain rewards or social approval, or because of their desire to adhere to internalized moral values (Bar-Tal, 1982; Eisenberg, 1986). In some circumstances in which people could help or share with others, there is no reason to feel empathy or sympathy because the potential recipient of aid does not feel distressed, or there are no cues regarding the recipient's emotional state. In such situations, people frequently may assist for egoistic reasons (Schoenrade, Batson, Brandt, & Loud, 1986); for example, people often assist friends, even when they are not distressed, because of the desire to maintain the friendship.

Guilt

Guilt refers to a "bad feeling one has about oneself because one is aware of harming someone" (Hoffman, 1984, p. 289). Such feelings may also mediate prosocial behavior (Hoffman, 1984). Children may first experience empathic distress when they observe someone who is physically injured, and this empathy may be transformed to guilt if they believe themselves responsible for the other's pain. Once children are aware that others can have internal states, empathic reactions to another who is in pain, is unhappy, or is experiencing other difficulties also may be transformed to guilt. Finally, when children develop the awareness that other people have an identity and continuing existence beyond the immediate situation, empathic responding to the other's general plight can be transformed into guilt if the empathizer feels responsible for the other's plight, or if the empathizer feels that he or she is in a relatively advantaged situation (Hoffman, 1982, 1984).

Although signs of conscience or guilt have been observed in 1- to 2-year-olds, there has been relatively little research on the role of guilt in prosocial behavior. Some children not only try to alleviate the distress they cause others but also exhibit guilty facial expressions or apologetic reactions. Moreover, children who exhibit signs of guilt are more likely than other children to assist when they observe another's distress, even though they did not cause it (Zahn-Waxler, Radke-Yarrow, & King, 1983).

When resolving hypothetical moral dilemmas, children and adolescents sometimes report that guilt reactions are important determinants of prosocial behavior (Eisenberg-Berg, 1979; Karylowski, 1982a,b; Thompson & Hoffman, 1980); and young children sometimes attribute guilt to hypothetical story characters who hurt others (Chapman et al., 1987). In experimental laboratory studies, adults who accidentally have harmed others (e.g., have broken a valued object or dropped a box of computer cards) are likely to provide assistance to the person they have harmed (e.g., Freedman, 1970; Freedman, Wallington, & Bless, 1967; Wallace & Sadalla, 1966). Such subsequent helping may represent an attempt to make reparation because of feelings of guilt.

It is likely not only that guilt reactions motivate subsequent helping but also that the anticipation of guilt motivates altruistic behavior (Bandura, 1977). This issue is difficult to investigate because guilt, like empathy, is an internal response. However, with the use of multimethod approaches to assess these variables, including facial expressions and physiological indices that are likely to give better assessments of internal emotional reactions, our understanding of the dynamics of empathy and guilt will increase (Eisenberg, Fabes, Bustamante, & Mathy, 1987; Eisenberg, Fabes, Bustamante, Mathy, Miller, & Lindholm, 1988).

10   Situational determinants

Almost all behavior, including moral behavior, is a function of the inter-action between the characteristics of the individual – personality traits, motives, needs, and physical and cognitive abilities – and features of the specific situation or circumstances (Krebs & Miller, 1985; Kurtines, 1984, 1986; Staub, 1978). On the one hand, the stability of prosocial behavior over time and across situations is believed to be the product of enduring characteristics or predispositions of the individual. On the other hand, it is obvious that our reactions are affected by transitory feelings (such as moods), features of the immediate situation (environmental circum-stances), and events that "just happen."

The term *situational determinants* is used to designate at least two kinds of influences: (1) striking, unique events that radically alter an individual's personality, life-style, or propensities toward various pat-terns of behavior; (2) temporary external conditions (such as suddenly encountering a bloody, injured child) and singular (or seldom repeated) experiences or transient moods and emotions. Even casual observation attests that such situational determinants often elicit or deter the expres-sion of prosocial tendencies. Variations in the individual's behavior from time to time or from situation to situation can be understood only by examining the role of the immediate context. Even the most selfish are likely to assist an elderly companion who has tripped or help a screaming toddler who is in danger of drowning in shallow water.

An example of the first type of situational determinant – a striking, unique event – is found in Victor Hugo's brilliant psychological novel *Les Miserables* (Hugo, 1862/1982). Jean Valjean, the hero, is a former

140

convict who is befriended by a bishop, from whom he steals some silver. When Valjean is apprehended by the police, the kind bishop declares that he gave Valjean the silver, and Valjean is freed. This one unexpected and overwhelming act of kindness changes Valjean completely; he becomes an extraordinarily charitable and considerate man who devotes his life to aiding the poor and victims of injustice. Essentially, Valjean underwent a conversion experience and felt that "if he were not henceforth the best of men, he would be the worst."

This fictional account of the impact of a single event on an individual has parallels in the biographies of some of the outstanding exemplars of altruistic behavior. Mahatma Gandhi, renowned for his self-sacrifice for the cause of human rights, made the decision to devote his life to improving the welfare of India's downtrodden and unjustly treated "untouchables" after he himself was a victim of discrimination. As a young lawyer in South Africa, he was put off a train when he refused to move to a section of the train designated for "coolies or coloreds" (as Indians were classified in South Africa) (Erikson, 1969).

For some individuals, serendipitous events may result in a marked increase in concern for the welfare of others. For example, a high-school student uncertain about her future vocation may attend a lecture by a charismatic nurse, a civil rights worker, or perhaps a lawyer who defends the poor, is passionate about that work, and is persuasive about the need for additional help in this area. Such a unique episode may alter the adolescent's scheme of values, leading to lifelong involvement in work on behalf of human rights or the sick and needy.

Such radical shifts in goals and behavior are infrequent and difficult to study; antecedents generally can be explored only by retrospective biographical accounts. The degree to which such a shift involves a complete restructuring of values, cognitions, motivations, and affects is unknown. Perhaps systematic studies of biographies and autobiographies of individuals who have undergone such dramatic changes in orientation and behavior could help us to better understand the processes underlying these changes; however, data of this sort are rare.

In contrast, situational determinants of the second type – the effects of the immediate social context, transitory events, or temporary conditions – have been studied more systematically and are better understood. The determinants that have been examined most thoroughly include the moods and characteristics of the potential beneficiary.

Mood

Positive mood

Both children and adults who are in a good mood typically are more helpful and will share more readily than will persons in a neutral (i.e., neither positive nor negative) mood. To illustrate, in a study of 7- and 8-year-olds, mood was manipulated by having three groups of children reminisce about different types of events. One group reminisced about happy events in their lives; another reminisced about sad events; a third (control) group simply counted numbers for the same length of time that the other children reminisced. Then all of the children had the opportunity to share anonymously with other children some of the money that they had earned by participating in the study. Those who reminisced about happy events and presumably were experiencing positive affect shared more money than did either the controls or the children who had reminisced about sad events (Rosenhan, Underwood, & Moore, 1974).

Feelings of success or accomplishment, especially success produced by one's own efforts or ability, are especially likely to enhance children's prosocial behavior. In a study by Bryant (1983), third-, fourth-, and fifth-grade boys played a game and won; one group was informed that their success at the game was due to skill, and another group was told that they were lucky. The former reported experiencing less unhappiness and shared more of their prize coupons with peers than did boys who believed that their winning had been due to chance.

Although the effects of positive mood have been noted in many studies (Cialdini, Baumann, & Kenrick, 1981; Rosenhan, Salovey, Karylowski, & Hargis, 1981; Shaffer, 1986), generalizations about the effects of positive mood on prosocial behavior must be qualified. For example, the effects of success on sharing are likely to be attenuated under competitive conditions. Children who are successful at competitive games are not as generous as nonwinners when the potential beneficiaries of the donation are competitors who failed to do well at the game (McGuire & Thomas, 1975).

The effects of positive mood on prosocial behavior appear to be ephemeral. In one study, adults' willingness to help a stranger increased immediately after being given a gift that presumably elicited positive affect, but this prosocial tendency declined soon and disappeared within 20 min (Isen, Clark, & Schwartz, 1976).

A variety of explanations have been offered for the correlation between positive affect and increased prosocial behavior, although none has yet been proved to be best. Positive mood may be associated with more optimism (Masters & Furman, 1976) or stronger feelings of competence and, consequently, less need to keep resources only for oneself (Cialdini, Kenrick, & Baumann, 1982). Alternatively, happy people may feel better off than others and therefore may feel it to be only fair, equitable, or socially responsible to share their good fortune with others (Isen, 1970; Rosenhan et al., 1981; Staub, 1978). Positive mood may also lead to an expansive social orientation and increased interest in, and liking for, others (Cialdini et al., 1982; Shaffer, 1986), as well as greater social responsiveness (Cunningham, Shaffer, Barbee, & Smith, 1986). In addition, people who are in a good mood may be better able to retrieve positive memories about past helping and therefore may be relatively more willing to assist (Isen, Shalker, Clark, & Karp, 1978; Shaffer & Smith, 1985). Moreover, by facilitating recall of social information (Isen, Herren, & Geva, 1986), positive mood may increase the likelihood of processing socially relevant reasons for helping.

Negative mood

The association between negative mood and prosocial behavior appears to be more complicated. Children may become less helpful and generous after experiencing failure or contemplating sad events in their own lives, especially if their prosocial actions are anonymous (Barden, Garber, Leiman, Ford, & Masters, 1985; Barnett, Howard, Melton, & Dino, 1982; Cialdini & Kenrick, 1976; Moore, Underwood, & Rosenhan, 1973). In contrast, in some circumstances, negative affective states actually increased children's sharing or did not affect prosocial behavior (Barnett & Bryan, 1974; Harris & Siebel, 1975; Rosenhan et al., 1974). Prosocial behavior increased when children who previously had failed at a task had an opportunity to assist needy others with the experimenter present; presumably these children felt that they could compensate for their loss of status due to failing by acting in a positive, socially desirable manner (Isen, Horn, & Rosenhan, 1973). In other studies, negative moods were positively related to helping when those moods were due to empathic sadness or sympathy for a needy other (see chapter 9) (see Eisenberg & Miller, 1987).

The bulk of the evidence suggests that negative affect (other than empathy or sympathy) increases anonymous prosocial behavior for adults (Carlson & Miller, 1987; Cialdini et al., 1982; Dovidio, 1984) and decreases it for children. To explain this pattern of findings, Cialdini, Darby, and Vincent (1973) have proposed a *negative-state-relief* model. They argue that adults usually assist others when they themselves are in a negative mood in order to feel better. Young children do not initially assist when in a negative mood. However, during the course of socialization, children learn that the performance of prosocial acts can relieve a negative mood, because such acts are frequently associated with approval and other rewards, with the result that prosocial behaviors are gradually experienced as reinforcing in themselves.

This hypothesis was supported by findings in a study in which children in three age groups (6–8, 10–12, and 15–18 years) were instructed to think of depressing personal experiences, whereas control groups of peers thought about neutral events. Subsequently the students were given an opportunity to donate the prize coupons they earned for participation to peers who did not have an opportunity to win any coupons. As predicted, the youngest children donated less when they felt sad, the 10-to-12-year-olds who felt sad donated the same amounts as children who did not think about sad events, and the oldest group donated more than did same-age controls when they were sad (Cialdini & Kenrick, 1976).

Other explanatory models have also been suggested (Carlson & Miller, 1987). For example, it has been proposed that negative mood increases helpfulness when attention is directed toward the misfortunes of others, but decreases helpfulness, or does not affect it, when one attends to one's own concerns (Barnett, King, & Howard, 1979; Rosenhan et al., 1981). Presumably, a focus on others' needs augments empathic or sympathetic responses (Thompson, Cowan, & Rosenhan, 1980). Such effects may be stronger for older children and adults (Cialdini et al., 1982).

Effects of incentive value and utility of a prosocial behavior

Children consider the costs and benefits associated with reinforcements and punishments administered by others when deciding whether to act in a prosocial manner or selfish manner (see chapter 6). In addition, when contemplating prosocial actions, children, like adults (Dovidio,

1984; Piliavin et al., 1981), appear to take into account both the cost of the prosocial behavior and its potential benefit for the beneficiary. For example, when kindergarteners and fourth-graders were given opportunities to share highly preferred, less preferred, and disliked toys, they shared the disliked toy most and the preferred toy least (Mosbacher, Gruen, & Rychlak, 1985). Similarly, second- and fifth-graders' readiness to give up recess time to assist peers injured in a car accident was highly negatively correlated with how much they liked recess (Eisenberg, Fabes, Miller, Fultz, Shell, Mathy, & Reno, 1989).

In addition, the payoff of a prosocial act for the potential beneficiary is related to children's and adults' willingness to help or share with another (e.g., Kerber, 1984; Krebs & Miller, 1985; Kurtines, 1984; Lynch & Cohen, 1978; see Dovidio, 1984). For example, children share more if the beneficiary is poor and help more if the beneficiary is doing poorly on a task (Kurtines & Schneider, 1983; Ladd, Lange, & Stremmel, 1983; Zinser & Lydiatt, 1976; Zinser, Perry, & Edgar, 1975). However, it is likely that the costs for helping are more important determinants of children's prosocial behavior than are the benefits of such behavior for others (e.g., Dovidio, 1984; Piliavin et al., 1981; Weyant, 1978).

Characteristics of the beneficiary

In making the decision whether or not to assist someone, adults generally consider the characteristics of the potential beneficiary. We are more likely to assist relatives, friends, helpless or dependent people, or victims of circumstances than strangers or people we consider unworthy (Berkowitz & Daniels, 1963; Schopler & Matthews, 1965; Wagner & Wheeler, 1969; see Dovidio, 1984). A variety of characteristics of the potential recipient also affect children's helping or sharing behavior: the recipient's needs, gender, relationship to the child, and demographic and social characteristics.

Relationship of the potential recipient to the benefactor

Not surprisingly, youngsters in the second year of life are more likely to offer an object or show or point out an object to a parent than to a sibling (Lamb, 1978a,b), and by age 2 years they would rather give toys to their parents than to strangers (Rheingold et al., 1976). By adolescence, children are more prosocial with familiar peers than with familiar adults other than parents (Zeldin, Small, & Savin-Williams, 1982).

Children may react preferentially to friends because they empathize with them more readily (Bengtsson & Johnson, 1987) or because friends are more likely to ask for things they want (Birch & Billman, 1986). Nonetheless, on some occasions, children help nonfriends more than they help friends. This occurs when they feel secure in their friendship (Staub & Noerenberg, 1981; see Berndt, 1982, 1987; Eisenberg & Pasternack, 1983), or when the children are involved in a competition in which the children's performances will be compared (Berndt, 1982). Furthermore, children may expect friends (but not strangers) to understand a decision to behave selfishly (Wright, 1942), and they feel less constrained to reciprocate friends' prosocial actions immediately or precisely, as compared with those of nonfriends (Clark, 1981; Staub & Sherk, 1970).

Both children and adults (Dovidio, 1984; Panofsky, 1976; Willis, Feldman, & Ruble, 1977) assist people who are similar to themselves somewhat more than they assist those who are dissimilar. Identical twins (ages 5 to 13) have been found to be more cooperative in their play than have fraternal twins, who are less similar (Segal, 1984). With increasing age, children seem to show less preferential prosocial behavior toward familiar individuals or those similar to themselves (i.e., family members, people from the same town or country, or of the same ethnic background) (Eisenberg, 1983). Perhaps it is easier to empathize or sympathize with similar individuals (Feshbach, 1978; Krebs, 1975), who are seen as more attractive and consequently are better liked (Byrne, 1971).

Gender and demographic characteristics of the potential recipient

Preschoolers ordinarily act more prosocially toward same-sex peers than toward other-sex peers (Charlesworth & Hartup, 1967; Eisenberg-Berg & Hand, 1979; Marcus & Jenny, 1977), but the tendency to favor one's own sex decreases with age (Ladd et al., 1983; Walters, Pearce, & Dahms, 1957; see Eisenberg & Pasternack, 1983). Indeed, adolescent and adult males help females more than they help males (females of this age are equally helpful to males and females) (Eagly & Crowley, 1986; Zeldin et al., 1982).

Many adults tend to discriminate against potential recipients of another race, primarily when they can attribute their failure to assist to factors other than race (Crosby, Bromley, & Saxe, 1980; Frey & Gaertner, 1986; Piliavin et al., 1981), but children appear to show less discrimination. In one study, Caucasian children donated more candy to black and Indian children than to Caucasians (Zinser, Perry, Bailey, & Lydiatt, 1976), whereas in other studies, white school-age children have helped a white adult more than a black adult (Katz, Katz, & Cohen, 1976) or have not differentiated in their sharing or helping with black and white peers (Panofsky, 1976). Clearly, more research is needed to determine the age at which children start to discriminate in their prosocial behavior against persons of other races, as well as ways to minimize such discrimination.

With respect to socioeconomic status, there is some evidence that middle-class boys tend to discriminate against working-class boys, helping them less on a task than they help other middle-class boys. Lower-class English boys and American boys from middle-class bureaucratic (rather than entrepreneurial) families did not discriminate in this way (Berkowitz, 1968; Berkowitz & Friedman, 1967).

Role of the potential recipient in the ongoing social interaction

Children are more helpful and generous toward potential recipients who have previously helped or shared with them, or those who might reciprocate in the future (Berkowitz & Friedman, 1967; Dreman, 1976; Dreman & Greenbaum, 1973; Staub & Sherk, 1970), although reciprocity considerations may be ignored if the potential recipient is unable to reciprocate (Peterson, 1980). With increasing age, children tend to devalue reciprocity-based prosocial behaviors (e.g., Baldwin & Baldwin, 1970; Peterson, Hartmann, & Gelfand, 1977; Suls et al., 1981); nonetheless, the tendency to assist people who can reciprocate may increase in frequency in the elementary-school years (Furby, 1978; Peterson, 1980).

Children who are prosocial to peers are themselves more likely to be recipients of sharing, helping, or cooperation (Marcus & Jenny, 1977; Staub & Feinberg, 1980). However, in one study, this reciprocity held only for help given voluntarily, not for help requested by others (Marcus & Jenny, 1977). Apparently, requested helping was perceived as being less internally motivated and therefore less worthy of reciprocation than was voluntary help.

Need state of the potential recipient

Children, even preschoolers, seem to prefer to assist dependent, needy others more than nonneedy others. For example, when given the opportunity to share with a rich person or a poor person, children share more candy with the poor person (Zinser & Lydiatt, 1976; Zinser et al., 1975), and friendless and needy children are more likely to be treated prosocially than are children with friends or children without a need (Fouts, 1972; Liebert, Fernandez, & Gill, 1969; Midlarsky & Hannah, 1985).

   The tendency to favor those in need or distress generally increases with age during childhood (Ladd et al., 1983), influenced by perceptions of the underlying causes of the potential beneficiary's need. Those whose need is caused by factors within their own control (e.g., laziness, carelessness) are not likely to be helped (Barnett, 1975; Berkowitz, 1972; Braband & Lerner, 1975; Meyer & Mulherin, 1980); see Eisenberg (1986) and Weiner (1986) for reviews. In one study, fifth-graders donated more money to other children who had no money (because the experimenter had not given them any, having run out of funds) than to children who had been careless and had lost money (Miller & Smith, 1977). However, it is likely that younger children base their helping on another's deservedness primarily when there are no other, more salient criteria (e.g., similarity to self) on which to base their decision making (Ladd et al., 1983).

Personality of the potential recipient

Popular children give and receive more help than do their less popular peers (Gottman et al., 1975; Masters & Furman, 1981; Raviv, Bar-Tal, Ayalon, & Raviv, 1980), and both children and adults share possessions more readily if they consider the potential recipients to be nice, friendly, and likable (Furby, 1978; Leung & Foster, 1985).

   In addition, children's styles of interaction affect the likelihood that they will receive assistance from peers. Sociable, assertive, helpful, generous, and responsive preschoolers are frequent targets of unsolicited acts of helping and sharing, whereas children who generally are targets of prosocial behavior only when they ask for it are characterized as frequently asking for help or for objects, sociable with teachers, and passive in response to their peers' prosocial acts (Eisenberg & Pasternack, 1983).

Other situational variables

An adult is more likely to help someone in distress (e.g., someone who has fainted or is having a seizure) if the adult is alone, rather than in a group, at the time (Latané & Nida, 1981). Failure to help when in a group may be due to fear of negative evaluation by other bystanders if one misinterprets the situation and offers help unnecessarily, to the belief that others in the group should take responsibility for helping, or to the belief that the situation is not critical because other bystanders have not tried to assist.

It is unclear whether or not children are also less likely to help when in a group. In one study, first- and second-graders were more likely to assist someone in distress if they were with a peer, rather than alone, whereas fourth- and sixth-graders were equally helpful in both circumstances. Perhaps the presence of a peer reduced young children's fears and inhibitions and thus increased their helping; older children may be inhibited by their concern about the peer's evaluation (Staub, 1970b). However, in another study, children in the first, fourth, and sixth grades who were with a peer helped more than did those who were not with a peer (Peterson, 1983b). The difference in the findings of these two studies may have been due to the difference in the degrees to which the members of the dyads – the potential helper and the peer – could interact. In the study in which children with peers helped more, the members of a dyad were separated by a screen and could not readily communicate, which may have reduced the likelihood that the older children would be concerned with the peer's approval (Peterson, 1983b).

In summary, it appears that the presence of others has an effect on children's helping behaviors, but this influence varies as a function of other aspects of the given situation. This is not surprising, given that children's prosocial actions in any particular situation are likely to vary as a function of not just one, but several, situational factors.

11 Conclusions

We have surveyed hundreds of studies. What do we know about the factors affecting the development of prosocial orientations and behaviors and the conditions that facilitate or undermine their development and expression? Some conclusions are relatively well established, based on a substantial body of research. Other conclusions must be drawn tentatively, because relevant investigations have yielded findings that are not consistent with each other. Still other issues, such as the interrelations of various influences (e.g., personal and situational factors) and their joint effects on prosocial functioning, have seldom been examined.

It seems appropriate to begin this concluding chapter with a summary of the robust, reliable findings, underscoring some of their implications. Some of the findings are so clear that we can make recommendations with regard to practical applications with confidence. For the most part, the research conducted in the last 12 years has served to reinforce our earlier conclusions in *The Roots of Caring, Sharing and Helping*. At the same time, new research has allowed us to analyze issues in more depth and to correct some prior misconceptions.

Of course, because no single determinant of prosocial behavior has an overriding influence on behavior in all situations, our conclusions and recommendations apply "in general," with the qualifier of "other things being equal." But, in reality, other things are almost never equal. Each antecedent functions as a part of a complex matrix of interacting factors that simultaneously exert their influences. In the domain of prosocial action, as in other areas of behavior, we cannot predict with certainty the reaction of any particular child in a particular situation. Nonetheless, the predictions we can make with regard to children as a group are substantially better than chance would yield.

150

Which children are most likely to assist, share, and comfort others? In general, they are relatively active, sociable, competent, assertive, advanced in role taking and moral judgment, and sympathetic. The parents of prosocial children also are likely to combine nurturant, supportive parenting practices with modeling of prosocial acts, discussions of the effects of such acts for others, inductive discipline, expectations of mature behavior, and early assignment of responsibility for others.

Predictions also can be made regarding situations in which children are most likely to be generous and helpful: when they feel happy, successful, or competent, and when the cost of prosocial action is low. In addition, children's prosocial actions in a given situation are affected by the characteristics of the potential recipient of assistance: Children generally assist more if the recipient of their help is loved or liked, has previously assisted the benefactor, and has an attractive personality.

The knowledge of determinants of prosocial behavior can be applied to training procedures. Parents, teachers, and religious educators frequently are in a position to, and desire to, stimulate prosocial development. To achieve their goals, they may be well advised to use several practices: modeling of helping, sharing, and comforting behaviors clearly and frequently; reasoning in disciplinary contexts and verbalizing the benefits of prosocial action for others; encouraging children to try to understand others' feelings and to respond emotionally to others; maintaining high standards for the child (including prosocial standards); providing opportunities for their children to engage in prosocial activities (e.g., by assigning them responsibilities for others). Creative educators can devise role-playing and sympathy-promoting class exercises and activities that are enjoyable to children and, at the same time, increase their prosocial proclivities. In addition, parents and educators can take action to try to encourage socially responsible television programming – programming in which children are exposed to more models of altruistic behavior and fewer acts of violence, aggression, and selfishness.

These are only a few examples. Other potentially useful procedures include implementation of structured activities that encourage cooperation in the classroom (Hertz-Lazarowitz & Sharan, 1984; Sharan, Hare, Webb, & Hertz-Lazarowitz, 1980; Solomon et al., 1987) and discussion groups in which moral issues are debated, cognitive conflict is induced, and higher-level moral reasoning is encouarged (Lockwood, 1978; Rest, 1979). All such interventions should, of course, be guided by research, and the effectiveness of the procedures should be evaluated repeatedly.

As we observed earlier, the study of prosocial behavior is relatively young; most of the research has been conduced in the last 20 years. Much information of practical and social utility has been accumulated, but there are many issues that have not yet been adequately examined and are not well understood. Certainly there are more gaps in our knowledge than there are definitive answers to questions.

One of the major deficiencies concerns the complex links among the various determinants of prosocial tendencies. In everyday life, behavior and reasoning are likely to be determined by a number of factors that may influence, and moderate, the effects of each other. Because it is so difficult to study the relative effects of multiple variables on behavior or reasoning simultaneously, it is not surprising that only a few researchers have tried to do so (Barrett & Yarrow, 1977; Hoffman, 1963; Suda & Fouts, 1980).

A model of prosocial behavior

In efforts to integrate research findings and to formulate questions for future work, some researchers have developed models of how the important determinants interrelate and jointly modify prosocial be-havior and reasoning (e.g., Piliavin et al., 1981; Schwartz & Howard, 1984). Figure 11.1 presents an oversimplified model of prosocial action; see Eisenberg (1986) for a more detailed version. This model was con-structed for heuristic purposes, with the hope of stimulating further thinking and research. Neither it nor any other existing model captures the full complexity of existing theory and research. For example, bio-logical factors, which are undoubtedly significant but little understood, are not included in the model.

The model pertains to prosocial action that is directed toward alle-viating another's need or distress or bettering another's situation – that is, altruistic behavior. Whether or not individuals attend to another in need is determined directly or indirectly by a variety of factors (Figure 11.1). Potential benefactors' socialization histories (e.g., exposure to

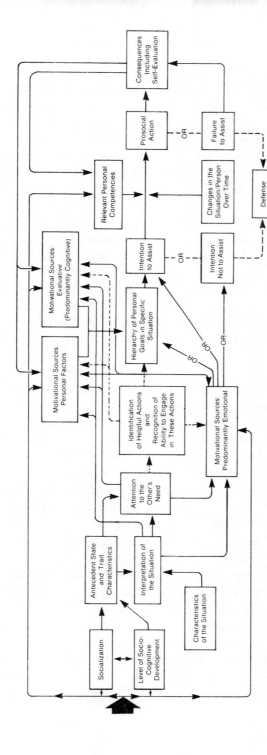

Figure 11.1. A model of prosocial behavior

prosocial models, reasoning, prosocial values and experiences) are viewed as having an effect on their cognitive functioning and on aspects of personality that are stable (traits) or are pertinent in the given situation (e.g., how much the person is other-oriented, and whether or not the person tends to use the role-taking abilities possessed). Moreover, situational cues, such as those related to the other's need, must be interpreted by potential benefactors, and their interpretations of such cues vary in part as a function of their personalities. For example, someone who is other-oriented or is sensitive to facial expressions is likely to interpret subtle cues of distress accurately. In addition, both personal characteristics and the individual's interpretation of situational cues determine whether or not a potential benefactor attends to another's need.

Attending to another's need is only the starting point of prosocial action, however. Before assisting, a person must decide that he or she intends to assist, and the decision will be a function of weighting and prioritizing various goals that are salient in the specific context. For example, the goal of relieving another's distress may conflict with the goal of protecting one's own resources or time. Moreover, the strengths of these various goals in a given situation ("Hierarchy of personal goals in specific situation" in the model) are determined by many factors: personal (e.g., one's personal values and preferences in general, or level of self-esteem), cognitive (e.g., one's estimate of the costs and benefits of providing assistance, or the reasons that the other is in need), and emotional (e.g., sympathetic or personal distress reactions). Often it is difficult to decide whether or not to assist, because of conflicting motives and, consequently, opposing goals. One may experience feelings of sympathy and also believe that helping will be costly to oneself. In this situation, the altruistic goal of alleviating the other's distress and the goal of taking care of oneself may conflict.

Even if people intend to act in a prosocial manner, they may not always do so, because they lack the prerequisite personality characteristics or the competence and skills to assist (or they may believe they do). For example, a shy child may not muster the courage to approach a peer who has fallen down, and an adolescent who knows little about cars may be unable to help a motorist in distress. In addition, even if people initially intend to help, the situation may change in ways that preclude their doing so. For example, a child who has fallen down may get help from someone else, or a distressed other may require more assistance than was initially evident (so the cost of helping increases).

There is one more step in our model after the actual performance (or lack thereof) of prosocial action. The act of assisting or not doing so has implications for future prosocial development and behavior. The actual experience of acting prosocially, as well as the attributions children make regarding themselves, will affect the likelihood of subsequent prosocial behavior. Children who view themselves as altruistic are likely to assist in the future, because people generally want to behave in ways that are consistent with the self-image (Eisenberg, 1986).

The model demonstrates the complexity of predicting whether or not a particular child will help, share, or comfort another in a specific situation. To predict behavior for a specific child, we would have to have good information about his or her socialization history, personality traits, emotional responding, values, needs and goals, cognitive functioning, competencies, and the ways in which the child resolves conflicts among various motives and goals. Moreover, we would have to know about the nuances of the actual situation that would affect how the child would react. Therefore, it is nearly impossible to predict the behavior of an individual child in a particular situation. Nonetheless, as we have seen, we are able to make some reasonable predictions about average behavior – about what most people will do – in some situations, as well as what people with specific personality traits or abilities will do in some situations. With increased knowledge about the ways in which the different factors that influence prosocial behavior interact, we should be able to refine and improve our ability to predict prosocial behavior.

Other gaps in theory and knowledge

Role of biology in prosocial behavior

Biological contributions to prosocial behavior were not included in our model, in part because so little information is available. Preliminary evidence suggests that genetic factors play a role in determining individual differences in prosocial behavior and sympathetic responsiveness. How do these factors influence aspects of prosocial responding? Is their influence mediated through genetically based differences in temperament? Children who differ in temperament – in such variables as tempo and responsiveness to social stimuli – may be socialized in different ways and consequently may differ in altruistic tendencies. Or perhaps genetic factors produce differences in children's capacities to experience empathy and sympathy, or in certain types of cognitive skills, which affect level of prosocial responding. Given the impressive advances in the study of the role of genetics in behavior (i.e., the field of behavioral genetics) in the past decade (*Child Development*, 1983; Plomin, 1986), it is likely that we will learn considerably more about the role of genetics in prosocial responding in the future.

Components of effective training programs

Some educators and researchers have been successful at enhancing prosocial behavior with training programs (see chapter 7), but it is often difficult to know why the training programs were effective. In most cases, a variety of potentially effective procedures have been implemented simultaneously, so that it is difficult to assess the relative effectiveness of different components of a program. For example, some interventions have involved procedures designed to enhance the understanding of others' emotional reactions and other role-taking skills, as well as sympathetic tendencies; under these circumstances, any effect of the interventions could be due to changes in cognitive or affective functioning, or both. Research is needed to separate the effects of the various components of the intervention package from one another and to evaluate the relative contribution of each specific procedure. This kind of information is necessary for designing cost-effective interventions to enhance prosocial behavior in natural settings such as at home or school.

It cannot be assumed that procedures that prove to be effective in laboratory studies (such as modeling; see chapters 6 and 7) will necessarily have a significant and lasting impact on behavior when introduced in a natural setting such as the home or school. In real-life settings, the effectiveness of a given procedure may be diluted by other factors operating in the context, (e.g., by a teacher's use of other procedures that might inhibit prosocial behavior). Thus, it is important to test in natural settings the effectiveness of those procedures that promote prosocial behavior in the laboratory.

Nonfamilial socializers

Although the past decade has brought some progress in understanding the influence of peers, teachers, neighbors, and others outside the home, we still know relatively little about how and to what degree these agents of socialization regulate children's prosocial tendencies. We know even less about the ways in which practices of familial and non-familial socializers jointly influence prosocial behavior. Can the reactions of peers and teachers undermine the achievements made in the family in regard to prosocial development? If a child is not encouraged to be prosocial at home, can extrafamilial influences overcome these home influences? To what degree are the effects of familial and extrafamilial socializers additive? These questions have not yet been adequately answered.

The roles of institutions other than the family in children's prosocial development are not fully understood. The structure of a school – specifically, the degree of its democratic orientation – has an impact on students' moral reasoning (Higgins et al., 1984). Do aspects of the school's structure and atmosphere, such as its emphasis on competition versus cooperation, also influence prosocial development? Institutions such as churches, camps, Girl Scouts, and athletic leagues may also contribute to the development of prosocial tendencies, but to date such possible influences have not been studied systematically.

In-depth studies of altruists

In-depth, multifaceted studies, both naturalistic and clinical, of individuals who have been outstanding exemplars of humanitarianism may provide unique opportunities to probe into the dynamics, motivations, and cognitive operations that direct prosocial actions. Detailed biographical studies of famous altruists such as Albert Schweitzer, Mahatma Gandhi, and Mother Teresa can be used to explore their personalities, motivations, socialization experiences, and cognitive functioning. Excellent models of this type of work are found in the field of psychohistory, particularly in Erik Erikson's psychoanalytic and social psychological analyses of the life and work of Mahatma Gandhi and Martin Luther. Unfortunately, however, the most essential data, such as objective and reliable evaluations of personalities and developmental histories, are not readily available. Consequently, only limited generalizations can be made, but the work could serve as a valuable source for generating hypotheses for further, more rigorous testing.

A fruitful, and more feasible, alternative approach is the intensive study of living people vigorously involved in humanitarian endeavors. Excellent examples of this approach are Rosenhan's fascinating study (1970) of freedom riders and Clary and Miller's study (1986) of crisis-counseling volunteers (see chapter 6). Another very exciting example of such work is Samuel and Pearl Oliner's study (1988) of people who rescued Jews from the Nazis during World War II. They have interviewed and administered personality tests to both rescuers and nonrescuers (controls) from the same vicinity as the rescuers. Analyses show that empathy or internalized altruistic values were related to rescuing behavior for some people, whereas feelings of obligation to a valued social group (such as a church or community group) and its explicit and implicit expectations seemed to play an important role for others. The great potential contribution of studies such as this stems from their focus on the individual as a whole being, embedded in his or her natural environment, so that the multiple interrelated and inter-acting factors, both personal and situational, that influence the altruist's reasoning and behavior can be examined.

A final word

Addressing the many important unanswered questions is a task for future research. For us, the social significance of this field of investi-gation cannot be overestimated, for it pertains to the quality of life and the morality of human interactions. Many agree that the present state of humankind's interrelationships is deplorable and that it is likely to deteriorate further. The world seems to be a never-ending arena for violence, injustice, inequality, and inhumanity.

Improvement in the quality of life must begin with changes in the motivations and behaviors of individuals, in greater concern for others, coupled with a willingness to devote considerable effort and energy to promoting the well-being of others. It is our thesis that fundamental constructive changes could be effected by means of application of knowledge derived from empirical research by behavioral scientists.

However, it is extremely difficult to implement interventions designed to produce change, and intervention efforts often are costly, disappointing, and discouraging.

But these costs and disappointments must be weighed against the potential social benefits to be gained from the application of well-established, reliable research findings. In our opinion, these benefits may be great. It would be a sad commentary on psychology and the other behavioral sciences if the training and capabilities of experts in these fields did not prove to be effective in helping to deal with urgent social psychological problems.

References

Adorno, T. W., Frenkel-Brunswick, E., Levinson, D. J., & Sanford, R. N. (1950). *The authoritarian personality*. New York: Harper.

Ahammer, I. M., & Murray, J. P. (1979). Kindness in the kindergarten: The relative influence of role playing and prosocial television in facilitating altruism. *International Journal of Behavioral Development*, *2*, 133–157.

Ainsworth, M. D. S. (1979). Attachment as related to mother–infant interaction. In J. S. Rosenblatt, R. A. Hinde, C. Beer, & M. Busnel (Eds.), *Advances in the study of behavior* (Vol. 9, pp. 2–51). New York: Academic Press.

Ainsworth, M. D. S., Blehar, M. C., Waters, E., & Wall, S. (1978). *Patterns of attachment: A psychological study of the strange situation*. Hillsdale, NJ: Lawrence Erlbaum Associates.

Ambron, S. R., & Irwin, D. M. (1975). Role taking and moral judgment in five and seven year olds. *Developmental Psychology*, *11*, 102.

Arbuthnot, J. (1973). Relationships between maturity of moral judgment and measures of cognitive abilities. *Psychological Reports*, *33*, 945–946.

Aronfreed, J. (1968). *Conduct and conscience: The socialization of internalized control over behavior*. New York: Academic Press.

Aronfreed, J. (1970). The socialization of altruistic and sympathetic behavior: Some theoretical and experimental analyses. In J. Macaulay & L. Berkowitz (Eds.), *Altruism and helping behavior* (pp. 103–126). New York: Academic Press.

Aronson, E., Blaney, N., Stephan, C., Sikes, J., & Snapp, M. (1978). *The jigsaw classroom*. Beverly Hills, CA: Sage.

Ascione, F. R., & Sanok, R. L. (1982). The role of peer and adult models in facilitating and inhibiting children's prosocial behavior. *Genetic Psychology Monographs*, *106*, 239–259.

Baldwin, A. L., Baldwin, C. P., Castillo-Vales, V., & Seegmiller, B. (1971). Cross-cultural similarities in the development of the concept of kindness. In W. W. Lambert & K. Weisbrod (Eds.), *Comparative perspectives in social psychology* (pp. 151–164). Boston: Little, Brown.

Baldwin, C. P., & Baldwin, A. L. (1970). Children's judgments of kindness. *Child Development*, *41*, 29–47.

Bandura, A. (1973). *Aggression: A social learning analysis*. Englewood Cliffs, NJ: Prentice-Hall.

Bandura, A. (1977). *Social learning theory*. Englewood Cliffs, NJ: Prentice-Hall.

Bandura, A. (1986). *The social foundation of thought and action: A social cognitive theory*. Englewood Cliffs, NJ: Prentice-Hall.

Bandura, A., Grusec, J. E., & Menlove, F. L. (1967). Vicarious extinction of avoidance behavior. *Journal of Personality and Social Psychology, 5,* 16–23.

Bandura, A., & Walters, R. H. (1963). *Social learning and personality development.* New York: Holt, Rinehart & Winston.

Bank, S., & Kahn, M. D. (1975). Sisterhood–brotherhood is powerful: Sibling subsystems and family therapy. *Family Process, 14,* 311–337.

Barden, R. C., Garber, J., Leiman, B., Ford, M. E., & Masters, J. C. (1985). Factors governing the effective remediation of negative affect and its cognitive and behavioral consequences. *Journal of Personality and Social Psychology, 49,* 1040–1053.

Barnett, K., Darcie, G., Holland, C. J., & Kobasigawa, A. (1982). Children's cognitions about effective helping. *Developmental Psychology, 18,* 267–277.

Barnett, M. A. (1975). Effects of competition and relative deservedness of the other's fate on children's generosity. *Developmental Psychology, 11,* 665–666.

Barnett, M. A., & Bryan, J. H. (1974). Effects of competition with outcome feedback on children's helping behavior. *Developmental Psychology, 10,* 838–842.

Barnett, M. A., Howard, J. A., Melton, E. M., & Dino, G. A. (1982). Effect of inducing sadness about self or other on helping behavior in high and low empathic children. *Child Development, 53,* 920–923.

Barnett, M. A., King, L. M., & Howard, J. A. (1979). Inducing affect about self or other: Effects on generosity in children. *Developmental Psychology, 15,* 164–167.

Barnett, M. A., & McMinimy, V. (1988). Influence of the reason for the other's affect on preschoolers' empathy response. *Journal of Genetic Psychology, 149,* 153–162.

Barnett, M. A., & Thompson, S. (1985). The role of perspective taking and empathy in children's Machiavellianism, prosocial behavior and motive for helping. *Journal of Genetic Psychology, 146,* 295–305.

Barrett, D. E. (1979). Relations between aggressive and prosocial behaviors in children. *Journal of Genetic Psychology, 134,* 317–318.

Barrett, D. E., & Yarrow, M. R. (1977). Prosocial behavior, social inferential ability, and assertiveness in young children. *Child Development, 48,* 475–481.

Bar-Tal, D. (1982). Sequential development of helping behavior: A cognitive-learning approach. *Developmental Review, 2,* 101–124.

Bar-Tal, D. (1984). American study of helping behavior: What? Why? and Where? In E. Staub, D. Bar-Tal, J. Karylowski, & J. Reykowski (Eds.), *The development and maintenance of prosocial behavior: International perspectives on positive morality* (pp. 5–27). New York: Plenum.

Bar-Tal, D., Korenfeld, D., & Raviv, A. (1985). Relationships between the development of helping behavior and the development of cognition, social perspective, and moral judgment. *Genetic, Social, and General Psychology Monographs, 11,* 23–40.

Bar-Tal, D., & Nissim, R. (1984). Helping behavior and moral judgment among adolescents. *British Journal of Developmental Psychology, 2,* 329–336.

Bar-Tal, D., Raviv, A., & Goldberg, M. (1982). Helping behavior among preschool children: An observational study. *Child Development, 53,* 396–402.

Bar-Tal, D., Raviv, A., & Leiser, T. (1980). The development of altruistic behavior: Empirical evidence. *Developmental Psychology, 16,* 516–524.

Batson, C. D. (1987). Prosocial motivation: Is it ever truly altruistic? In L. Berkowitz (Ed.), *Advances in experimental social psychology* (pp. 65–122). New York: Academic Press.

Batson, C. D., Bolen, M. H., Cross, J. A., & Neuringer-Benefiel, H. E. (1986). Where is the altruism in the altruistic personality? *Journal of Personality and Social Psychology, 50,* 212–220.

Battistich, V., Solomon, D., Watson, M., Solomon, J., & Schaps, E. (in press). Effects of an elementary school program to enhance prosocial behavior on children's cognitive problem-solving skills and strategies. *Journal of Applied Developmental Psychology*.

Baumrind, D. (1967). Child care practices anteceding three patterns of preschool behavior. *Genetic Psychological Monographs*, *75*, 43–88.

Baumrind, D. (1971). Current patterns of parental authority. *Developmental Psychology Monographs*, *4*, 1–103.

Baumrind, D. (1973). The development of instrument competence through socialization. In A. D. Pick (Ed.), *Minnesota symposia on child psychology* (Vol. 7, pp. 3–46). Minneapolis: University of Minnesota Press.

Baumrind, D. (1988). *Familial antecedents of social competence in middle childhood*. Unpublished manuscript.

Bem, D. J., & Allen, A. (1974). On predicting some of the people some of the time. *Psychological Review*, *81*, 506–520.

Bengtsson, H., & Johnson, L. (1987). Cognitions related to empathy in 5 to 11 year-old children. *Child Development*, *58*, 1001–1012.

Benson, N. C., Hartmann, D. P., & Gelfand, D. M. (1981, April). *Intentions and children's moral judgments*. Paper presented at the biennial meeting of the Society for Research in Child Development, Boston.

Benson, P. L., Dehority, J., Garman, L., Hanson, E., Hochschwender, M., Lebold, C., Rohr, R., & Sullivan J. (1980). Interpersonal correlates of nonspontaneous helping behavior. *Journal of Social Psychology*, *110*, 87–95.

Berg, N. E., & Mussen, P. (1975). Origins and development of concepts of justice. *Journal of Social Issues*, *31*, 183–201.

Bergin, C. A. C. (1987, April). *Relations among prosocial behaviors in toddlers*. Paper presented at the biennial meeting of the Society for Research in Child Development, Baltimore.

Berkowitz, L. (1968). Responsibility, reciprocity, and social distance in help giving: An experimental investigation of English social class differences. *Journal of Experimental Social Psychology*, *4*, 46–63.

Berkowitz, L. (1972). Social norms, feelings, and other factors affecting helping and altruism. In L. Berkowitz (Ed.), *Advances in experimental social psychology* (Vol. 6, pp. 63–108). New York: Academic Press.

Berkowitz, L., & Daniels, L. R. (1963). Responsibility and dependency. *Journal of Abnormal and Social Psychology*, *66*, 429–436.

Berkowitz, L., & Friedman, P. (1967). Some social class differences in helping behavior. *Journal of Personality and Social Psychology*, *5*, 217–225.

Berman, P. W. (1980). Are women more responsive than men to the young? A review of developmental and situational variables. *Psychological Bulletin*, *88*, 668–695.

Berman, P. W. (1987). Children caring for babies: Age and sex differences in response to infant signals and to the social context. In N. Eisenberg (Ed.), *Contemporary topics in development psychology* (pp. 141–164). New York: Wiley.

Berndt, T. J. (1982). The features and effects of friendship in early adolescence. *Child Development*, *53*, 1447–1460.

Berndt, T. J. (1987). The distinctive features of conversations between friends: Theories, research, and implications for sociomoral development. In W. M. Kurtines & J. L. Gewirtz (Eds.), *Moral development through social interaction* (pp. 281–300). New York: Wiley.

Bethleheim, D. W. (1973). Cooperation, competition and altruism among school children in Zambia. *International Journal of Psychology*, *8*, 125–135.

Birch, L. L., & Billman, J. (1986). Preschool children's food sharing with friends and acquaintances. *Child Development*, *57*, 387–395.

Blaney, N. T., Stephan, C., Rosenfield, D., Aronson, E., & Sikes, J. (1977). Interdependence in the classroom: A field study. *Journal of Educational Psychology*, *69*, 139–176.

Blasi, A. (1980). Bridging moral cognition and moral action: A critical review of the literature. *Psychological Bulletin*, *88*, 1–45.

Block, J. H. (1973). Conceptions of sex role: Some cross-cultural and longitudinal perspectives. *American Psychologist*, *28*, 512–526.

Block, J., & Block, J. H. (1973, January). *Ego development and the provenance of thought: A longitudinal study of ego and cognitive development in young children.* Progress report for the National Institute of Mental Health (grant no. MH16080).

Borke, H. (1971). Interpersonal perception of young children: Egocentricism or empathy? *Developmental Psychology*, *5*, 263–269.

Borke, H. (1975). Piaget's mountains revisited: Changes in the egocentric landscape. *Developmental Psychology*, *11*, 240–243.

Boyd, R., & Richardson, P. J. (1985). *Culture and the evolutionary process.* University of Chicago Press.

Braband, J., & Lerner, M. J. (1975). "A little time and effort"...Who deserves what from whom. *Personality and Social Psychology Bulletin*, *1*, 177–179.

Breger, L. (1973). *From instinct to identity.* Englewood Cliffs, NJ: Prentice-Hall.

Bronfenbrenner, U. (1970). *Two worlds of childhood: U.S. and U.S.S.R.* New York: Russell Sage Foundation

Bryan, J. H., & Walbek, N. H. (1970). The impact of words and deeds concerning altruism upon children. *Child Development*, *41*, 747–757.

Bryant, B. K. (1983). Context of success, affective arousal, and generosity: The neglected role of negative affect in success experience. *American Educational Research Journal*, *20*, 553–562.

Bryant, B. K., & Crockenberg, S. B. (1980). Correlates and dimensions of prosocial behavior: A study of female siblings with their mothers. *Child Development*, *51*, 529–544.

Buckley, N., Siegel, L., & Ness, S. (1979). Egocentrism, empathy and altruistic behavior in young children. *Developmental Psychology*, *15*, 329–330.

Burleson, B. R. (1982). The development of comforting strategies in childhood and adolescence. *Child Development*, *53*, 1578–1588.

Burton, R. V. (1963). Generality of honesty reconsidered. *Psychological Review*, *70*, 481–499.

Byrne, D. (1971). *The attraction paradigm.* New York: Academic Press.

Campbell, D. T. (1961). The mutual methodological relevance of anthropology and psychology. In F. L. K. Hsu (Ed.), *Psychological anthropology* (pp. 333–352). Homewood, IL: Dorsey Press.

Campbell, D. T. (1975). On the conflicts between biological and social evolution and between psychology and moral tradition. *American Psychologist*, *30*, 1103–1126.

Campbell, D. T. (1982). Legal and primary group social controls. *Journal of Social and Biological Structures*, *5*, 431–438.

Campbell, D. T. (1983). The two distinct routes beyond kin selection to ultrasociality:

Implications for the humanities and social sciences. In D. L. Bridgeman (Ed.), *The nature of prosocial development* (pp. 11–41). New York: Academic Press.

Carlson, M., & Miller, N. (1987). Explanation of the relation between negative mood and helping. *Psychological Bulletin, 102,* 91–108.

Cauble, M. A. (1976). Formal operations, ego identity, and principled morality: Are they related? *Developmental Psychology, 12,* 363–364.

Chapman, M., Zahn-Waxler, C., Cooperman, G., & Iannotti, R. (1987). Empathy and responsibility in the motivation of children's helping. *Developmental Psychology, 23,* 140–145.

Charlesworth, R., & Hartup, W. W. (1967). Positive social reinforcement in the nursery school peer group. *Child Development, 38,* 993–1002.

Child Development (1983). Special issue on developmental behavioral genetics, *54*(2).

Cialdini, R. B., Baumann, D. J., & Kenrick, D. T. (1981). Insights from sadness: A three-step model of the development of altruism as hedonism. *Developmental Review, 1,* 207–223.

Cialdini, R. B., Darby, B. L., & Vincent, J. E. (1973). Transgression and altruism: A case for hedonism. *Journal of Experimental Social Psychology, 9,* 502–516.

Cialdini, R. B., & Fultz, J. (1988). *Mega-analysis. An idea whose time should pass.* Unpublished manuscript, Arizona State University.

Cialdini, R. B., & Kenrick, D. T. (1976). Altruism as hedonism: A social development perspective on the relationship of negative mood state and helping. *Journal of Personality and Social Psychology, 34,* 907–914.

Cialdini, R. B., Kenrick, D. T., & Baumann, D. J. (1982). Effects of mood on prosocial behavior in children and adults. In N. Eisenberg (Ed.), *The development of prosocial behavior* (pp. 339–359). New York: Academic Press.

Cicirelli, V. G. (1976). Mother–child and sibling–sibling interactions on a problem-solving task. *Child Development, 47,* 588–596.

Clark, M. S. (1981). Noncomparability to benefits given and received: A cue to the existence of friendship. *Social Psychology Quarterly, 44,* 375–381.

Clary, E. G., & Miller, J. (1986). Socialization and situational influences on sustained altruism. *Child Development, 57,* 1358–1369.

Cohen, E. A., Gelfand, D. M., & Hartmann, D. P. (1981). Causal reasoning as a function of behavioral consequences. *Child Development, 52,* 514–522.

Colby, A., & Kohlberg, L. (1984). Invariant sequence and internal consistency in moral judgment stages. In W. M. Kurtines & J. L. Gewirtz (Eds.), *Morality, moral behavior and moral development* (pp. 41–51) New York: Wiley.

Colby, A., & Kohlberg, L. (1987). *The measurement of moral judgment.* Cambridge University Press.

Collins, W. A., & Getz, S. K. (1976). Children's social responses following modeled reactions to provocation: Prosocial effects of a television drama. *Journal of Personality, 44,* 488–500.

Conger, J. J. (1977). *Adolescence and youth: Psychological development in a changing world* (2nd ed.). New York: Harper.

Cox, N. (1974). Prior help, ego development, and helping behavior. *Child Development, 75,* 594–603.

Crosby, F., Bromley, S., & Saxe, L. (1980). Recent unobtrusive studies of black and white discrimination and prejudice: A literature review. *Psychological Bulletin, 87,* 546–563.

Cunningham, M. R., Shaffer, D. R., Barbee, A. P., & Smith, J. (1986, August). *Dual processes in the relationship of mood to altruism: Helping for you and for me*. Paper presented at the annual convention of the American Psychological Association, Washington, DC.

Damon, W. (1983). *Social and personality development*. New York: Norton.

Daniels, D., Plomin, R., & Greenhalgh, J. (1984). Correlates of difficult temperament in infancy. *Child Development, 55*, 1184–1194.

Denham, S. A. (1986). Social cognition, prosocial behavior, and emotion in preschoolers: Contextual validation. *Child Development, 57*, 194–201.

Dennis, W. (1965). *The Hopi child*. New York: Wiley.

DePalma, D. J. (1974). Effects of social class, moral orientation and severity of punishment of boys' moral responses to transgression and generosity. *Developmental Psychology, 10*, 890–900.

Devereux, E. C., Shouval, R., Bronfenbrenner, U., Rodgers, R. R., Kav-Venaki, S., Kiely, E., & Karson, E. (1974). Socialization practices of parents, teachers and peers in Israel: The kibbutz versus the city. *Child Development, 45*, 269–281.

DeVoe, M. W., Render, G. F., & Collins, J. R. (1979). Microtechnology processes and cooperative behavior of third grade children. *Journal of Experimental Education, 47*, 296–301.

DiVitto, B., & McArthur, L. Z. (1978). Developmental differences in the use of distinctiveness, consensus, and consistency information in making causal judgments. *Developmental psychology, 14*, 474–482.

Dlugokinski, E. L., & Firestone, I. J. (1974). Other centeredness and susceptibility to charitable appeals: Effects of perceived discipline. *Developmental Psychology, 10*, 21–28.

Doland, D. J., & Adelberg, K. (1967). The learning of sharing behavior. *Child Development, 38*, 695–700.

Dovidio, J. F. (1984). Helping behavior and altruism: An empirical and conceptual overview. In L. Berkowitz (Ed.), *Advances in experimental social psychology* (Vol. 17, pp. 361–427). New York: Academic Press.

Dreman, S. B. (1976). Sharing behavior in Israeli school children: Cognitive and social learning factors. *Child Development, 47*, 186–194.

Dreman, S. B., & Greenbaum, C. W. (1973). Altruism or reciprocity: Sharing behavior in Israeli kindergarten children. *Child Development, 44*, 61–68.

Dunn, J. (1983). Sibling relationships in early childhood. *Child Development, 54*, 787–811.

Dunn, J., & Kendrick, C. (1979). Interaction between young siblings in the context of family relationships. In M. Lewis & L. A. Rosenblum (Eds.), *The child and its family* (pp. 143–168). New York: Plenum.

Dunn, J., & Kendrick, C. (1982). Siblings and their mothers: Developing relationships within the family. In M. C. Lamb & B. Sutton-Smith (Eds.), *Sibling relationships* (pp. 39–60). Hillsdale, NJ: Lawrence Erlbaum Associates.

Dunn, J., & Munn, P. (1986). Siblings and the development of prosocial behaviors. *International Journal of Behavioral Development, 9*, 265–284.

Eagly, A. H., & Crowley, M. (1986). Gender and helping behavior: A meta-analytic review of the social psychological literature. *Psychological Bulletin, 100*, 283–308.

Easterbrooks, M. A., & Lamb, M. E. (1979). The relationship between quality of infant-mother attachment and infant competence in initial encounters with peers. *Child Development, 50*, 380–387.

Eisenberg, N. (1982). The development of reasoning about prosocial behavior. In N. Eisenberg (Ed.), *The development of prosocial behavior* (pp. 219–249). New York: Academic Press.

Eisenberg, N. (1983). Children's differentiations among potential recipients of aid. *Child Development, 3*, 594–602.

Eisenberg, N. (1986). *Altruistic emotion, cognition and behavior.* Hillsdale, NJ: Lawrence Erlbaum Associates.

Eisenberg, N., Boehnke, K., Schuhler, P., & Silbercisen, R. K. (1985). The development of prosocial behavior and cognition in German children. *Journal of Cross-Cultural Psychology, 16*, 69–82.

Eisenberg, N., Cameron, E., & Tryon, K. (1984). Prosocial behavior in the preschool years: Methodological and conceptual issues. In E. Staub, D. Bar-Tal, J. Karylowski, & J. Reykowski (Eds.), *The development and maintenance of prosocial behavior: International perspectives on positive morality* (pp. 101–115). New York: Plenum.

Eisenberg, N., Cameron, E., Tryon, K., & Dodez, R. (1981). Socialization of prosocial behavior in the preschool classroom. *Developmental Psychology, 17*, 773–782.

Eisenberg, N., Cialdini, R. B., McCreath, H., & Shell, R. (1987). Consistency-based compliance: When and why do children become vulnerable? *Journal of Personality and Social Psychology, 52*, 1174–1181.

Eisenberg, N., Fabes, R. A., Bustamante, D., & Mathy, R. M. (1987). Physiological indices of empathy. In N. Eisenberg & J. Strayer (Eds.), *Empathy and its development* (pp. 380–385). Cambridge University Press.

Eisenberg, N., Fabes, R. A., Bustamante, D., Mathy, R. M., Miller, P. A., & Lindholm, E. (1988). Differentiation of vicariously induced emotional reactions in children. *Developmental Psychology, 24*, 766–775.

Eisenberg, N., Fabes, R. A., Miller, P. A., Fultz, J., Shell, R., Mathy, R. M., & Reno, R. (in press). The relation of sympathy and personal distress to prosocial behavior: A multimethod study. *Journal of Personality and Social Psychology.*

Eisenberg, N., & Giallanza, S. (1984). The relation of mode of prosocial behavior and other proprietary behaviors to toy dominance. *Child Study Journal, 14*, 115–121.

Eisenberg, N., & Lennon, R. (1983). Sex differences in empathy and related capacities. *Psychological Bulletin, 94*, 100–131.

Eisenberg, N., Lennon, R., & Roth, K. (1983). Prosocial development in childhood: A longitudinal study. *Developmental Psychology, 19*, 846–855.

Eisenberg, N., McCreath, H., & Ahn, R. (1988). Vicarious emotional responsiveness and prosocial behavior: Their interrelations in young children. *Personality and Social Psychology Bulletin, 14*, 298–311.

Eisenberg, N., & Miller, P. (1987). The relation of empathy to prosocial and related behaviors. *Psychological Bulletin, 101*, 91–119.

Eisenberg, N., Miller, P., & Shell, R. (1988). Prosocial moral reasoning in early adolescence. Work in progress.

Eisenberg, N., & Pasternack, J. F. (1983). Inequities in children's prosocial behavior: Whom do children assist? In R. L. Leahy (Ed.), *The child's construction of social inequity* (pp. 179–205). New York: Academic Press.

Eisenberg, N., Pasternack, J. F., Cameron, E., & Tryon, K. (1984). The relation of quantity and mode of prosocial to moral cognitions and social style. *Child Development, 55*, 1479–1485.

Eisenberg, N., & Shell, R. (1986). Prosocial moral judgment and behavior in children: The mediating role of cost. *Personality and Social Psychology Bulletin, 12*, 426–433.

Eisenberg, N., Shell, R., Pasternack, J., Lennon, R., Beller, R., & Mathy, R. M. (1987). Prosocial development in middle childhood: A longitudinal study. *Developmental*

Psychology, *23*, 712–718.

Eisenberg, N., & Strayer, J. (1987). Critical issues in the study of empathy. In N. Eisenberg & J. Strayer (Eds.), *Empathy and its development* (pp. 3–13). Cambridge University Press.

Eisenberg, N., Tietjen, A., Silbereisen, R. K., Schuhler, P., Hertz-Lazarowitz, R., Fuchs, I., & Boehnke, K. (1986). Prosocial moral judgment: Cross-cultural research. In N. Eisenberg (Ed.), *Altruistic emotion, cognition, and behavior* (pp. 161–172). Hillsdale, NJ: Lawrence Erlbaum Associates.

Eisenberg-Berg, N. (1979). Development of children's prosocial moral judgment. *Developmental Psychology*, *15*, 128–137.

Eisenberg-Berg, N., & Geisheker, E. (1979). Content of preachings and power of the model/preacher: The effect on children's generosity. *Developmental Psychology*, *15*, 168–175.

Eisenberg-Berg, N., & Hand, M. (1979). The relationship of preschoolers' reasoning about prosocial moral conflicts to prosocial behavior. *Child Development*, *50*, 356–363.

Eisenberg-Berg, N., & Lennon, R. (1980). Altruism and the assessment of empathy in the preschool years. *Child Development*, *51*, 552–557.

Eisenberg-Berg, N., & Roth, K. (1980). The development of children's prosocial moral judgment: A longitudinal follow-up. *Developmental Psychology*, *16*, 375–376.

Ekstein, R. (1972). Psychoanalysis and education for the facilitation of positive human qualities. *Journal of Social Issues*, *28*, 71–86.

Elder, J. L. D. (1983, April). *Role-taking and prosocial behavior revisited: The effects of aggregation.* Paper presented at the biennial meeting of the Society for Research in Child Development, Detroit.

Elliott, R., & Vasta, R. (1970). The modeling of sharing: Effects associated with vicarious reinforcement, symbolization, age, and generalization. *Journal of Experimental Child Psychology*, *10*, 8–15.

Epstein, S. (1979). The stability of behavior: 1. On predicting most of the people most of the time. *Journal of Personality and Social Psychology*, *37*, 1097–1126.

Erikson, E. (1969). *Gandhi's truth.* New York: Norton.

Eron, L. D. (1987). The development of aggressive behavior from the perspective of a developing behaviorism. *American Psychologist*, *42*, 435–442.

Eron, L. D., Lefkowitz, M. M., Huesmann, L. R., & Walder, L. O. (1972). Does television violence cause aggression? *American Psychologist*, *27*, 253–263.

Eysenck, H. J. (1960). The development of moral values in children: The contribution of learning theory. *British Journal of Educational Psychology*, *30*, 11–21.

Eysenck, H. J. (1976). The biology of morality. In T. Lickona (Ed.), *Moral development and behavior: Theory, research and social issues* (pp. 108–123). New York: Holt, Rinehart & Winston.

Fagot, B. I. (1977). Consequences of moderate cross-gender behavior in preschool children. *Child Development*, *48*, 902–907.

Fagot, B. I. (1978). The influence of sex of child on parental reactions to toddler children. *Child Development*, *49*, 459–465.

Fenichel, O. (1945). *The psychoanalytic theory of neurosis.* New York: Norton.

Feshbach, N. (1973, July). *The relationship of child rearing factors to children's aggression, empathy, and relative positive and negative social behaviors.* Paper presented at a conference on the determinants and origins of aggressive behavior, Monte Carlo, Monaco.

Feshbach, N. D. (1978). Studies of empathic behavior in children. In B. A. Maher (Ed.),

Progress in experimental personality research (Vol. 8, pp. 1–47). New York: Academic Press.

Feshbach, N. (1979). Empathy training: A field study in affective education. In S. Feshbach & A. Fraczek (Eds.), *Aggression and behavior change: Biological and social processes* (pp. 234–249). New York: Praeger.

Feshbach, N. D., & Feshbach, S. (1982). Empathy training and the regulation of aggression: Potentialities and limitations. *Academic Psychological Bulletin, 4*, 399–413.

Feshbach, N. D., & Feshbach, S. (1983). *Learning to care: Classroom activities for social and affective development.* Glenview, IL: Scott, Foresman.

Feshbach, N. D., & Roe, K. (1968). Empathy in six- and seven-year-olds. *Child Development, 39*, 133–145.

Flavell, J. H., Botkin, P., Fry, C., Wright, J., & Jarvis, P. (1968). *The development of role-taking and communication skills in children.* New York: Wiley.

Flugel, J. C. (1945). *Man, morals, and society.* London: Duckworth and Penguin Books.

Fouts, G. T. (1972). Charity in children: The influence of "charity" stimuli and an audience. *Journal of Experimental Child Psychology, 13*, 303–309.

Freedman, J. L. (1970). Transgression, compliance and guilt. In J. R. Macaulay & L. Berkowitz (Eds.), *Altruism and helping behavior* (pp. 155–161). New York: Academic Press.

Freedman, J. L., Wallington, S. A., & Bless, E. (1967). Compliance without pressure: The effect of guilt. *Journal of Personality and Social Psychology, 7*, 117–124.

Freud, A. (1937). *The ego and mechanisms of defense.* London: Hogarth.

Freud, S. (1953). Civilization and its discontents. In J. Strackey (Ed.), *The standard edition of the complete works of Sigmund Freud* (Vol. 21). London: Hogarth (originally published 1930).

Freud, S. (1960). *Group psychology and the analysis of the ego* (translated by James Strachey). New York: Bantam Books (originally published 1921).

Freud, S. (1959). The passing of the Oedipus complex. In *Collected papers* (Vol. 11). New York: Basic Books (originally published 1924).

Frey, D. L., & Gaertner, S. L. (1986). Helping and the avoidance of inappropriate interracial behavior: A strategy that perpetuates a nonprejudiced self-image. *Journal of Personality and Social Psychology, 50*, 1083–1090.

Friedrich, L. K., & Stein, A. H. (1973). Aggressive and prosocial television programs and the natural behavior of preschool children. *Monographs of the Society for Research in Child Development, 38* (4, Serial No. 151), 1–64.

Friedrich, L. K., & Stein, A. H. (1975). Prosocial television and young children: The effects of verbal labeling and role playing on learning and behavior. *Child Development, 46*, 27–38.

Friedrich-Cofer, L. K., & Huston, A. C. (1986). Television violence and aggression: The debate continues. *Psychological Bulletin, 100*, 364–371.

Fuchs, I., Eisenberg, N., Hertz-Lazarowitz, R., & Sharabany, R. (1986). Kibbutz, Israeli city, and American children's moral reasoning about prosocial moral conflicts. *Merrill-Palmer Quarterly, 32*, 37–50.

Furby, L. (1978). Sharing: Decisions and moral judgments about letting others use one's possessions. *Psychological Reports, 43*, 595–609.

Furman, W., Rahe, D. F., & Hartup, W. W. (1979). Rehabilitation of socially withdrawn preschool children through mixed-age and same-age socialization. *Child Development, 50*, 915–922.

Gelfand, D. M., Hartmann, D. P., Cromer, C. C., Smith, C. L., & Page, B. C. (1975).

The effects of instructional prompts and praise on children's donation rates. *Child Development, 46,* 980–983.

Gergen, K. J., Gergen, M. M., & Meter, K. (1972). Individual orientations to prosocial behavior. *Journal of Social Issues, 28,* 105–130.

Glover, E. (1968). *The birth of the ego.* London: George Allen & Unwin.

Goldsmith, H. H. (1983). Genetic influences on personality from infancy to adulthood. *Child Development, 54,* 331–355.

Goranson, R. E., & Berkowitz, L. (1966). Reciprocity and responsibility reactions to prior help. *Journal of Personality and Social Psychology, 3,* 227–232.

Gottman, J., Gonso, J., & Rasmussen, B. (1975). Social interaction, social competence, and friendship in children. *Child Development, 46,* 709–718.

Gottman, J. M., & Parkhurst, J. T. (1980). A developmental theory of friendship and acquaintanceship processes. In W. A. Collins (Ed.), *Development of cognition, affect, and social relations. The Minnesota symposium on child psychology* (Vol. 13, pp. 197–253). Hillsdale, NJ: Lawrence Erlbaum Associates.

Gould, S. J. (1976). Biological potential vs. biological determinism. *Natural History, 85,* 12–22.

Grant, J. E., Weiner, A., & Rushton, J. P. (1976). Moral judgment and generosity in children. *Psychological Reports, 39,* 451–454.

Graves, N. B., & Graves, T. D. (1983). The cultural context of prosocial development: An ecological model. In D. L. Bridgeman (Ed.), *The nature of prosocial development* (pp. 243–264). New York: Academic Press.

Grieger, T., Kauffman, J. M., & Grieger, R. M. (1976). Effects of peer reporting on cooperative play and aggression of kindergarten children. *Journal of School Psychology, 14,* 307–313.

Grueneich, R. (1982). Issues in the developmental study of how children use intention and consequence information to make moral evaluations. *Child Development, 53,* 29–43.

Grusec, J. E. (1971). Power and internalization of self-denial. *Child Development, 42,* 93–105.

Grusec, J. E. (1981). Socialization processes and altruism. In J. P. Rushton & R. M. Sorrentino (Eds.), *Altruism and helping behavior* (pp. 139–166). Hillsdale, NJ: Lawrence Erlbaum Associates.

Grusec, J. E. (1982). The socialization of altruism. In N. Eisenberg (Ed.), *The development of prosocial behavior* (pp. 65–90). New York: Academic Press.

Grusec, J. E., Kuczynski, L., Rushton, J. P., & Simutis, Z. M. (1978). Modeling, direct instruction, and attributions: Effects on altruism. *Developmental Psychology, 14,* 51–57.

Grusec, J. E., & Redler, E. (1980). Attribution, reinforcement, and altruism: A developmental analysis. *Developmental Psychology, 16,* 525–534.

Grusec, J. E., Saas-Kortsaak, P., & Simutis, Z. M. (1978). The role of example and moral exhortation in the training of altruism. *Child Development, 49,* 920–923.

Grusec, J. E., & Skubiski, L. (1970). Model nurturance, demand characteristics of the modeling experiment and altruism. *Journal of Personality and Social Psychology, 14,* 352–359.

Guttman, J., Bar-Tal, D., & Leiser, T. (1979). *The effect of various reward situations on children's helping behavior.* Unpublished manuscript, Tel-Aviv University.

Haan, N., Weiss, R., & Johnson, V. (1982). The role of logic in moral reasoning and development. *Developmental Psychology, 18,* 245–256.

Hallie, P. (1979). *Lest innocent blood be shed: The story of the Chambon and how goodness happened there*. New York: Harper & Row.

Hampson, R. B. (1984). Adolescent prosocial behavior: Peer group and situational factors associated with helping. *Journal of Personality and Social Psychology, 46*, 153–162.

Handlon, B. J., & Gross, P. (1959). The development of sharing behavior. *Journal of Abnormal and Social Psychology, 59*, 425–428.

Hansen, R., Goldman, B. D., & Baldwin, M. (1975, June). *Towards a taxonomy of altruism: An observational study of spontaneous prosocial behavior among young children*. Paper presented at the annual meeting of the Canadian Psychological Association, Quebec City.

Harris, M. B., & Siebel, C. E. (1975). Affect, aggression, and altruism. *Developmental Psychology, 11*, 623–627.

Harris, S., Mussen, P., & Rutherford, E. (1976). Some cognitive, behavioral, and personality correlates of maturity of moral judgment. *Journal of Genetic Psychology, 128*, 123–135.

Hartmann, D. P., Gelfand, D. M., Smith, C. L., Paul, S. C., Cromer, C. C., Page, B. C., & LeBenta, D. V. (1976). Factors affecting the acquisition and elimination of children's donating behavior. *Journal of Experimental Child Psychology, 21*, 328–338.

Hartshorne, H., & May, M. A. (1928). *Studies in the nature of character. Vol. 1: Studies in deceit*. New York: Macmillan.

Hartshorne, H., May, M. A., & Maller, J. B. (1929). *Studies in the nature of character. Vol. 2: Studies in self-control*. New York: Macmillan.

Hartshorne, H., May, M. A., & Shuttleworth, F. K. (1930). *Studies in the nature of character. Vol. 3: Studies in the organization of character*. New York: Macmillan.

Hartup, W. W. (1983). Peer relations. In P. H. Mussen (Ed.), *Handbook of child development. Vol. 4, Socialization, personality and social development* (4th ed., pp. 103–196). New York: Wiley.

Hartup, W. W., & Coates, B. (1967). Imitation of a peer as a function of reinforcement from the peer group and rewardingness of the model. *Child Development, 38*, 1003–1016.

Hay, D. F., Nash, A., & Pedersen, J. (1981). Responses of six-month-olds to the distress of their peers. *Child Development, 52*, 1071–1075.

Hayes, D. J., Felton, R. R., & Cohen, R. R. (1985). A natural occurrence of foster parenting by a female mountain bluebird. *Auk*, 191–193.

Heider, F. (1958). *The psychology of interpersonal relations*. New York: Wiley.

Hertz-Lazarowitz, R., & Sharan, S. (1984). Enhancing prosocial behavior through co-operative learning in the classroom. In E. Staub, D. Bar-Tal, J. Karylowski, & J. Reykowski (Eds.), *The development and maintenance of prosocial behavior: International perspectives on positive morality* (pp. 423–443). New York: Plenum.

Higgins, A., Power, C., & Kohlberg, L. (1984). The relationship of moral atmosphere to judgments of responsibility. In W. M. Kurtines & J. L. Gewirtz (Eds.), *Morality, moral behavior, and moral development* (pp. 74–106). New York: Wiley.

Hill, J. (1984). Human altruism and sociocultural fitness. *Journal of Social and Biological Structures, 7*, 17–35.

Hoffman, M. L. (1963). Parent discipline and the child's consideration for others. *Child Development, 34*, 573–588.

Hoffman, M. L. (1975a). Altruistic behavior and the parent–child relationship. *Journal of Personality and Social Psychology, 31*, 937–943.

Hoffman, M. L. (1975b). Developmental synthesis of affect and cognition and its implications for altruistic motivation. *Developmental Psychology, 11,* 607–622.

Hoffman, M. L. (1975c). Sex differences in moral internalization and values. *Journal of Personality and Social Psychology, 32,* 720–729.

Hoffman, M. (1981). Is altruism part of human nature? *Journal of Personality and Social Psychology, 40,* 121–137.

Hoffman, M. L. (1982). The measurement of empathy. In C. E. Izard (Ed.), *Measuring emotions in infants and children* (pp. 279–296). Cambridge: Cambridge University Press.

Hoffman, M. L. (1984). Empathy, its limitations, and its role in a comprehensive moral theory. In W. M. Kurtines & J. L. Gewirtz (Eds.), *Morality, moral behavior, and moral development* (pp. 283–302). New York: Wiley.

Hoffman, M. L., & Saltzstein, H. D. (1967). Parent discipline and the child's moral development. *Journal of Personality and Social Psychology, 5,* 45–57.

Hudson, L. M., Forman, E. A., & Brion-Meisels, S. (1982). Role taking as a predictor of prosocial behavior in cross-age tutors. *Child Development, 53,* 1320–1329.

Hugo, V. (1982). *Les miserables.* London: Penguin (originally published 1862).

Iannotti, R. J. (1975, April). *The effect of role-taking experiences on role-taking, altruism, empathy, and aggression.* Paper presented at the biennial meeting of the Society for Research on Child Development, Denver.

Iannotti, R. J. (1985). Naturalistic and structured assessments of prosocial behavior in preschool children: The influence of empathy and perspective taking. *Developmental Psychology, 21,* 46–55.

Ickes, W. J., & Kidd, R. F. (1976). An attributional analysis of helping behavior. In J. H. Harvey, W. J. Ickes, & R. F. Kidd (Eds.), *New directions in attribution research* (Vol. 1, pp. 311–334). Hillsdale, NJ: Lawrence Erlbaum Associates.

Isen, A. M. (1970). Success, failure, and reaction to others: The warm glow of success. *Journal of Personality and Social Psychology, 15,* 294–301.

Isen, A. M., Clark, M., & Schwartz, M. F. (1976). Duration of the effect of mood on helping: "Footprints in the sands of time." *Journal of Personality and Social Psychology, 34,* 385–393.

Isen, A. M., Herren, L. T., & Geva, N. (1986, August). *The effect of positive affect on recall of social information.* Paper presented at the annual meeting of the American Psychological Association, Washington, DC.

Isen, A. M., Horn, N., & Rosenhan, D. L. (1973). Effects of success and failure on children's generosity. *Journal of Personality and Social Psychology, 27,* 239–247.

Isen, A. M., Shalker, T. E., Clark, M., & Karp, L. (1978). Affect, accessibility of material in memory, and behavior: A cognitive loop? *Journal of Personality and Social Psychology, 36,* 1–12.

Israel, A. C., & Brown, M. S. (1979). Effects of directiveness of instructions and surveillance on the production and persistence of children's donations. *Journal of Experimental Child Psychology, 27,* 250–261.

Israel, A. C., & Raskin, P. A. (1979). Directiveness of instructions and modeling: Effects on production and persistence on children's donations. *Journal of Genetic Psychology, 135,* 269–277.

Johnson, D. B. (1982). Altruistic behavior and the development of the self in infants. *Merrill-Palmer Quarterly, 28,* 379–388.

Johnson, N. (1973). Quoted in Liebert, R. M., Neale, J. M., & Davidson, E. S. (1973). *The early window.* New York: Pergamon.

Kagan, J. (1958). The concept of identification. *Psychological Review, 65,* 296–305.

Kagan, S., & Knight, G. P. (1981). Social motives among Anglo-American and Mexican-American children: Experimental and projective measures. *Journal of Research in Personality, 15*, 93–106.

Kagan, S., Knight, G. P., & Martinez-Romero, S. (1982). Culture and the development of conflict resolution style. *Journal of Cross-Cultural Psychology, 13*, 43–58.

Kagan, S., & Madsen, M. C. (1971). Cooperation and competition of Mexican, Mexican-American, and Anglo children of two ages. *Developmental Psychology, 5*, 32–39.

Kagan, S., Zahn, G. L., & Gealy, J. (1977). Competition and school achievement among Anglo-American and Mexican-American children. *Journal of Educational Psychology, 69*, 432–441.

Kaplan, R. W. (1984). Empathy or altruistic surrender. *Dynamic Psychotherapy, 2*, 123–131.

Karniol, R. (1978). Children's use of intention cues in evaluating behavior. *Psychological Bulletin, 85*, 76–85.

Karylowski, J. (1982a). Doing good to feel good v. doing good to make others feel good: Some child-rearing antecedents. *School Psychology International, 3*, 149–156.

Karylowski, J. (1982b). Two types of altruistic behavior: Doing good to feel good or to make the other feel good. In V. J. Derlega & J. Grzelak (Eds.), *Cooperation and helping behavior: Theories and research* (pp. 397–413). New York: Academic Press.

Katz, P. A., Katz, I., & Cohen, S. (1976). White children's attitudes toward blacks and the physically handicapped: A developmental study. *Journal of Educational Psychology, 82*, 20–24.

Keasey, C. B. (1978). Children's development awareness and usage of intentionality and motives. In H. E. Howe, Jr. (Ed.), *Nebraska symposium on motivation* (Vol. 25, pp. 219–260). Lincoln: University of Nebraska Press.

Kelley, H. H. (1967). Attribution theory in social psychology. In D. Levine (Ed.), *Nebraska symposium on motivation* (Vol. 15). Lincoln: University of Nebraska Press.

Kerber, K. W. (1984). The perception of nonemergency helping situations: Costs, rewards, and the altruistic personality. *Journal of Personality, 52*, 177–187.

Kiselica, M. S., & Levin, G. R. (1987, April). *Young children's responses to a crying peer.* Paper presented at the biennial meeting of the Society for Research in Child Development, Baltimore.

Kluckhohn, C. (1954). Culture and behavior. In G. Lindzey (Ed.), *Handbook of social psychology* (Vol. 11, pp. 921–976). Cambridge, MA: Addison-Wesley.

Kluckhohn, C., & Murray, H. A. (Eds.). (1948). *Personality in nature, society, and culture.* New York: Knopf.

Knight, G. P., & Kagan, S. (1977). Acculturation of prosocial and competitive behaviors among second- and third-generation Mexican-American children. *Journal of Cross-Cultural Psychology, 8*, 273–284.

Knight, G. P., Kagan, S., & Buriel, R. (1982). Perceived parental practices and prosocial development. *Journal of Genetic Psychology, 141*, 57–65.

Kohlberg, L. (1969). Stage and sequence: The cognitive-developmental approach to socialization. In D. A. Goslin (Ed.), *Handbook of socialization theory and research* (pp. 325–480). Chicago: Rand McNally.

Kohlberg, L. (1976). Moral stage and moralization: The cognitive-developmental approach. In T. Lickona (Ed.), *Moral development and behavior: Theory, research, and social issues* (pp. 84–107). New York: Holt, Rinehart & Winston.

Kohlberg, L. (1981). *The philosophy of moral development: Moral stages and the idea of justice.* New York: Harper & Row.

Kohlberg, L. (1984). *Essays on moral development. Vol. 11: The psychology of moral development.* New York: Harper & Row.

Kohlberg, L., & Candee, D. (1984). The relationship of moral judgment to moral action. In W. M. Kurtines & J. L. Gewirtz (Eds.), *Morality, moral behavior, and moral development* (pp. 52–73). New York: Wiley.

Krebs, D. (1975). Empathy and altruism. *Journal of Personality and Social Psychology, 32,* 1134–1146.

Krebs, D., & Gillmore, J. (1982). The relationship among the first stages of cognitive development, role-taking abilities, and moral development. *Child Development, 53,* 877–886.

Krebs, D. L., & Miller, D. T. (1985). Altruism and aggression. In G. Lindzey & E. Aronson (Eds.), *Handbook of social psychology* (Vol. II, 3rd ed., pp. 1–71). New York: Random House.

Krebs, D., & Sturrup, B. (1982). Role-taking ability and altruistic behavior in elementary school children. *Journal of Moral Education, 11,* 94–100.

Kuczynski, L. (1982). Intensity and orientation of reasoning: Motivational determinants of children's compliance to verbal rationales. *Journal of Experimental Child Psychology, 34,* 357–370.

Kuhn, D., Langer, J., Kohlberg, L., & Haan, N. S. (1977). The development of formal operations in logical and moral judgments. *Genetic Psychology Monographs, 95,* 97–188.

Kurdek, L. A. (1977). Structural components and intellectual correlates of cognitive perspective taking in first- through fourth-grade children. *Child Development, 48,* 1503–1511.

Kurdek, L. A. (1978). Perspective taking as the cognitive basis of children's moral development: A review of the literature. *Merrill-Palmer Quarterly, 24,* 3–27.

Kurtines, W. M. (1984). Moral behavior as rule-governed behavior: A psychosocial role-theoretical approach to moral behavior and development. In W. M. Kurtines & J. L. Gewirtz (Eds.), *Morality, moral behaviors, and moral development* (pp. 303–324). New York: Wiley.

Kurtines, W. M. (1986). Moral behavior as rule-governed behavior: Person and situation effects on moral decision making. *Journal of Personality and Social Psychology, 50,* 784–791.

Kurtines, W. M., & Schneider, P. J. (1983, August). *Sharing and giving as rule-governed behavior: A psychological role-theoretical approach to pro- and anti-social behavior.* Paper presented at the annual meeting of the American Psychological Association, Anaheim, CA.

Ladd, G. W., Lange, G., & Stremmel, A. (1983). Personal and situational influences on children's helping behavior: Factors that mediate compliant helping. *Child Development, 54,* 488–501.

Lamb, M. E. (1978a). Interactions between eighteen-month-olds and their preschool-aged siblings. *Child Development, 49,* 51–59.

Lamb, M. E. (1978b). The development of sibling relationships in infancy: A short-term longitudinal study. *Child Development, 49,* 1189–1196.

Lamb, M. E. (1982). Sibling relationships across the lifespan. In M. E. Lamb & B. Sutton-Smith (Eds.), *Sibling relationships* (pp. 1–12). Hillsdale, NJ: Lawrence Erlbaum Associates.

Lamb, M. E., & Roopnarine, J. L. (1979). Peer influences on sex-role development in preschoolers. *Child Development, 50,* 1219–1222.

Larrieu, J. A. (1984a, March). *Children's commitment to others, social efficacy, and prosocial behavior*. Paper presented at the biennial meeting of the Southwestern Society for Research in Human Development, Denver.

Larrieu, J. A. (1984b, March). *Prosocial values, assertiveness, and sex: Predictors of children's naturalistic helping*. Paper presented at the biennial meeting of the Southwestern Society for Research in Human Development, Denver.

Larrieu, J., & Mussen, P. (1986). Some personality and motivational correlates of children's prosocial behavior. *Journal of Genetic Psychology, 147*, 529–542.

Latané, B., & Darley, J. (1970). *The unresponsive bystander: Why doesn't he help?* New York: Appleton.

Latané, B., & Nida, S. (1981). Ten years of research on group size and helping. *Psychological Bulletin, 89*, 308–324.

Leahy, R. L. (1979). Development of conceptions of prosocial behavior: Information affecting rewards given for altruism and kindness. *Developmental Psychology, 15*, 34–37.

Lennon, R., & Eisenberg, N. (1987). Emotional displays associated with preschoolers' prosocial behavior. *Child Development, 58*, 992–1000.

Lennon, R., Eisenberg, N., & Carroll, J. (1986). The relation between empathy and prosocial behavior in the preschool years. *Journal of Applied Developmental Psychology, 7*, 219–224.

Leung, J. J., & Foster, S. F. (1985). Helping the elderly: A study on altruism in children. *Child Study Journal, 15*, 293–309.

Levitt, M. J., Weber, R. A., Clark, M. C., & McDonnell, P. (1985). Reciprocity of exchange in toddler sharing behavior. *Developmental Psychology, 21*, 122–123.

Liben, L. S. (1978). Perspective-taking skills in young children: Seeing the world through rose colored glasses. *Developmental Psychology, 14*, 87–92.

Lickona, T. (1976). Research on Piaget's theory of moral development. In T. Lickona (Ed.), *Moral development and behavior: Theory, research, and social issues* (pp. 219–240). New York: Holt, Rinehart & Winston.

Liebert, R. M., Fernandez, L. E., & Gill, L. (1969). Effects of a "friendless" model on imitation and prosocial behavior. *Psychonomic Science, 16*, 81–82.

Liebert, R. M., Neale, J. M., & Davidson, E. S. (1973). *The early window: Effects of television on children and youth*. New York: Pergamon Press.

Lipscomb, T. J., Larrieu, J. A., McAllister, H. A., & Bregman, N. J. (1982). Modeling and children's generosity: A developmental perspective. *Merrill-Palmer Quarterly, 28*, 275–282.

Lockwood, A. L. (1978). The effects of values clarification and moral development curriculum on school-age subjects: A critical review of recent research. *Review of Educational Research, 48*, 325–364.

Londerville, S., & Main, M. (1981). Security of attachment, compliance, and maternal training methods in the second year of life. *Developmental Psychology, 17*, 298–299.

London, P. (1970). The rescuers: Motivational hypotheses about Christians who saved Jews from the Nazis. In J. Macaulay & L. Berkowitz (Eds.), *Altruism and helping behavior* (pp. 241–250). New York: Academic Press.

Long, G. T., & Lerner, M. J. (1974). Deserving the "personal contract" and altruistic behavior by children. *Journal of Personality and Social Psychology, 29*, 551–556.

Lumsden, C. J. (1988). Psychological development: Epigenetic rules and gene-culture coevolution. In K. B. MacDonald (Ed.), *Sociobiological perspectives on human development* (pp. 234–267). New York: Springer-Verlag.

Lumsden, C. J., & Wilson, E. O. (1981). *Genes, mind, and culture: The co-evolutionary process.* Cambridge, MA: Harvard University Press.

Lynch, J. G., & Cohen, J. L. (1978). The use of subjective expected utility theory as an aid to understanding variables that influence helping behavior. *Journal of Personality and Social Psychology*, *36*, 1138–1151.

Maccoby, E. E. (1968). The development of moral values and behavior in childhood. In J. A. Clausen (Ed.), *Socialization and society* (pp. 227–269). New York: Wiley.

MacDonald, K. (1984). An ethological-social learning theory of the development of altruism: Implications for human sociobiology. *Ethology and Sociobiology*, *5*, 97–109.

McGuire, J. M., & Thomas, M. H. (1975). Effects of sex, competence, and competition on sharing behavior in children. *Journal of Personality and Social Psychology*, *32*, 490–494.

McGuire, K. D., & Weisz, J. R. (1982). Social cognition and behavior correlates of preadolescent chumship. *Child Development*, *53*, 1478–1484.

MacLean, P. D. (1982, May). *Evolutionary brain roots of family, play, and the isolation call.* Paper presented at the annual meeting of the American Psychiatric Association, Toronto.

Madsen, M. C. (1967). Cooperative and competitive motivation of children in three Mexican sub-cultures. *Psychological Reports*, *20*, 1307–1320.

Madsen, M. C. (1971). Developmental and cross-cultural differences in the cooperative and competitive behavior of young children. *Journal of Cross-Cultural Psychology*, *2*, 365–371.

Madsen, M. C., & Shapiro, A. (1970). Cooperative and competitive behavior of urban Afro-American, Anglo-American, Mexican-American, and Mexican village children. *Developmental Psychology*, *3*, 16–20.

Madsen, M. C., & Yi, S. (1975). Cooperation and competition of urban and rural children in the Republic of Korea. *International Journal of Psychology*, *10*, 269–274.

Main,M., & George, C. (1985). Responses of abused and disadvantaged toddlers to distress in agemates: A study in the day care setting. *Developmental Psychology*, *21*, 407–412.

Malinowski, C. I., & Smith, C. P. (1985). Moral reasoning and moral conduct. *Journal of Personality and Social Psychology*, *49*, 1016–1027.

Marcus, R. F. (1986). Naturalistic observation of cooperation, helping, and sharing and their associations with empathy and affect. In C. Zahn-Waxler, E. M. Cummings, & R. Iannotti (Eds.), *Altruism and aggression: Biological and social origins* (pp. 256–279). Cambridge University Press.

Marcus, R. F., & Jenny, B. (1977). A naturalistic study of reciprocity in the helping behavior of young children. *Alberta Journal of Educational Research*, *23*, 195–206.

Marin, G., Mejia, B., & DeOberle, C. (1975). Cooperation as a function of place of residence in Colombian children. *Journal of Social Psychology*, *95*, 127–128.

Marsh, D. T. (1982). The development of interpersonal problem solving among elementary school children. *Journal of Genetic Psychology*, *140*, 107–118.

Marsh, D. T., Serafica, F. C., & Barenboim, C. (1981). Interrelationships among perspective taking, interpersonal problem solving and interpersonal functioning. *Journal of Genetic Psychology*, *138*, 37–48.

Maruyama, G., Fraser, S. C., & Miller, N. (1982). Personal responsibility and altruism in children. *Journal of Personality and Social Psychology*, *42*, 659–664.

Masters, J. C., & Furman, W. (1976). Effects of affective state on noncontinent outcome expectancies and beliefs in internal and external control. *Developmental Psychology*, *12*, 481–482.

Masters, J. C., & Furman, W. (1981). Popularity, individual friendship selection, and specific peer interaction among children. *Developmental Psychology*, *17*, 344–350.

Matthews, K. A., Batson, C. D., Horn, J., & Rosenman, R. H. (1981). "Principles in his nature which interest him in the fortune of others...": The heritability of empathic concern for others. *Journal of Personality*, *49*, 237–247.

Mead, M. (1935). *Sex and temperament in three primitive societies*. New York: Morrow.

Mednick, S. A., Gabrielli, W. F., & Hutchings, B. (1984). Genetic influences in criminal convictions: Evidence from an adoption cohort. *Science*, *224*, 891–894.

Meyer, J. P., & Mulherin, A. (1980). From attribution to helping: An analysis of the mediating effects of affect and expectancy. *Journal of Personality and Social Psychology*, *39*, 201–210.

Midlarsky, E. (1984). Competence and helping: Notes toward a model. In E. Staub, D. Bar-Tai, J. Karylowski, & J. Reykowski (Eds.). *Development and maintenance of prosocial behavior: International perspectives on positive morality* (pp. 291–308). New York: Plenum.

Midlarsky, E., & Bryan, J. H. (1972). Affect expressions and children's imitative altruism. *Journal of Experimental Research on Personality*, *6*, 195–203.

Midlarsky, E., & Hannah, M. E. (1985). Competence, reticence, and helping by children and adolescents. *Developmental Psychology*, *21*, 534–541.

Miller, A. G. (1973). Integration and acculturation of cooperative behavior among Blackfoot Indian and non-Indian Canadian children. *Journal of Cross-Cultural Psychology*, *4*, 374–380.

Miller, A. G., & Thomas, R. (1972). Cooperation and competition among Blackfoot Indian and urban Canadian children. *Child Development*, *43*, 1104–1110.

Miller, D. T., & Smith, J. (1977). The effect of own deservingness and deservingness of others on children's helping behavior. *Child Development*, *48*, 617–620.

Moir, D. J. (1974). Egocentrism and the emergency of conventional morality in pre-adolescent girls. *Child Development*, *45*, 299–309.

Moore, B. S., & Eisenberg, N. (1984). The development of altruism. In G. Whitehurst (Ed.), *Annals of child development* (pp. 107–174). Greenwich, CT: JAI Press.

Moore, B. S., Underwood, B., & Rosenhan, D. L. (1973). Affect and altruism. *Developmental Psychology*, *8*, 99–104.

Mosbacher, B. J., Gruen, G. E., & Rychlak, J. F. (1985). Incentive value: The overlooked dimension in childhood sharing. *Journal of Genetic Psychology*, *146*, 197–204.

Munroe, R. L., & Munroe, R. H. (1977). Cooperation and competition among East African and American children. *Journal of Social Psychology*, *10*, 145–146.

Murphy, L. B. (1937). *Social behavior and child personality*. New York: Columbia University Press.

Mussen, P., & Eisenberg-Berg, N. (1977). *Caring, sharing, and helping: The roots of prosocial behavior in children*. San Francisco: Freeman.

Mussen, P., Rutherford, E., Harris, S., & Keasey, C. (1970). Honesty and altruism among preadolescents. *Developmental Psychology*, *3*, 169–194.

Nadler, A., Romek, E., & Shapiro-Friedman, A. (1979). Giving in the kibbutz: Pro-social behavior of city and kibbutz children as affected by social responsibility and social pressure. *Journal of Cross-Cultural Psychology*, *10*, 57–72.

Nelsen, E. A., Grinder, R. E., & Biaggio, A. M. (1969). Relationships among behavioral, cognitive development, and self-report measures of morality and personality.

Multivariate Behavioral Research, *4*, 483–500.

Nelson, L., & Madsen, M. C. (1969). Cooperation and competition in four-year-olds as a function of reward contingency and subculture. *Developmental Psychology*, *1*, 340–344.

Nisan, M., & Kohlberg, L. (1982). Universality and variation in moral judgment: A longitudinal and cross-sectional study in Turkey. *Child Development*, *53*, 865–876.

O'Connor, M., Dollinger, S., Kennedy, S., & Pelletier-Smetko, P. (1979). Prosocial behavior and psychopathology in emotionally disturbed boys. *American Journal of Orthopsychiatry*, *49*, 301–310.

O'Connor, R. (1969). Modification of social withdrawal through symbolic modeling. *Journal of Applied Behavior Analysis*, *2*, 15–22.

Olden, C. (1958). Notes on the development of empathy. *Psychoanalytic Study of the Child*, *13*, 505–518.

Oliner, S. P., & Oliner, P. M. (1988). *The altruistic personality: Rescuers of Jews in Nazi Europe.* New York: Free Press.

Olson, S. L., Johnson, J., Belleau, K., Parks, J., & Barrett, E. (1983, April). *Social competence in preschool children: Interrelations with sociometric status, social problem-solving, and impulsivity.* Paper presented at the biennial meeting of the Society for Research in child Development, Detroit.

Panksepp, J. (1986). The psychobiology of prosocial behaviors: Separation distress, play, and altruism. In C. Zahn-Waxler, E. M. Cummings, & R. Iannotti (Eds.), *Altruism and aggression: Biological and social origins* (pp. 19–57). Cambridge University Press.

Panofsky, A. D. (1976). The effect of similarity/dissimilarity of race and personal interests on empathy and altruism in second graders (doctoral dissertation, University of California, Los Angeles). *Dissertation Abstracts International*, *37*, 200A.

Parke, R. D., & Slaby, R. G. (1983). The development of aggression. In P. H. Mussen (Ed.), *Handbook of child psychology, Vol. 4: Socialization, personality, and social development* (pp. 547–641) (E. M. Hetherington, Ed.). New York: Wiley.

Patterson, G. R. (1982). *Coercive family processes.* Eugene, OR: Castilla Press.

Patterson, G. R., Littman, R. A., & Bricker, W. (1967). Assertive behavior in children: A step toward a theory of aggression. *Monographs of the Society for Research in Child Development*, *32*(5, Serial No. 113).

Payne, F. D. (1980). Children's prosocial conduct in structural situations and as viewed by others: Consistency, convergence and relationships with person variables. *Child Development*, *51*, 1252–1259.

Pearl, R. (1985). Children's understanding of others' need for help: Effects of problem explicitness and type. *Child Development*, *56*, 735–745.

Pepler, D., Corter, C., & Abramovitch, R. (1982). Social relations among children: Comparison of siblings and peer interaction. In K. Rubin & H. S. Ross (Eds.), *Peer relationships and social skills in childhood* (pp. 209–227). New York: Springer-Verlag.

Peterson, L. (1980). Developmental changes in verbal and behavioral sensitivity to cues of social norms of altruism. *Child Development*, *51*, 830–838.

Peterson, L. (1983a). Influence of age, task competence, and responsibility focus on children's altruism. *Developmental Psychology*, *19*, 141–148.

Peterson, L. (1983b). Role of donor competence, donor age, and peer presence on helping on an emergency. *Development Psychology*, *19*, 873–880.

Peterson, L., & Gelfand, D. M. (1984). Causal attributions of helping as a function of age and incentives. *Child Development*, 55, 504–511.

Peterson, L., Hartmann, D. P., & Gelfand, D. M. (1977). Developmental change in the effects of dependency and reciprocity cues on children's moral judgments and donation rates. *Child Development*, 48, 1331–1339.

Piaget, J. (1965). *The moral judgment of the child*. New York: Free Press (originally published 1932).

Piliavin, J. A., Dovidio, J. F., Gaertner, S. L., & Clark, R. D., III (1981). *Emergency intervention*. New York: Academic Press.

Plomin, R. (1986). *Development, genetics, and psychology*, Hillsdale, NJ: Lawrence Erlbaum Associates.

Power, T. G., & Parke, R. D. (1986). Patterns of early socialization: Mother- and father-infant interaction in the home. *International Journal of Behavioral Development*, 9, 331–341.

Radke-Yarrow, M., & Zahn-Waxler, C. (1984). Roots, motives, and patterns in children's prosocial behavior. In E. Staub, D. Bar-Tal, J. Karylowski, & J. Reykowski (Eds.), *The development and maintenance of prosocial behavior: International perspectives on positive morality* (pp. 81–99). New York: Plenum.

Radke-Yarrow, M., Zahn-Waxler, C., & Chapman, M. (1983). Prosocial dispositions and behavior. In P. Mussen (Ed.), *Manual of child psychology. Vol. 4: Socialization, personality, and social development* (pp. 469–545) (E. M. Hetherington, Ed.). New York: Wiley.

Raviv, A., & Bar-Tal, D. (1981). Demographic correlates of adolescents' helping behavior. *Journal of Youth and Adolescence*, 10, 45–53.

Raviv, A., Bar-Tal, D., Ayalon, H., & Raviv, A. (1980). Perception of giving and receiving help by group members. *Representative Research in Social Psychology*, 11, 140–151.

Raviv, A., Bar-Tal, D., & Lewis-Levin, T. (1980). Motivations for donation behavior by boys of three different ages. *Child Development*, 51, 610–613.

Reisenzein, R. (1986). A structural equation analysis of Weiner's attribution-affect model of helping behavior. *Journal of Personality and Social Psychology*, 50, 1123–1133.

Rest, J. R. (1979). *Development in judging moral issues*. Minneapolis: University of Minnesota Press.

Rheingold, H. L. (1982). Little children's participation in the work of adults, a nascent prosocial behavior. *Child Development*, 53, 114–125.

Rheingold, H. L., Hay, D. F., & West, M. J. (1976). Sharing in the second year of life. *Child Development*, 47, 1148–1158.

Ribal, J. E. (1963). Social character and meaning of selfishness and altruism. *Sociology and Social Research*, 47, 311–321.

Rice, M. E., & Grusec, J. E. (1975). Saying and doing: Effects on observer performance. *Journal of Personality and Social Psychology*, 32, 584–593.

Rohner, R. P. (1975). *They love me, they love me not*. HRAF Press.

Romer, D., Gruder, C. L., & Lizzardo, T. (1986). A person-situation approach to altruistic behavior. *Journal of Personality and Social Psychology*, 51, 1001–1012.

Rosenhan, D. (1970). The natural socialization of altruistic autonomy. In J. Macaulay & L. Berkowitz (Eds.), *Altruism and helping behavior* (pp. 251–268). New York: Academic Press.

Rosenhan, D. L. (1972). Learning theory and prosocial behavior. *Journal of Social Issues*, 28, 151–164.

Rosenhan, D. L., Salovey, P., Karylowski, J., & Hargis, K. (1981). Emotion and altruism. In J. P. Rushton & R. M. Sorrentino (Eds.), *Altruism and helping behavior:*

Social, personality, and developmental perspectives (pp. 233–248). Hillsdale, NJ: Lawrence Erlbaum Associates.

Rosenhan, D. L., Underwood, B., & Moore, B. S. (1974). Affect moderates self-gratification and altruism. *Journal of Personality and Social Psychology, 30*, 546–552.

Rosenhan, D. L., & White, G. M. (1967). Observation and rehearsal as determinants of prosocial behavior. *Journal of Personality and Social Psychology, 5*, 424–431.

Rubin, K. H., & Schneider, F. W. (1973). The relationship between moral judgment, egocentrism, and altruistic behavior. *Child Development, 44*, 661–665.

Rushton, J. P. (1975). Generosity in children: Immediate and long term effects of modeling, preaching, and moral judgment. *Journal of Personality and Social Psychology, 31*, 459–466.

Rushton, J. P. (1979). Effects of prosocial television and film material on the behavior of viewers. In L. Berkowitz (Ed.), *Advances in experimental social psychology* (Vol. 12, pp. 321–351). New York: Academic Press.

Rushton, J. P. (1980). *Altruism, socialization, and society.* Englewood Cliffs, NJ: Prentice-Hall.

Rushton, J. P. (1981). Television as a socializer. In J. P. Rushton & R. M. Sorrentino (Eds.), *Altruism and helping behavior* (pp. 91–108). Hillsdale, NJ: Lawrence Erlbaum Associates.

Rushton, J. P., Brainerd, C. J., & Pressley, M. (1983). Behavioral development and construct validity: The principle of aggregation. *Psychological Bulletin, 94*, 18–38.

Rushton, J. P., Chrisjohn, R. D., & Fekken, G. C. (1981). The altruistic personality and the self-report altruism scale. *Personality and Individual Differences, 2*, 1–11.

Rushton, J. P., Fulker, D. W., Neale, M. C., Nias, D. K. B., & Eysenck, H. J. (1986). Altruism and aggression: The heritability of individual differences. *Journal of Personality and Social Psychology, 50*, 1192–1198.

Rushton, J. P., & Littlefield, C. (1979). The effects of age, amount of modeling, and a success experience on seven- to eleven-year-old children's generosity. *Journal of Moral Education, 9*, 55–56.

Rushton, J. P., Littlefield, C. H., & Lumsden, C. J. (1986). Gene–culture coevaluation of complex social behavior: Human altruism and mate choice. *Proceedings of the National Academy of Sciences, 83*, 7340–7343.

Rushton, J. P., & Teachman, G. (1978). The effects of positive reinforcement, attributions, and punishment on model induced altruism in children. *Personality and Social Psychology Bulletin, 4*, 322–325.

Rushton, J. P., & Wheelwright, M. (1980). Validation of donating to charity as a measure of children's altruism. *Psychological Reports, 47*, 803–806.

Rushton, J. P., & Wiener, J. (1975). Altruism and cognitive development in children. *British Journal of Social and Clinical Psychology, 14*, 341–349.

Rutherford, E., & Mussen, P. (1968). Generosity in nursery school boys. *Child Development, 39*, 755–765.

Sawyer, J. (1966). The altruism scale: A measure of cooperative, individualistic and competitive interpersonal orientation. *American Journal of Sociology, 71*, 407–416.

Scarr, S., & Kidd, K. K. (1983). Developmental behavioral genetics. In P. Mussen (Ed.), *Handbook of child psychology. Vol. 2: Infancy and developmental psychology* (pp. 344–433) (M. M. Haith & J. J. Campos, Eds.). New York: Wiley.

Schopler, J., & Matthews, M. W. (1965). The influence of the perceived causal locus of partner's dependence on the use of interpersonal power. *Journal of Personality and Social Psychology, 2*, 609–612.

Schroenrade, P. A., Batson, C. D., Brandt, J. R., & Loud, R. E., Jr. (1986). Attachment, accountability and motivation to benefit another not in distress. *Journal of Personality and Social Psychology, 51,* 357–363.

Schwartz, S. H., & Howard, J. A. (1984). Internalized values as motivators of altruism. In E. Staub, D. Bar-Tal, J. Karylowski, & J. Reykowski (Eds.), *The development and maintenance of prosocial behavior: International perspectives on positive morality* (pp. 229–255). New York: Plenum.

Segal, N. L. (1984). Cooperation, competition, and altruism within twin sets: A re-appraisal. *Ethology and Sociobiology, 5,* 163–177.

Selman, R. (1971). The relation of role taking to the development of moral judgment in children. *Child Development, 42,* 79–91.

Selman, R. L. (1980). *The growth of interpersonal understanding: Developmental and clinical analysis.* New York: Academic Press.

Settlage, C. F. (1972). Cultural values and the superego in late adolescence. *Psychoanalytic Study of the Child, 27,* 74–97.

Shaffer, D. R. (1986). Is mood-induced altruism a form of hedonism? *Humboldt Journal of Social Relations, 13,* 195–216.

Shaffer, D. R., & Smith, J. E. (1985). Effects of preexisting moods on observers' reactions to helpful and nonhelpful models. *Motivation and Emotion, 9,* 101–122.

Shantz, C. V. (1983). Social cognition. In P. H. Mussen (Ed.), *Handbook of child psychology: Cognitive development* (Vol. 3, pp. 495–555). New York: Wiley.

Shapira, A., & Lomranz, J. (1972). Cooperative and competitive behavior of rural Arab children in Israel. *Journal of Cross-Cultural Psychology, 3,* 353–359.

Shapira, A., & Madsen, M. C. (1969). Cooperative and competitive behavior of kibbutz and urban children in Israel. *Child Development, 40,* 609–617.

Shapira, A., & Madsen, M. C. (1974). Between- and within-group cooperation and competition among kibbutz and nonkibbutz children. *Developmental Psychology, 10,* 140–145.

Sharan, S., Hare, P., Webb, C. D., & Hertz-Lazarowitz, R. (Eds.). (1980). *Cooperation in education.* Provo, UT: Brigham Young University Press.

Shigetomi, C. C., Hartmann, D. P., & Gelfand, D. M. (1981). Sex differences in children's altruistic behaviors and reputations for helpfulness. *Developmental Psychology, 17,* 434–437.

Shure, M. B. (1980). *Interpersonal problem solving in ten-year-olds.* Final grant report to the National Institute of Mental Health (grant no. R01 MH 27741).

Shure, M. B. (1982). Interpersonal problem solving: A cog in the wheel of social cognition. In F. C. Serafica (Ed.), *Social-cognitive development in context* (pp. 133–166). New York: Guilford Press.

Singleton, L. C., & Asher, S. R. (1977). Peer preferences and social interaction among third-grade children in an integrated school district. *Journal of Educational Psychology, 69,* 330–336.

Slaby, R. G., & Crowley, C. G. (1977). Modification of cooperative and aggression through teacher attention to children's speech. *Journal of Experimental Child Psychology, 23,* 442–458.

Small, S. A., Zeldin, R. S., & Savin-Williams, R. C. (1983). In search of personality traits: A multimethod analysis of naturally occurring prosocial and dominance behavior. *Journal of Personality, 51,* 1–16.

Snarey, J. R. (1985). Cross-cultural universality of socio-moral development: A critical review of Kohlbergian research. *Psychological Bulletin, 97,* 202–232.

Solomon, D., Schaps, E., & Watson, M. (1987, April). *Effects of a comprehensive school-based program on children's prosocial behavior.* Paper presented at a meeting of the American Educational Research Association, Washington, DC.

Solomon, D., Watson, M., Battistich, V., & Schaps, E. (1986, April). *Promoting prosocial behavior in schools: An interim report on a five-year longitudinal intervention program.* Paper presented at a meeting of the American Education Research Association, San Francisco.

Solomon, D., Watson, M., Schaps, E., Battistich, V., & Solomon, J. (in press). Cooperative learning as part of a comprehensive program designed to promote prosocial development. In S. Sharan (Ed.), *Current research on cooperative learning.* New York: Praeger.

Sommerlad, E. A., & Bellingham, W. P. (1972). Cooperation–competition: A comparison of Australian and European and Aboriginal school children. *Journal of Cross-Cultural Psychology, 3,* 149–157.

Spiro, M. E. (1965). *Kibbutz: Venture in Utopia.* New York: Schocken Books.

Spivack, G., Platt, J. J., & Shure, M. B. (1976). *The problem solving approach to adjustment.* San Francisco: Jossey-Bass.

Spivack, G., & Shure, M. B. (1974). *Social adjustment of young children.* San Francisco: Jossey-Bass.

Sprafkin, J. M., Liebert, R. M., & Poulos, R. W. (1975). Effects of a prosocial example on children's helping. *Journal of Experimental Child Psychology, 20,* 119–126.

Sroufe, A. (1983). Infant caregiver attachment and patterns of adaptation in preschool: The roots of maladaption and competence. In M. Perlmutter (Ed.), *Minnesota symposium on child development* (Vol. 16, pp. 41–79). Hillsdale, NJ: Lawrence Erlbaum Associates.

Stanhope, L., Bell, R. Q., & Parker-Cohen, N. Y. (1987). Temperament and helping behavior in preschool children. *Developmental Psychology, 23,* 347–353.

Staub, E. (1970a). A child in distress: The effects of focusing responsibility on children on their attempts to help. *Developmental Psychology, 2,* 152–153.

Staub, E. (1970b). A child in distress: The influence of age and number of witnesses on children's attempts to help. *Journal of Personality and Social Psychology, 14,* 130–140.

Staub, E. (1971a). Helping a person in distress: The influence of implicit and explicit rules of conduct on children and adults. *Journal of Personality and Social Psychology, 17,* 137–145.

Staub, E. (1971b). A child in distress: The influence of nurturance and modeling on children's attempts to help. *Developmental Psychology, 5,* 124–132.

Staub, E. (1971c). The use of role playing and induction in children's learning of helping and sharing behavior. *Child Development, 42,* 805–817.

Staub, E. (1978). *Positive social behavior and morality: Social and personal influences* (Vol. 1). New York: Academic Press.

Staub, E. (1979). *Positive social behavior and morality: Socialization and development* (Vol. 2). New York: Academic Press.

Staub, E., & Feinberg, H. K. (1980, September). *Regularities in peer interaction, empathy, and sensitivity to others.* Paper presented at the annual meeting of the American Psychological Association, Montreal.

Staub, E., & Noerenberg, H. (1981). Property rights, deservingness, reciprocity, friendship: The transactional character of children's sharing behavior. *Journal of Personality and Social Psychology, 40,* 271–289.

Staub, E., & Sherk, L. (1970). Need for approval, children's sharing behavior, and reciprocity in sharing. *Child Development, 41,* 243–252.

Strain, P. S., Cooke, T. P., & Apolloni, T. (1976). The role of peers in modifying classmates' social behavior: A review. *Journal of Special Education, 10,* 351–356.

Strayer, F. F., Wareing, S., & Rushton, J. P. (1979). Social constraints on naturally occurring preschool altruism. *Ethology and Sociobiology, 1,* 3–11.

Strayer, J. (1980). A naturalistic study of empathic behaviors and their relation to affective states and perspective-taking skills in preschool children. *Child Development, 51,* 815–822.

Suda, W., & Fouts, G. (1980). Effects of peer presence on helping in introverted and extroverted children. *Child Development, 51,* 1272–1275.

Sullivan, H. S. (1940). *Conceptions of modern psychiatry.* New York: Norton.

Suls, J., Witenberg, S., & Gutkin, D. (1981). Evaluating reciprocal and nonreciprocal prosocial behavior: Developmental changes. *Personality and Social Psychology Bulletin, 7,* 25–31.

Summers, M. (1987, April). *Imitation, dominance, agonism and prosocial behavior: A meta-analysis of sibling behavior.* Paper presented at the biennial meeting of the Society for Research in Child Development, Baltimore.

Surber, C. F. (1982). Separable effects of motives, consequences, and presentation order on children's moral judgments. *Developmental Psychology, 18,* 257–266.

Thomas, D. R. (1975). Cooperation and competition among Polynesian and European children. *Child Development, 46,* 948–953.

Thompson, R. A., & Hoffman, M. L. (1980). Empathy and the development of guilt in children. *Developmental Psychology, 16,* 155–156.

Thompson, W. C., Cowan, C. L., & Rosenhan, D. L. (1980). Focus of attention mediates the impact of negative mood on altruism. *Journal of Personality and Social Psychology, 38,* 291–300.

Tietjen, A. (1986). Prosocial reasoning among children and adults in a Papua New Guinea society. *Developmental Psychology, 22,* 861–868.

Toda, M., Shinotsuka, H., McClintock, C. G., & Stech, F. J. (1978). Development of competitive behavior as a function of culture, age, and social comparison. *Journal of Personality and Social Psychology, 36,* 825–839.

Toi, M., & Batson, C. D. (1982). More evidence that empathy is a source of altruistic motivation. *Journal of Personality and Social Psychology, 43,* 281–292.

Tomlinson-Keasey, C., & Keasey, C. B. (1974). The mediating role of cognitive development in moral judgment. *Child Development, 45,* 291–298.

Trivers, R. L. (1971). The evolution of reciprocal altruism. *Quarterly Review of Biology, 46,* 35–57.

Trivers, R. (1983). The evolution of cooperation. In D. L. Bridgeman (Ed.), *The nature of prosocial development* (pp. 95–112). New York: Academic Press.

Turiel, E., Edwards, C. P., & Kohlberg, L. (1978). Moral development in Turkish children, adolescents, and young adults. *Journal of Cross-Cultural Psychology, 9,* 75–85.

Turiel, E. (in press). Multifaceted social reasoning and educating for character, culture, and development. In L. Nucci & A. Higgins (Eds.), *Moral development and character education: A dialogue.* Berkeley, CA: McCutchen.

Turnbull, C. M. (1972). *The mountain people.* New York: Simon & Schuster.

Ugurel-Semin, R. (1952). Moral behavior and moral judgment of children. *Journal of Abnormal and Social Psychology, 47,* 463–474.

Underwood, B., & Moore, B. S. (1982a). The generality of altruism in children. In N. Eisenberg (Ed.), *The development of prosocial behavior* (pp. 25–52). New York: Academic Press.

Underwood, B., & Moore, B. (1982b). Perspective-taking and altruism. *Psychological Bulletin, 91*, 143–173.

Wagner, C., & Wheeler, L. (1969). Model, need and cost effects in helping behaviors. *Journal of Personality and Social Psychology, 12*, 111–116.

Walker, L. J. (1980). Cognitive and perspective-taking prerequisites for moral development. *Child Development, 51*, 131–139.

Walker, L. J., & Richards, B. S. (1979). Stimulating transitions in moral reasoning as a function of cognitive development. *Developmental Psychology, 15*, 95–103.

Wallace, J., & Sadalla, E. (1966). Behavioral consequences of transgression: 1. The effects of social recognition. *Journal of Experimental Research in Personality, 1*, 187–194.

Walters, J., Pearce, D., & Dahms, L. (1957). Affectional and aggressive behavior of preschool children. *Child Development, 28*, 15–26.

Waters, E., Wippman, J., & Sroufe, L. A. (1979). Attachment, positive affect, and competence in the peer group: Two studies in construct validation. *Child Development, 50*, 821–829.

Weiner, B. (1980). A cognitive(attribution)-emotion-action model of motivated behavior: An analysis of judgments of help giving. *Journal of Personality and Social Psychology, 39*, 186–200.

Weiner, B. (1986). *An attributional theory of motivation and emotion.* New York: Springer-Verlag.

Weissbrod, C. S. (1976). Noncontingent warmth induction, cognitive style, and children's imitative donation and rescue effort behaviors. *Journal of Personality and Social Psychology, 34*, 274–281.

Weston, D. R., & Main, M. (1980, April). *Infant responses to the crying of an adult actor in the laboratory: Stability and correlates of "concerned attention."* Paper presented at the Second International Conference on Infant Studies, New Haven.

Weyant, J. M. (1978). Effect of mood states, costs, and benefits on helping. *Journal of Personality and Social Psychology, 36*, 1169–1176.

White, C. B., Bushnell, N., & Regnemer, J. L. (1978). Moral development in Bahamian school children: A 3-year examination of Kohlberg's stages of moral development. *Developmental Psychology, 14*, 58–65.

Whiting, B. B., & Whiting, J. W. M. (1975). *Children of six cultures: A psychocultural analysis.* Cambridge, MA: Harvard University Press.

Whiting, J. W. M., & Whiting, B. B. (1973). Altruistic and egoistic behavior in six cultures. In L. Nader & T. Maretzki (Eds.), *Cultural illness and health.* Washington, DC: American Anthropological Association.

Willis, J. B., Feldman, N. S., & Ruble, D. N. (1977). Children's generosity as influenced by deservedness of reward and type of recipient. *Journal of Educational Psychology, 69*, 33–35.

Wilson, E. O. (1975a). Human decency is animal. *New York Times Magazine*, October 12, 38–50.

Wilson, E. O. (1975b). *Sociobiology: The new synthesis.* Cambridge, MA: Harvard University Press.

Wilson E. O. (1978). *On human nature.* Cambridge, MA: Harvard University Press.

Wispe, L. (1986). The distinction between sympathy and empathy: To call forth a concept, a word is needed. *Journal of Personality and Social Psychology, 50,* 314–421.

Wright, B. A. (1942). Altruism in children and the perceived conduct of others. *Journal of Abnormal and Social Psychology, 37,* 218–233.

Wright, D. (1971). *The psychology of moral behavior.* Middlesex, UK: Penguin Books.

Yarrow, M. R., Scott, P. M., & Waxler, C. Z. (1973). Learning concern for others. *Developmental Psychology, 8,* 240–260.

Yarrow, M. R., & Waxler, C. Z. (1976). Dimensions and correlates of prosocial behavior in young children. *Child Development, 47,* 118–125.

Zahn-Waxler, C., Iannotti, R., & Chapman, M. (1982). Peers and prosocial development. In K. H. Rubin & H. S. Ross (Eds.), *Peer relationships and social skills in childhood* (pp. 133–162). New York: Springer-Verlag.

Zahn-Waxler, C., & Radke-Yarrow, M. (1982). The development of altruism: Alternative research strategies. In N. Eisenberg (Ed.), *The development of prosocial behavioral* (pp. 109–137). New York: Academic Press.

Zahn-Waxler, C., Radke-Yarrow, M., & King, R. A. (1979). Child rearing and children's prosocial initiations toward victims of distress. *Child Development, 50,* 319–330.

Zahn-Waxler, C., Radke-Yarrow, M., & King, R. (1983). Early altruism and guilt. *Academic Psychology Bulletin, 5,* 247–260.

Zarabatany, L., Hartmann, D. P., Gelfand, D. M., & Vinciguerra, P. (1985). Gender differences in altruistic reputation: Are they artifactual? *Developmental Psychology, 21,* 97–101.

Zeldin, R. S., Small, S. A., & Savin-Williams, R. C. (1982). Prosocial interactions in two mixed-sex adolescent groups. *Child Development, 53,* 1492–1498.

Zinser, O., & Lydiatt, E. W. (1976). Mode of recipient definition, affluence of the recipient, and sharing behavior in preschool children. *Journal of Genetic Psychology, 129,* 261–266.

Zinser, O., Perry, J. S., Bailey, R. G., & Lydiatt, E. W. (1976). Racial recipients, value of donations, and sharing behavior in children. *Journal of Genetic Psychology, 129,* 29–35.

Zinser, O., Perry, J. S., & Edgar, R. M. (1975). Affluence of the recipient, value of donations, and sharing behavior in preschool children. *Journal of Psychology, 89,* 301–305.

Name index

Subject index